Building Machine Learning Systems with Python
Third Edition

Explore machine learning and deep learning techniques for building intelligent systems using scikit-learn and TensorFlow

Luis Pedro Coelho
Willi Richert
Matthieu Brucher

BIRMINGHAM - MUMBAI

Building Machine Learning Systems with Python

Third Edition

Commissioning Editor: Sunith Shetty
Acquisition Editor: Divya Poojari
Content Development Editor: Dattatraya More
Technical Editor: Varsha Shivhare
Copy Editor: Safis Editing
Project Coordinator: Shweta H Birwatkar
Proofreader: Safis Editing
Indexer: Aishwarya Gangawane
Graphics: Jisha Chirayil
Production Coordinator: Arvindkumar Gupta

First published: July 2013

Second edition: March 2015

Third edition: July 2018

Production reference: 2280718

Published by Packt Publishing Ltd.
Livery Place
35 Livery Street
Birmingham
B3 2PB, UK.

ISBN 978-1-78862-322-3

www.packtpub.com

`mapt.io`

Mapt is an online digital library that gives you full access to over 5,000 books and videos, as well as industry leading tools to help you plan your personal development and advance your career. For more information, please visit our website.

Why subscribe?

- Spend less time learning and more time coding with practical eBooks and Videos from over 4,000 industry professionals

- Improve your learning with Skill Plans built especially for you

- Get a free eBook or video every month

- Mapt is fully searchable

- Copy and paste, print, and bookmark content

PacktPub.com

Did you know that Packt offers eBook versions of every book published, with PDF and ePub files available? You can upgrade to the eBook version at `www.PacktPub.com` and as a print book customer, you are entitled to a discount on the eBook copy. Get in touch with us at `service@packtpub.com` for more details.

At `www.PacktPub.com`, you can also read a collection of free technical articles, sign up for a range of free newsletters, and receive exclusive discounts and offers on Packt books and eBooks.

Contributors

About the authors

Luis Pedro Coelho is a computational biologist who analyzes DNA from microbial communities to characterize their behavior. He has also worked extensively in bioimage informatics—the application of machine learning techniques for the analysis of images of biological specimens. His main focus is on the processing and integration of large-scale datasets. He has a PhD from Carnegie Mellon University and has authored several scientific publications. In 2004, he began developing in Python and has contributed to several open source libraries. He is currently a faculty member at Fudan University in Shanghai.

Willi Richert has a PhD in machine learning/robotics, where he has used reinforcement learning, hidden Markov models, and Bayesian networks to let heterogeneous robots learn by imitation. Now at Microsoft, he is involved in various machine learning areas, such as deep learning, active learning, or statistical machine translation. Willi started as a child with BASIC on his Commodore 128. Later, he discovered Turbo Pascal, then Java, then C++—only to finally arrive at his true love: Python.

Matthieu Brucher is a computer scientist who specializes in high-performance computing and computational modeling and currently works for JPMorgan in their quantitative research branch. He is also the lead developer of Audio ToolKit, a library for real-time audio signal processing. He has a PhD in machine learning and signals processing from the University of Strasbourg, two Master of Science degrees—one in digital electronics and signal processing and another in automation – from the University of Paris XI and Supelec, as well as a Master of Music degree from Bath Spa University.

About the reviewers

Alberto Boschetti is a data scientist with expertise in signal processing and statistics. He holds a PhD in telecommunication engineering and currently lives and works in London. In his work projects, he faces challenges ranging from NLP, behavioral analysis, and machine learning to deep nets and distributed processing. He is very passionate about his job and always tries to stay updated about the latest developments in data science technologies, attending meet-ups, conferences, and other events.

Gerold Hintz is an applied scientist who specializes in NLP. He obtained an MSc in Computer Science from Darmstadt University of Technology in 2014, focusing on machine learning and minoring in linguistics. He worked as a researcher in the field of computational semantics, applying unsupervised methods to paraphrasing tasks. He likes to study both natural languages and programming languages, and has a particular interest in the intersection of these fields.

Packt is searching for authors like you

If you're interested in becoming an author for Packt, please visit `authors.packtpub.com` and apply today. We have worked with thousands of developers and tech professionals, just like you, to help them share their insight with the global tech community. You can make a general application, apply for a specific hot topic that we are recruiting an author for, or submit your own idea.

Table of Contents

Preface

Machine learning allows models or systems to learn without being explicitly programmed. You will see how to use the best library support available, including, scikit-learn, TensorFlow, and many others, to build efficient, smart systems.

Who this book is for

Building Machine Learning Systems with Python is for data scientists, machine learning developers, and Python developers who want to learn how to build increasingly complex machine learning systems. You will use Python's machine learning capabilities to develop effective solutions. Prior knowledge of Python programming is expected.

What this book covers

Chapter 1, *Getting Started with Python Machine Learning*, introduces the basic idea of machine learning and TensorFlow with a very simple example. Despite its simplicity, it will challenge us with the risk of overfitting.

Chapter 2, *Classifying with Real-world Examples*, uses real data to explore classification by training a computer to be able to distinguish between different classes of flowers.

Chapter 3, *Regression*, explains how to use regression to handle data, a classic topic that is still relevant today. You will also learn about advanced regression techniques such as Lasso and ElasticNet.

Chapter 4, *Classification I – Detecting Poor Answers*, demonstrates how to use the bias-variance trade-off to debug machine learning models, though this chapter is mainly about using logistic regression to ascertain whether a user's answer to a question is good or bad.

Chapter 5, *Dimensionality Reduction*, explores what other methods exist to help us to downsize data so that it is chewable by our machine learning algorithms.

Chapter 6, *Clustering – Finding Related Posts*, demonstrates how powerful the bag of words approach is by applying it to find similar posts without really understanding them.

Chapter 7, *Recommendations*, builds recommendation systems based on customer product ratings. We will also see how to build recommendations from shopping data without the need for ratings data (which users do not always provide).

`Chapter 8`, *Artificial Neural Networks and Deep Learning*, deals with the fundamentals and examples of CNN and RNN using TensorFlow.

`Chapter 9`, *Classification II – Sentiment Analysis*, explains how Naïve Bayes works, and how to use it to classify tweets to see whether they are positive or negative.

`Chapter 10`, *Topic Modeling*, moves beyond assigning each post to a single cluster to assigning posts to several topics, as real texts can deal with multiple topics.

`Chapter 11`, *Classification III – Music Genre Classification*, sets the scene of someone having scrambled our huge music collection, our only hope of creating order being to let a machine learner classify our songs. It turns out that it is sometimes better to trust someone else's expertise to create features ourselves. The chapter also covers the conversion of speech into text.

`Chapter 12`, *Computer Vision*, demonstrates how to apply classification in the specific context of handling images by extracting features from data. We also see how these methods can be adapted to find similar images in a collection, and the applications of CNN and GAN using TensorFlow.

`Chapter 13`, *Reinforcement Learning*, covers the fundamentals of reinforcement learning and Deep Q networks on Atari game playing.

`Chapter 14`, *Bigger Data*, explores some approaches to dealing with larger data by taking advantage of multiple cores or computing clusters. It also introduces cloud computing (using Amazon Web Services as our cloud provider).

To get the most out of this book

This book assumes you know Python and how to install a library using `easy_install` or `pip`. We do not rely on any advanced mathematics, such as calculus or matrix algebra. We are using the following versions throughout the book, but you should be fine with any more recent ones:

- Python 3.5
- NumPy 1.13.3
- SciPy 1.0.0
- scikit-learn latest version

All examples are available as Jupyter notebooks in our code bundle (`https://github.com/PacktPublishing/Building-Machine-Learning-Systems-with-Python-Third-edition`).

Download the example code files

You can download the example code files for this book from your account at `www.packtpub.com`. If you purchased this book elsewhere, you can visit `www.packtpub.com/support` and register to have the files emailed directly to you.

You can download the code files by following these steps:

1. Log in or register at `www.packtpub.com`.
2. Select the **SUPPORT** tab.
3. Click on **Code Downloads & Errata**.
4. Enter the name of the book in the **Search** box and follow the onscreen instructions.

Once the file is downloaded, please make sure that you unzip or extract the folder using the latest version of:

- WinRAR/7-Zip for Windows
- Zipeg/iZip/UnRarX for Mac
- 7-Zip/PeaZip for Linux

The code bundle for the book is also hosted on GitHub at `https://github.com/PacktPublishing/Building-Machine-Learning-Systems-with-Python-Third-edition`. In case there's an update to the code, it will be updated on the existing GitHub repository.

We also have other code bundles from our rich catalog of books and videos available at `https://github.com/PacktPublishing/`. Check them out!

Download the color images

We also provide a PDF file that has color images of the screenshots/diagrams used in this book. You can download it here: `https://www.packtpub.com/sites/default/files/downloads/BuildingMachineLearningSystemswithPythonThirdedition_ColorImages.pdf`.

Conventions used

There are a number of text conventions used throughout this book.

`CodeInText`: Indicates code words in text, database table names, folder names, filenames, file extensions, pathnames, dummy URLs, user input, and Twitter handles. Here is an example: "If you don't have Jupyter already, simply install it with `pip install jupyter` and then run it with Jupyter Notebook."

A block of code is set as follows:

```
from sklearn.datasets import load_boston
boston = load_boston()
```

Any command-line input or output is written as follows:

```
>>> import numpy
>>> numpy.version.full_version
1.13.3
```

Bold: Indicates a new term, an important word, or words that you see onscreen. For example, words in menus or dialog boxes appear in the text like this. Here is an example: "We select **Launch Instance**, which leads to the following screen, asking us to select the operating system to use."

Warnings or important notes appear like this.

Tips and tricks appear like this.

Get in touch

Feedback from our readers is always welcome.

General feedback: Email `feedback@packtpub.com` and mention the book title in the subject of your message. If you have questions about any aspect of this book, please email us at `questions@packtpub.com`.

Errata: Although we have taken every care to ensure the accuracy of our content, mistakes do happen. If you have found a mistake in this book, we would be grateful if you would report this to us. Please visit www.packtpub.com/submit-errata, selecting your book, clicking on the Errata Submission Form link, and entering the details.

Piracy: If you come across any illegal copies of our works in any form on the Internet, we would be grateful if you would provide us with the location address or website name. Please contact us at copyright@packtpub.com with a link to the material.

If you are interested in becoming an author: If there is a topic that you have expertise in and you are interested in either writing or contributing to a book, please visit authors.packtpub.com.

Reviews

Please leave a review. Once you have read and used this book, why not leave a review on the site that you purchased it from? Potential readers can then see and use your unbiased opinion to make purchase decisions, we at Packt can understand what you think about our products, and our authors can see your feedback on their book. Thank you!

For more information about Packt, please visit packtpub.com.

Getting Started with Python Machine Learning

Machine learning teaches machines to learn to carry out tasks by themselves. It is that simple. The complexity comes with the details, and that is most likely the reason you are reading this book.

Maybe you have too much data and too little insight. Maybe you hope that, by using machine learning algorithms, you can solve this challenge, so you started digging into the algorithms. But perhaps after a while you became puzzled: which of the myriad of algorithms should you actually choose?

Alternatively, maybe you are simply more generally interested in machine learning and you have been reading blogs and articles about it for some time. Everything seemed to be magic and cool, so you started your exploration and fed some data into a decision tree or a support vector machine. However, after you successfully applied these to some other data, perhaps you wondered: was the whole setting right? Did you get optimal results? How do you know that there are no better algorithms? Or whether your data was the right kind?

Welcome to the club! All of us authors were once at those stages, looking for information that tells the stories behind the theoretical textbooks about machine learning. It turned out that much of that information was black art, not usually taught in standard text books. So, in a sense, we wrote this book to our younger selves. A book that not only gives a quick introduction to machine learning, but also teaches the lessons we learned during our careers in the field. We hope that it will also give you a smoother entry into one of the most exciting fields in computer science.

Machine learning and Python – a dream team

The goal of machine learning is to teach machines (software) to carry out tasks by providing them with a couple of examples (that is, examples of how to do or not do the task). Let's assume that each morning when you turn on your computer, you perform the same task of moving emails around so that only emails belonging to the same topic end up in the same folder. After some time, you might feel bored and think of automating this chore. One way would be to start analyzing your brain and write down all the rules and decisions that your brain processes while you are shuffling your emails. However, this will be quite cumbersome and always imperfect. While you will miss some rules, you will overspecify others. A better and more future-proof way of doing this would be to automate this process by choosing a set of email meta information and body/folder name pairs and letting an algorithm come up with the best rule set. The pairs would be your training data, and the resulting rule set (also called a model) could then be applied to future emails that you have not yet seen. This is machine learning in its simplest form.

Of course, machine learning is not a brand new field in itself. Quite the contrary: its success in recent years can be attributed to the pragmatic way that it uses rock-solid techniques and insights from other successful fields, such as statistics. In these fields, the purpose is for us humans to get insights into the data—for example, by learning more about the underlying patterns and relationships within it. As you read more and more about successful applications of machine learning (you have checked out www.kaggle.com already, haven't you?), you will see that applied statistics is a common field among machine learning experts.

As you will see later, the process of coming up with a decent machine learning approach is never easy. Instead, you will find yourself going back and forth in your analysis, trying out different versions of your input data on diverse sets of machine learning algorithms. It is this exploratory nature that lends itself perfectly to Python. Being an interpreted, high-level programming language, it seems that Python has been designed exactly for this process of trying out different things. What is more, it even does this fast. Sure, it is slower than C or many other natively compiled programming languages. Nevertheless, with the myriad of easy-to-use libraries that are often written in C, you don't have to sacrifice speed for agility.

What the book will teach you – and what it will not

This book will give you a broad overview of what types of learning algorithms are currently most used in the diverse fields of machine learning, and what to watch out for when applying them. From our own experience, however, we know that doing the cool stuff—that is, using and tweaking machine learning algorithms, such as support vector machines, nearest neighbor searches, or ensembles thereof—will only consume a tiny fraction of the overall time that a good machine learning expert will spend doing the same thing. Looking at the following typical workflow, we can see that most of the time will be spent on rather mundane tasks:

- Reading the data and cleaning it
- Exploring and understanding the input data
- Analyzing how to best present the data to the learning algorithm
- Choosing the right model and learning algorithm
- Measuring the performance correctly

When talking about exploring and understanding the input data, we will need to use a bit of statistics and basic math. However, while doing this, you will see that those topics that seemed so dry in your math class can actually be really exciting when you use them to look at interesting data.

The journey starts when you read in the data. When you have to answer questions such as, "How do I handle invalid or missing values?", you will see that this is more an art than a precise science, and a very rewarding art, as doing this part correctly will open your data to more machine learning algorithms and hence increase the likelihood of success.

With the data ready and waiting in your program's data structures, you will want to get a real feeling for what animal you are working with. Do you have enough data to answer your questions? If not, you might want to think about additional ways to get more of it. Perhaps you even have too much data. In that case, you probably want to think about how to best extract a sample of it.

Often, you will not feed the data directly into your machine learning algorithm. Instead, you will find that you can refine parts of the data before training. Oftentimes, the machine learning algorithm will reward you with increased performance. You will even find that a simple algorithm with refined data generally outperforms a very sophisticated algorithm with raw data. This part of the machine learning workflow is called **feature engineering**, and, most of the time, it is a very exciting and rewarding challenge. You will immediately see the results of your previous creative and intelligent efforts.

Choosing the right learning algorithm, then, is not simply a shoot-out of the three or four that are in your toolbox (there will be more; you will see). It is more a thoughtful process of weighing different performance and functional requirements. Do you need a fast result and are willing to sacrifice quality? Or would you rather spend more time to get the best possible result? Do you have a clear idea of future data, or should you be a bit more conservative on that side?

Finally, measuring performance is the part of the process that has the most potential pitfalls for the aspiring machine learner. There are easy mistakes to avoid, such as testing your approach with the same data on which you have trained. But there are more difficult ones as well, such as using imbalanced training data. Again, the data is the part that determines whether your undertaking will fail or succeed.

We see that only the fourth point deals with the fancy algorithms. Nevertheless, we hope that this book will convince you that the other four tasks are not simply chores, but can be equally exciting. Our hope is that, by the end of the book, you will have truly fallen in love with data instead of learning algorithms.

To that end, we will not overwhelm you with the theoretical aspects of the diverse machine learning algorithms, as there are already excellent books in that area (you will find pointers in the appendix). Instead, we will try to provide you with an understanding of the underlying approaches in the individual chapters—just enough for you to get an idea and be able to undertake your first steps. Hence, this book is by no means the definitive guide to machine learning—it is more of a starter kit. We hope that it ignites your curiosity enough to keep you eager in trying to learn more and more about this interesting field.

In the rest of this chapter, we will set up and get to know the basic Python libraries of NumPy and SciPy, and then train our first machine learning algorithm using scikit-learn. During this, we will introduce basic machine learning concepts that will be used throughout the book. The rest of the chapters will then go into more detail about the five steps described earlier, highlighting different aspects of machine learning in Python using diverse application scenarios.

How to best read this book

While we have tried to provide all the code required to convey the book's ideas, we don't want to bore you with repetitive code snippets. Instead, we have created self-contained Jupyter notebooks (`http://jupyter.org`) that you can find via Git from `https://github.com/PacktPublishing/Building-Machine-Learning-Systems-with-Python-Third-edition`.

If you don't have Jupyter already, simply install it with `pip install jupyter` and then run it with `jupyter notebook`. It provides a much richer experience; for example, it directly integrates charts into it. Once you have cloned the Git repository of the book's code, you can simply follow along by hitting *Shift + Enter*. As a bonus, you will find that it has interactive widgets that let you play with the code:

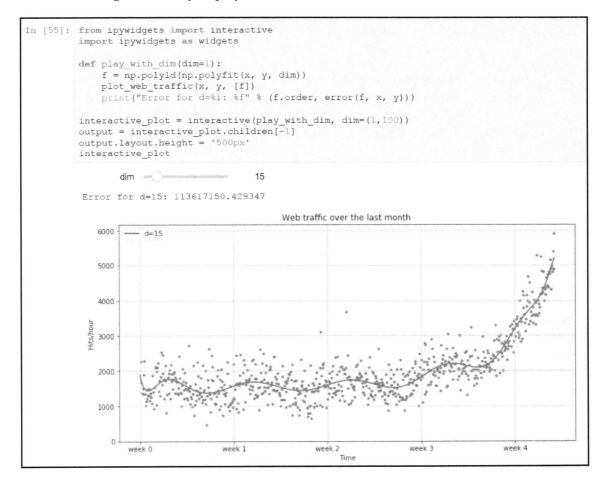

```
In [55]:  from ipywidgets import interactive
          import ipywidgets as widgets

          def play_with_dim(dim=1):
              f = np.poly1d(np.polyfit(x, y, dim))
              plot_web_traffic(x, y, [f])
              print("Error for d=%i: %f" % (f.order, error(f, x, y)))

          interactive_plot = interactive(play_with_dim, dim=(1,100))
          output = interactive_plot.children[-1]
          output.layout.height = '500px'
          interactive_plot
```

```
          dim  ⟶○⋯⋯⋯⋯⋯⋯⋯⋯⋯⋯⋯        15

          Error for d=15: 113617150.429347
```

What to do when you are stuck

We have tried to convey every idea necessary to reproduce the steps throughout this book. Nevertheless, there will be situations where you are stuck. The reasons might range from simple typos over odd combinations of package versions to problems in understanding.

There are many different ways to get help. Most likely, your problem will already have been raised and solved in the following excellent Q&A sites:

- `http://stats.stackexchange.com`: This Q&A site is named Cross Validated, similar to MetaOptimize, but is focused more on statistical problems.
- `http://stackoverflow.com`: This Q&A site is much like the previous one, but with a broader focus on general programming topics. It contains, for example, more questions on some of the packages that we will use in this book, such as SciPy or Matplotlib.
- `https://freenode.net/`: This is the IRC channel focused on machine learning topics. It is a small but very active and helpful community of machine learning experts.

As stated at the beginning, this book is intended to help you get started quickly on your machine learning journey. Therefore, we highly encourage you to build up your own list of machine learning-related blogs and check them out regularly. This is the best way to get to know what works and what doesn't.

The only blog we want to highlight right here (though there there are more in the appendix) is `http://blog.kaggle.com`, the blog of the company, Kaggle, which hosts machine learning competitions. Typically, they encourage the winners of the competitions to write down how they approached the competition, what strategies did not work, and how they arrived at the winning strategy. Even if you don't read anything else, this is a must.

Getting started

Assuming that you have Python already installed (anything at least as recent as 3 should be fine), we need to install NumPy and SciPy for numerical operations, as well as Matplotlib for visualization.

Introduction to NumPy, SciPy, Matplotlib, and TensorFlow

Before we can talk about concrete machine learning algorithms, we have to talk about how best to store the data we will chew through. This is important as the most advanced learning algorithm will not be of any help to us if it will never finish. This may be simply because the mere process of accessing the data is too slow, or maybe its representation forces the operating system to swap all day. Add to this the fact that Python is an interpreted language (a highly optimized one, though) that is slow for many numerically heavy algorithms compared to C or Fortran. So we might ask why on earth so many scientists and companies are betting their fortune on Python even in highly computation-intensive areas.

The answer is that, in Python, it is very easy to offload number crunching tasks to the lower layer in the form of C or Fortran extensions, and that is exactly what NumPy and SciPy do (see `https://scipy.org`). NumPy provides the support of highly optimized multidimensional arrays, which are the basic data structure of most state-of-the-art algorithms. SciPy uses those arrays to provide a set of fast numerical recipes. Matplotlib (`http://matplotlib.org`) is probably the most convenient and feature-rich library to plot high-quality graphs using Python. Finally, TensorFlow is one of the leading neural network packages for Python (we will explain what this package is about in a subsequent chapter).

Installing Python

Luckily, for all major operating systems—that is, Windows, Mac, and Linux—there are targeted installers for NumPy, SciPy, Matplotlib, and TensorFlow. If you are unsure about the installation process, you might want to install the Anaconda Python distribution (which you can access at `https://www.anaconda.com/download`), which is maintained and developed by Travis Oliphant, a founding contributor of SciPy. Luckily, Anaconda is already fully compatible with Python 3—the Python version we will be using throughout this book.

The main Anaconda channel comes with three flavors of TensorFlow (use the Intel channel at your own risk, that is an older version of TensorFlow). The main flavor, `tensorflow`, is compiled for all platforms and runs on the CPU. If you have a Haswell CPU or a more recent Intel one, you can use the `tensorflow-mkl` package. Finally, if you have an Nvidia GPU with a compute capability of 3.0 or higher, you can use `tensorflow-gpu`.

Chewing data efficiently with NumPy and intelligently with SciPy

Let's walk quickly through some basic NumPy examples and then take a look at what SciPy provides on top of it. On the way, we will get our feet wet with plotting using the marvelous `matplotlib` package.

For an in-depth explanation, you might want to take a look at some of the more interesting examples of what NumPy has to offer at `https://docs.scipy.org/doc/numpy/user/quickstart.html`.

You will also find the *NumPy Beginner's Guide - Second Edition* by Ivan Idris, from Packt Publishing, very valuable. Additional tutorial style guides can be found at `http://www.scipy-lectures.org`, and the official SciPy tutorial can be found at `http://docs.scipy.org/doc/scipy/reference/tutorial`.

In this book, we will use NumPy in version 1.13.3 and SciPy in version 1.0.0.

Learning NumPy

So, let's import NumPy and play with it a bit. For that, we need to start the Python interactive shell:

```
>>> import numpy
>>> numpy.version.full_version
1.13.3
```

As we do not want to pollute our namespace, we certainly should not use the following code:

```
>>> from numpy import *
```

If we do this, then, for instance, `numpy.array` will potentially shadow the array package that is included in standard Python. Instead, we will use the following convenient shortcut:

```
>>> import numpy as np
>>> a = np.array([0,1,2,3,4,5])
>>> a
array([0, 1, 2, 3, 4, 5])
>>> a.ndim
1
>>> a.shape
(6,)
```

With the previous code snippet, we created an array in the same way that we would create a list in Python. However, the NumPy arrays have additional information about the shape. In this case, it is a one-dimensional array of six elements. That's no surprise so far.

We can now transform this array into a two-dimensional matrix:

```
>>> b = a.reshape((3,2))
>>> b
array([[0, 1],
       [2, 3],
       [4, 5]])
>>> b.ndim
2
>>> b.shape
(3, 2)
```

It is important to realize just how much the NumPy package is optimized. For example, doing the following avoids copies wherever possible:

```
>>> b[1][0] = 77
>>> b
array([[ 0, 1],
       [77, 3],
       [ 4, 5]])
>>> a
array([ 0, 1, 77, 3, 4, 5])
```

In this case, we have modified the value 2 to 77 in b, and we immediately see the same change reflected in a, as well. Keep in mind that whenever you need a true copy, you can always perform the following:

```
>>> c = a.reshape((3,2)).copy()
>>> c
array([[ 0, 1],
       [77, 3],
```

```
            [ 4,  5]])
>>> c[0][0] = -99
>>> a
array([ 0,  1, 77,  3,  4,  5])
>>> c
array([[-99,  1],
       [ 77,  3],
       [  4,  5]])
```

Note that, here, c and a are totally independent copies.

Another big advantage of NumPy arrays is that the operations are propagated to the individual elements. For example, multiplying a NumPy array will result in an array of the same size (including all of its elements) being multiplied:

```
>>> d = np.array([1,2,3,4,5])
>>> d*2
array([ 2,  4,  6,  8, 10])
```

This is also true for other operations:

```
>>> d**2
array([ 1,  4,  9, 16, 25])
```

Contrast that with ordinary Python lists:

```
>>> [1,2,3,4,5]*2
[1, 2, 3, 4, 5, 1, 2, 3, 4, 5]
>>> [1,2,3,4,5]**2
Traceback (most recent call last):
  File "<stdin>", line 1, in <module>
TypeError: unsupported operand type(s) for ** or pow(): 'list' and 'int'
```

Of course, by using NumPy arrays, we sacrifice the agility Python lists offer. Simple operations, such as adding or removing elements, are a bit complex for NumPy arrays. Luckily, we have both at our hands, and we will use the right one for the task at hand.

Indexing

Part of the power of NumPy comes from the versatile ways in which its arrays can be accessed.

In addition to normal list indexing, it allows you to use arrays themselves as indices by performing the following:

```
>>> a[np.array([2,3,4])]
array([77, 3, 4])
```

Coupled with the fact that conditions are also propagated to individual elements, we gain a very convenient way to access our data, using the following:

```
>>> a>4
array([False, False, True, False, False, True], dtype=bool)
>>> a[a>4]
array([77, 5])
```

By performing the following command, we can trim outliers:

```
>>> a[a>4] = 4
>>> a
array([0, 1, 4, 3, 4, 4])
```

As this is a frequent use case, there is a special `clip` function for it, clipping the values at both ends of an interval with one function call:

```
>>> a.clip(0,4)
array([0, 1, 4, 3, 4, 4])
```

Handling nonexistent values

The power of NumPy's indexing capabilities comes in handy when preprocessing data that we have just read in from a text file. Most likely, this will contain invalid values that we will mark as not being real numbers, using numpy.NAN, as shown in the following code:

```
>>> # let's pretend we have read this from a text file:
>>> c = np.array([1, 2, np.NAN, 3, 4])
array([ 1., 2., nan, 3., 4.])
>>> np.isnan(c)
array([False, False, True, False, False], dtype=bool)
>>> c[~np.isnan(c)]
array([ 1., 2., 3., 4.])
>>> np.mean(c[~np.isnan(c)])
2.5
```

Comparing the runtime

Let's compare the runtime behavior of NumPy to normal Python lists. In the following code, we will calculate the sum of all squared numbers from 1 to 1,000 and see how much time it will take. We will perform it 10,000 times and report the total time so that our measurement is accurate enough:

```
import timeit

normal_py_sec = timeit.timeit('sum(x*x for x in range(1000))',
                                number=10000)
naive_np_sec = timeit.timeit('sum(na*na)',
                                setup="import numpy as np;
na=np.arange(1000)",
                                number=10000)
good_np_sec = timeit.timeit('na.dot(na)',
                                setup="import numpy as np; na=np.arange(1000)",
                                number=10000)

print("Normal Python: %f sec" % normal_py_sec)
print("Naive NumPy: %f sec" % naive_np_sec)
print("Good NumPy: %f sec" % good_np_sec)
```

Executing this will output

```
Normal Python: 1.571072 sec
Naive NumPy: 1.621358 sec
Good NumPy: 0.035686 sec
```

We can make two interesting observations from this code. Firstly, just using NumPy as data storage (naive NumPy) takes longer, which is surprising since it seems it should be much faster, as it is written as a C extension. One reason for this increased processing time is that the access of individual elements from Python itself is rather costly. Only when we are able to apply algorithms inside the optimized extension code do we get speed improvements. The other observation is quite a tremendous one: using the dot () function of NumPy, which does exactly the same, allows us to be more than 44 times faster. In summary, in every algorithm we are about to implement, we should always look at how we can move loops over individual elements from Python to some of the highly optimized NumPy or SciPy extension functions.

However, this speed comes at a price. Using NumPy arrays, we no longer have the incredible flexibility of Python lists, which can hold basically anything. NumPy arrays always have only one data type:

```
>>> a = np.array([1,2,3])
>>> a.dtype
dtype('int32')
```

If we try to use elements of different types, such as the ones shown in the following code, NumPy will do its best to correct them to be the most reasonable common data type:

```
>>> np.array([1, "stringy"])
array(['1', 'stringy'], dtype='<U11')
>>> np.array([1, "stringy", {1, 2, 3}])
array([1, 'stringy', {1, 2, 3}], dtype=object)
```

Learning SciPy

On top of the efficient data structures of NumPy, SciPy offers a magnitude of algorithms for working on those arrays. Whatever numerical heavy algorithm you take from current books on numerical recipes, you will most likely find support for them in SciPy in one way or another. Whether it is matrix manipulation, linear algebra, optimization, clustering, spatial operations, or even fast Fourier transformation, the toolbox is readily filled. Therefore, it is a good habit to always inspect the `scipy` module before you start implementing a numerical algorithm.

For convenience, the complete namespace of NumPy is also accessible via SciPy. So, from now on, we will use NumPy's machinery via the SciPy namespace. You can check this by easily comparing the function references of any base function, such as the following:

```
>>> import scipy, numpy
>>> scipy.version.full_version
1.0.0
>>> scipy.dot is numpy.dot
True
```

The diverse algorithms are grouped into the following toolboxes:

SciPy packages	Functionalities
`cluster`	Hierarchical clustering (`cluster.hierarchy`) Vector quantization/K-means (`cluster.vq`)
`constants`	Physical and mathematical constants Conversion methods
`fftpack`	Discrete Fourier transform algorithms
`integrate`	Integration routines
`interpolate`	Interpolation (linear, cubic, and so on)
`io`	Data input and output
`linalg`	Linear algebra routines using the optimized `BLAS` and `LAPACK` libraries
`ndimage`	n-dimensional image package
`odr`	Orthogonal distance regression
`optimize`	Optimization (finding minima and roots)
`signal`	Signal processing
`sparse`	Sparse matrices
`spatial`	Spatial data structures and algorithms
`special`	Special mathematical functions, such as Bessel or Jacobian
`stats`	Statistics toolkit

The toolboxes that are most pertinent to our goals are `scipy.stats`, `scipy.interpolate`, `scipy.cluster`, and `scipy.signal`. For the sake of brevity, we will briefly explore some features of the `stats` package and explain the others when they show up in the individual chapters.

Fundamentals of machine learning

In machine learning, what we are doing is asking a question and answering it. From the samples we have, we create a question that is the learning aspect of the model. Answering the question involves using the model for new samples.

Asking a question

If the workflow involves preprocessing the features, followed by model training, and finally model usage, then the preprocessing features step can be linked to the assumptions that we make when asking a question. For instance, the question can be, "Are these images of cats, knowing that cats have two ears, two eyes, a nose, a mouth, and whiskers?"

Our assumptions here are linked to how the images will be preprocessed to get the number of ears, eyes, noses, mouths, and whiskers. This data will be fed into the model during training so that we get answers.

Getting answers

Once the model is trained, we use the same features to get our answer. Of course, with the question we asked earlier, if we feed in images of cats, we will get a positive answer. But if we feed in an image of a tiger, a lion, or a dog, we will also get a positive identification. So the question we asked is not, "Are these images of cats?", but really, "Are these images of cats, knowing that cats have two ears, two eyes, a nose, a mouth, and whiskers?". Our definition of a cat was wrong and lead us to wrong answers.

This is where know-how and practice are important. Designing the right model to answer the question you have been asked is something that anyone can do once this important point has been understood.

Our first (tiny) application of machine learning

Let's get our hands dirty and take a look at our hypothetical web start-up, MLaaS, which sells the service of providing machine learning algorithms via HTTP. With the increasing success of our company, the demand for better infrastructure also increases so that we can serve all incoming web requests successfully. We don't want to allocate too many resources as that would be too costly. On the other hand, we will lose money if we have not reserved enough resources to serve all incoming requests. Now, the question is, when will we hit the limit of our current infrastructure, which we estimated to have a capacity of about 100,000 requests per hour? We would like to know in advance when we have to request additional servers in the cloud to serve all the incoming requests successfully without paying for unused ones.

Reading in the data

We have collected the web statistics for the last month and aggregated them in a file named `ch01/data/web_traffic.tsv` (`.tsv` because it contains tab-separated values). They are stored as the number of hits per hour. Each line contains the hour and the number of web hits in that hour. The hours are listed consecutively.

Using SciPy's `genfromtxt()`, we can easily read in the data using the following code:

```
>>> data = np.genfromtxt("web_traffic.tsv", delimiter="\t")
```

We have to specify tabs as the delimiter so that the columns are correctly determined. A quick check shows that we have correctly read in the data:

```
>>> print(data[:10])
[[  1.00000000e+00  2.27333105e+03]
 [  2.00000000e+00  1.65725549e+03]
 [  3.00000000e+00  nan]
 [  4.00000000e+00  1.36684644e+03]
 [  5.00000000e+00  1.48923438e+03]
 [  6.00000000e+00  1.33802002e+03]
 [  7.00000000e+00  1.88464734e+03]
 [  8.00000000e+00  2.28475415e+03]
 [  9.00000000e+00  1.33581091e+03]
 [  1.00000000e+01  1.02583240e+03]]
>>> print(data.shape)
(743, 2)
```

As you can see, we have 743 data points with 2 dimensions.

Preprocessing and cleaning the data

It is more convenient for SciPy to separate the dimensions into two vectors, each the size of 743 data points. The first vector, x, will contain the hours, and the other, y, will contain the web hits in that particular hour. This splitting is done using the special index notation of SciPy, by which we can choose the columns individually:

```
x = data[:,0]
y = data[:,1]
```

There are many more ways in which data can be selected from a SciPy array. Check out https://docs.scipy.org/doc/numpy/user/quickstart.html for more details on indexing, slicing, and iterating.

One caveat is that we still have some values in *y* that contain invalid values, such as nan. The question is what we can do with them. Let's check how many hours contain invalid data by running the following code:

```
>>> np.sum(np.isnan(y))
8
```

As you can see, we are missing only 8 out of 743 entries, so we can afford to remove them. Remember that we can index a SciPy array with another array. The Sp.isnan(y) phrase returns an array of Booleans indicating whether an entry is a number or not. Using ~, we logically negate that array so that we choose only those elements from *x* and *y* where *y* contains valid numbers:

```
>>> x = x[~np.isnan(y)]
>>> y = y[~np.isnan(y)]
```

To get the first impression of our data, let's plot the data in a scatter plot using matplotlib. Matplotlib contains the pyplot package, which tries to mimic MATLAB's interface, which is a very convenient and easy-to-use interface, as you can see in the following code:

```
import matplotlib.pyplot as plt

def plot_web_traffic(x, y, models=None):
    '''
    Plot the web traffic (y) over time (x).
    If models is given, it is expected to be a list of fitted models,
    which will be plotted as well (used later in this chapter).
    '''
    plt.figure(figsize=(12,6)) # width and height of the plot in inches
    plt.scatter(x, y, s=10)
    plt.title("Web traffic over the last month")

    plt.xlabel("Time")
    plt.ylabel("Hits/hour")
    plt.xticks([w*7*24 for w in range(5)],
                ['week %i' %(w+1) for w in range(5)])
    if models:
        colors = ['g', 'k', 'b', 'm', 'r']
        linestyles = ['-', '-.', '--', ':', '-']

        mx = sp.linspace(0, x[-1], 1000)
```

```
        for model, style, color in zip(models, linestyles, colors):
            plt.plot(mx, model(mx), linestyle=style, linewidth=2, c=color)

        plt.legend(["d=%i" % m.order for m in models], loc="upper left")
    plt.autoscale(tight=True)
    plt.grid()
```

The main command here is `plt.scatter(x, y, s=10)`, which plots the web traffic in y over the individual days in x. With s=10 we are setting the line width. Then we are dressing up the chart a bit (title, labels, grid, and so on) and finally we provide the possibility to add additional models to it.

 You can find more tutorials on plotting at `http://matplotlib.org/users/pyplot_tutorial.html`.

You can run this function with the following:

```
>>> plot_web_traffic(x, y)
```

We will see what happens if you are in a Jupyter notebook session and have run the following command:

```
>>> %matplotlib inline
```

In one of the cells of the notebook, Jupyter will automatically show the generated graphs inline, using the following code:

```
>>> plot_web_traffic(x, y)
```

If you are in a normal command shell, you will have to save the graph to disk and then display it later with an image viewer:

```
>>> plt.savefig("web_traffic.png"))
```

In the resulting chart, we can see that while in the first weeks the traffic stayed more or less the same, the last week shows a steep increase:

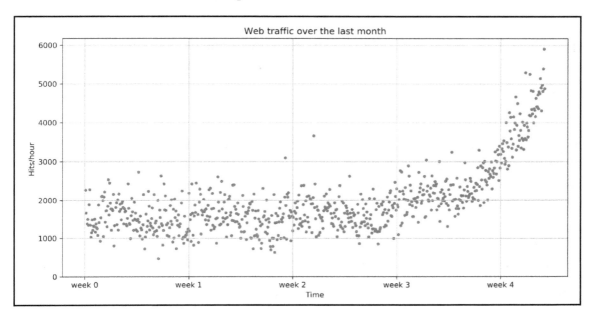

Choosing the right model and learning algorithm

Now that we have a first impression of the data, we return to the initial question: how long will our server be able to handle the incoming web traffic? To answer this, we have to do the following:

1. Find the real model behind the noisy data points
2. Use the model to find the point in time where our infrastructure won't handle the load anymore and has to be extended

Before we build our first model

When we talk about models, you can think of them as simplified theoretical approximations of complex reality. As such, there is always some inferiority involved, also called the approximation error. This error will guide us in choosing the right model among the many choices we have. We will calculate this error as the squared distance of the model's prediction to the real data; for example, for a learned model function, f, the error is calculated as follows:

```
def error(f, x, y):
    return np.sum((f(x)-y)**2)
```

The vectors x and y contain the web stats data that we extracted earlier. It is the beauty of NumPy's vectorized functions, which we exploit here with f(x). The trained model is assumed to take a vector and return the results again as a vector of the same size so that we can use it to calculate the difference to y.

Starting with a simple straight line

Let's assume for a second that the underlying model is a straight line. Then the challenge is how to best put that line into the chart so that it results in the smallest approximation error. SciPy's polyfit() function does exactly that. Given data x and y and the desired order of the polynomial (a straight line has an order of 1), it finds the model function that minimizes the error function defined earlier:

```
fp1 = np.polyfit(x, y, 1)
```

The polyfit() function returns the parameters of the fitted Model function, fp1:

```
>>> print("Model parameters: %s" % fp1)
Model parameters: [ 2.59619213 989.02487106]
```

This means the best straight line fit is the following function:

```
f(x) = 2.59619213 * x + 989.02487106
```

We then use poly1d() to create a model function from the model parameters:

```
>>> f1 = np.poly1d(fp1)
>>> print(error(f1, x, y))
317389767.34
```

We can now use `f1()` to plot our first trained model. We have already implemented `plot_web_traffic` in a way that lets us easily add additional models to plot. In addition, we pass a list of models, of which we currently have only one:

```
plot_web_traffic(x, y, [f1])
```

This will produce the following plot:

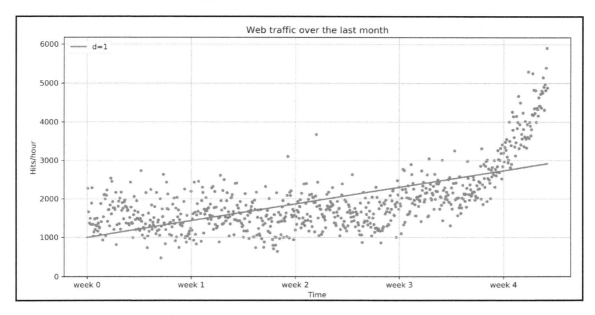

It seems like the first four weeks are not that far off, although we can clearly see that there is something wrong with our initial assumption that the underlying model is a straight line. Also, how good or how bad actually is the error of `319,531,507.008`?

The absolute value of the error is seldom of use in isolation. However, when comparing two competing models, we can use their errors to judge which one of them is better. Although our first model clearly is not the one we would use, it serves a very important purpose in the workflow. We will use it as our baseline until we find a better one. Whatever model we come up with in the future, we will compare it against the current baseline.

Toward more complex models

Let's now fit a more complex model, a polynomial of degree 2, to see whether it better understands our data:

```
>>> f2p = np.polyfit(x, y, 2)
>>> print(f2p)
[ 1.05605675e-02 -5.29774287e+00 1.98466917e+03]
>>> f2 = np.poly1d(f2p)
>>> print(error(f2, x, y))
181347660.764
```

With `plot_web_traffic(x, y, [f1, f2])` we can see how a function of degree 2 manages to model our web traffic data:

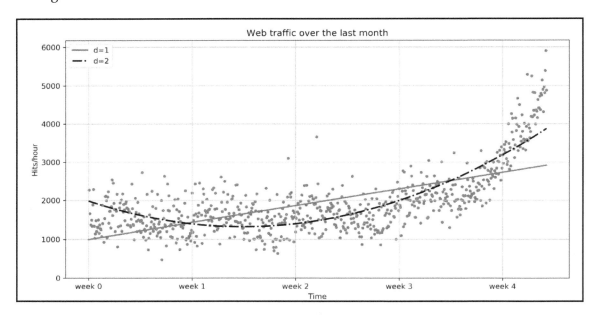

The error is `181,347,660.764`, which is almost half the error of the straight-line model. This is good, but unfortunately this comes at a price: we now have a more complex function, meaning that we have one more parameter to tune inside `polyfit()`. The fitted polynomial is as follows:

```
f(x) = 0.0105605675 * x**2 - 5.29774287 * x + 1984.66917
```

So, if more complexity gives better results, why not increase the complexity even more? Let's try it for degrees 3, 10, and 100:

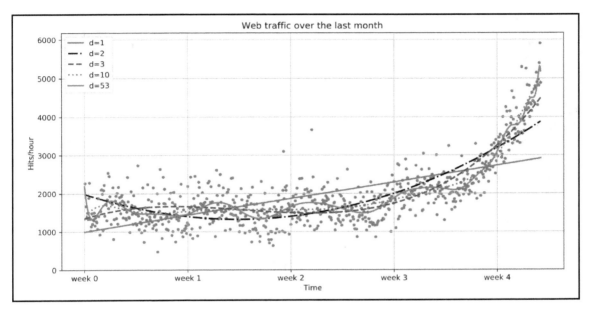

Interestingly, we do not see **d = 100** for the polynomial that had been fitted with 100 degrees, but instead **d = 53**. This has to do with the warning we get when fitting 100 degrees:

```
RankWarning: Polyfit may be poorly conditioned
```

This means that, because of numerical errors, `polyfit` cannot determine a good fit with 100 degrees. Instead, it figured that 53 would be good enough.

It seems like the curves capture the fitted data better the more complex they get. The errors seem to tell the same story:

```
>>> print("Errors for the complete data set:")
>>> for f in [f1, f2, f3, f10, f100]:
...     print("td=%i: %f" % (f.order, error(f, x, y)))
...
```

The errors for the complete dataset are as follows:

- d=1: 319,531,507.008126
- d=2: 181,347,660.764236
- d=3: 140,576,460.879141
- d=10: 123,426,935.754101
- d=53: 110,768,263.808878

However, taking a closer look at the fitted curves, we start to wonder whether they also capture the true process that generated that data. Framed differently, do our models correctly represent the underlying mass behavior of customers visiting our website? Looking at the polynomials of degree 10 and 53, we see wildly oscillating behavior. It seems that the models are fitted too much to the data. So much so that the graph is now capturing not only the underlying process, but also the noise. This is called **overfitting**.

At this point, we have the following choices:

- Choose one of the fitted polynomial models
- Switch to another more complex model class
- Think differently about the data and start again

Out of the five fitted models, the first-order model is clearly too simple, and the models of order 10 and 53 are clearly overfitting. Only the second- and third-order models seem to somehow match the data. However, if we extrapolate them at both borders, we see them going berserk.

Switching to a more complex class also doesn't seem to be the right way to go. Which arguments would back which class? At this point, we realize that we have probably not fully understood our data.

Stepping back to go forward - another look at our data

So, we step back and take another look at the data. It seems that there is an inflection point between weeks 3 and 4. Let's separate the data and train two lines using week 3.5 as a separation point:

```
>>> inflection = int(3.5*7*24) # calculate the inflection point in hours
>>> xa = x[:inflection] # data before the inflection point
>>> ya = y[:inflection]
>>> xb = x[inflection:] # data after
>>> yb = y[inflection:]

>>> fa = sp.poly1d(sp.polyfit(xa, ya, 1))
>>> fb = sp.poly1d(sp.polyfit(xb, yb, 1))

>>> fa_error = error(fa, xa, ya)
>>> fb_error = error(fb, xb, yb)
>>> print("Error inflection=%f" % (fa_error + fb_error))

Error inflection=132950348.197616
```

From the first line (straight), we train with the data up to week 3, and in the second line (dashed), we train with the remaining data:

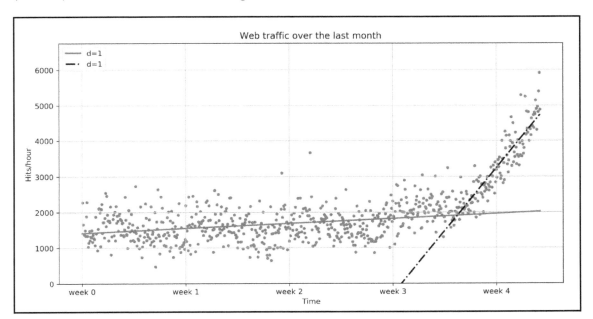

Clearly, the combination of these two lines seems to be a much better fit to the data than anything we have modeled before. But still, the combined error is higher than the higher order polynomials. Can we trust the error at the end?

Asked differently, why do we trust the straight line fitted only during the last week of our data more than any of the more complex models? It is because we assume that it will capture future data better. If we plot the models into the future, we can see how right we are (**d = 1** is again our initial straight line):

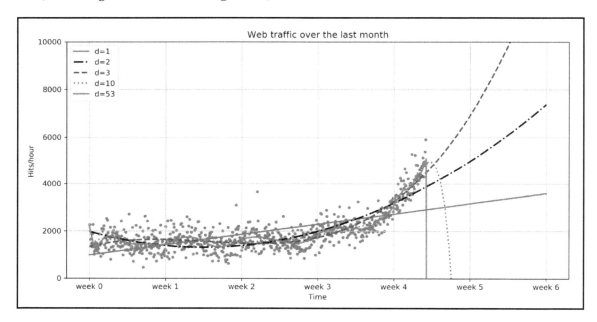

The models of degree 10 and 53 don't seem to expect a bright future of our start-up. They tried so hard to model the given data correctly that they are clearly useless to extrapolate beyond. This is called overfitting.

On the other hand, the lower degree models seem not to be capable of capturing the data well enough. This is called **underfitting**.

So, let's play fair to models of degree 2 and more and look at how they behave if we fit them only to the data of the last week. After all, we believe that the last week says more about the future than the data prior to it. The result can be seen in the following psychedelic chart, which further shows how bad the problem of overfitting is:

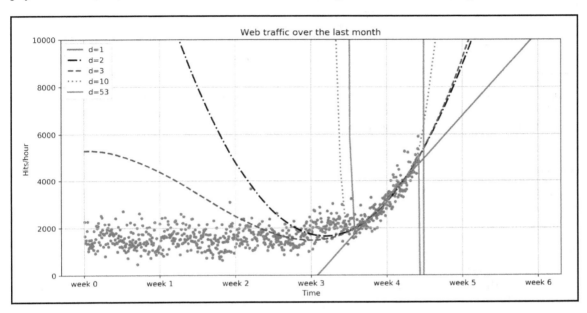

See following commands:

```
>>> fb1 = np.poly1d(np.polyfit(xb, yb, 1))
>>> fb2 = np.poly1d(np.polyfit(xb, yb, 2))
>>> fb3 = np.poly1d(np.polyfit(xb, yb, 3))
>>> fb10 = np.poly1d(np.polyfit(xb, yb, 10))
>>> fb100 = np.poly1d(np.polyfit(xb, yb, 100))

>>> print("Errors for only the time after inflection point")
>>> for f in [fb1, fb2, fb3, fb10, fb100]:
...     print("td=%i: %f" % (f.order, error(f, xb, yb)))

>>> plot_web_traffic(x, y, [fb1, fb2, fb3, fb10, fb100],
...     mx=np.linspace(0, 6 * 7 * 24, 100),
...     ymax=10000)
```

Following table shows errors and time after inflection point:

Errors	Time after inflection point
d = 1	22140590.598233
d = 2	19764355.660080
d = 3	19762196.404203
d = 10:	18942545.482218
d = 53:	18293880.824253

Still, judging from the errors of the models when trained only on the data from week 3.5 and later, we should still choose the most complex one (note that we also calculate the error when trained only on datapoints that occur after the inflection point).

Training and testing

If we only had some data from the future that we could use to measure our models against, then we should be able to judge our model choice only on the resulting approximation error.

Although we cannot look into the future, we can and should simulate a similar effect by holding out a part of our data. Let's remove, for instance, a certain percentage of the data and train on the remaining one. Then, we use the held-out data to calculate the error. As the model has been trained without knowing the held-out data, we should get a more realistic picture of how the model will behave in the future.

The test errors for the models trained only on the time after the inflection point now show a completely different picture:

- d=1: 6492812.705336
- d=2: 5008335.504620
- d=3: 5006519.831510
- d=10: 5440767.696731
- d=53: 5369417.148129

Have a look at the following plot:

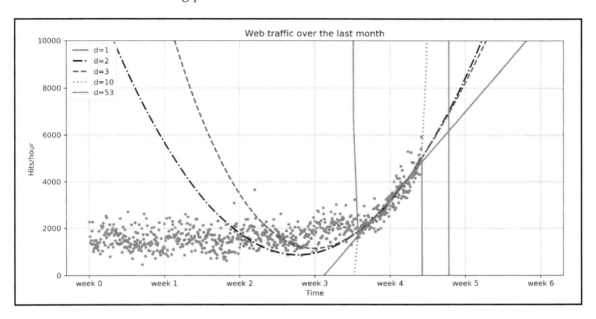

It seems the model with the degrees 2 and 3 has the lowest test error, which is the error that is shown when measured using data that the model did not see during training. This gives us hope that we won't get bad surprises when future data arrives. However, we are not fully done yet.

We will see in the next plot why we cannot simply pick the model with the lowest error:

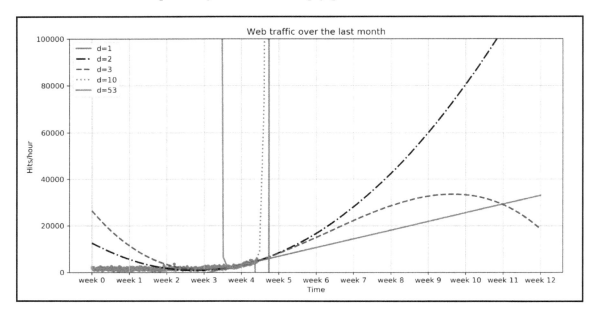

The model with degree 3 does not foresee a future in which we will ever get 100,000 hits per hour. So we stick with degree 2.

Answering our initial question

We have finally arrived at some models that we think can represent the underlying process best. It is now a simple matter of finding out when our infrastructure will reach 100,000 requests per hour. We have to calculate when our model function reaches the value of 100,000. Because both models (degree 2 and 3) were so close together, we will do it for both.

With a polynomial of degree 2, we could simply compute the inverse of the function and calculate its value at 100,000. Of course, we would like to have an approach that is easily applicable to any model function.

This can be done by subtracting 100,000 from the polynomial, which results in another polynomial, and finding its root. SciPy's `optimize` module has the `fsolve` function to achieve this, when provided an initial starting position with the x0 parameter. As every entry in our input data file corresponds to one hour, and we have `743` of them, we set the starting position to some value after that. Let `fbt2` be the winning polynomial of degree 2:

```
>>> fbt2 = np.poly1d(np.polyfit(xb[train], yb[train], 2))
>>> print("fbt2(x)= n%s" % fbt2)
fbt2(x)=
         2
0.05404 x - 50.39 x + 1.262e+04

>>> print("fbt2(x)-100,000= n%s" % (fbt2-100000))
fbt2(x)-100,000=
         2
0.05404 x - 50.39 x - 8.738e+04

>>> from scipy.optimize import fsolve
>>> reached_max = fsolve(fbt2-100000, x0=800)/(7*24)

>>> print("100,000 hits/hour expected at week %f" % reached_max[0])
100,000 hits/hour expected at week 10.836350
```

It is expected to have 100,000 hits/hour at week `10.836350`, so our model tells us that, given the current user behavior and traction of our start-up, it will take a couple more weeks for us to reach our capacity threshold.

Of course, there is a certain uncertainty involved with our prediction. To get a real picture of it, one could draw in more sophisticated statistics to find the variance we can expect when looking further and further into the future.

There are also the user and underlying user behavior dynamics that we cannot model accurately. However, at this point, we are fine with the current prediction as it is good enough to answer our initial question of when we would have to increase the capacity of our system. If we then monitor our web traffic closely, we will see in time when we have to allocate new resources.

Summary

Congratulations! You just learned two important things, of which the most important is that, as a typical machine learning operator, you will spend most of your time understanding and refining the data—exactly what we just did in our first, tiny machine learning example. We hope that this example helped you to start switching your mental focus from algorithms to data.

Then, you learned how important it is to have the correct experiment setup, and that it is vital to not mix up training and testing. Admittedly, the use of polynomial fitting is not the coolest thing in the machine learning world; we chose it so that you would not be distracted by the coolness of some shiny algorithm when we conveyed those two most important messages we mentioned earlier.

So, let's move on to `Chapter 2`, *Classifying with Real-world Examples*, we are on the topic of classification. Now, we will apply the concepts on a very specific, but very important, type of data, namely text.

Classifying with Real-World Examples

2

The topic of this chapter is **classification**. In this setting of machine learning, you provide the system with examples of different classes of objects that you are interested in and then ask it to generalize to new examples where the class is not known. This may seem abstract, but you have probably already used this form of machine learning as a consumer, even if you were not aware of it: your email system will likely have the ability to automatically detect spam. That is, the system will analyze all incoming emails and mark them as either spam or not spam. Often, you, the end user, will be able to manually tag emails as spam or not, in order to improve its spam detection ability. This is exactly what we mean by classification: you provide examples of spam and and non-spam emails and then use an automated system to classify incoming emails. This is one of the most important machine learning modes and is the topic of this chapter.

Working with text such as emails requires a specific set of techniques and skills, and we discuss those later in the book. For the moment, we will work with a smaller, easier-to-handle dataset. The example question for this chapter is: can a machine distinguish between flower species based on images? We will use two datasets where measurements of flower morphology are recorded along with the species for several specimens.

We will explore these small datasets in order to focus on the high-level concepts. The important elements of this chapter are the following:

- What classification is
- How scikit-learn can be used for classification and which classifier is a good solution for most problems
- How to strictly evaluate a classifier and avoid fooling ourselves

The Iris dataset

The Iris dataset is a classic dataset from the 1930s; it is one of the first modern examples of statistical classification.

The dataset is a collection of morphological measurements of several iris flowers. These measurements will enable us to distinguish multiple species of flower. Today, species are identified by their DNA fingerprints, but in the 1930s, DNA's role in genetics had not yet been discovered.

The following four attributes of each plant were measured:

- Sepal length
- Sepal width
- Petal length
- Petal width

In general, we call the individual numeric measurements we use to describe our data **features**. These features can be directly measured or computed from intermediate data.

This dataset has four features. Additionally, for each plant, the species is recorded. The problem we want to solve is: "given these examples, if we see a new flower out in the field, could we make a good prediction about its species from its measurements?

This is the **classification** problem: given labeled examples, can we design a rule to be later applied to other examples?

Later in the book, we will look at problems dealing with text. For the moment, the Iris dataset serves our purposes well. It is small (150 examples, four features each) and can be easily visualized and manipulated.

Visualization is a good first step

Datasets later in the book will grow to thousands of features. With only four features in our starting example, we can easily plot all two-dimensional projections on a single page and build predictions, which can then be extended to large datasets with many more features. As we saw in `Chapter 3`, *Regression*, visualizations are excellent in the initial exploratory phase of the analysis as they allow you to learn the general features of your problem as well as catch problems that occurred with data collection early.

Each subplot in the following plot shows all points projected into two of the dimensions. The outlying group (triangles) are the Iris Setosa plants, while Iris Versicolor plants are in the center (circle) and Iris Virginica are plotted with *x* marks. We can see that there are two large groups. One is of Iris Setosa and another is a mixture of Iris Versicolor and Iris Virginica:

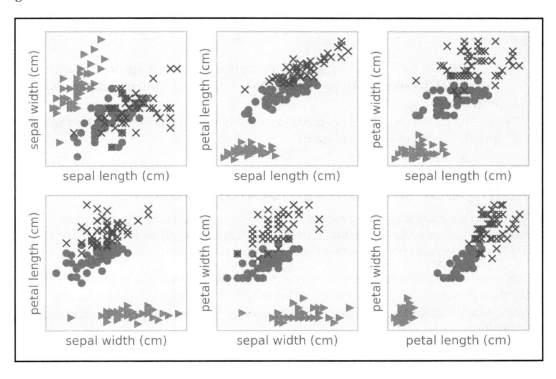

Here is the code to load the dataset (you can find the plotting code in the online repository):

```
from sklearn.datasets import load_iris
data = load_iris()
features = data.data
feature_names = data.feature_names
target = data.target
target_names = data.target_names
labels = target_names[target]
```

Classifying with scikit-learn

Python is an excellent language for machine learning because of its excellent libraries. In particular, scikit-learn has become the standard library for many machine learning tasks, including classification. We are going to use its implementation of decision trees in this section and in other classifiers. Fortunately, classifiers in scikit-learn follow the same API, thus making it easy to change from one to another. These objects have the following two essential methods:

- `fit(features, labels)`: This is the learning step and fits the parameters of the model. It takes a list-like object with features and another with labels as arguments.
- `predict(features)`: This method can only be called after fit and returns a prediction for one or more inputs.

Building our first classification model

If the goal is to separate the three types of flowers, we can immediately make a few suggestions just by looking at the data. For example, petal length seems to be able to separate Iris Setosa from the other two flower species on its own.

Intuitively, we can build a simple model in our heads: if the petal width is smaller than about 1, then this is an Iris Setosa flower; otherwise it is either Iris Virginica or Iris Versicolor. Machine learning is when we write code to look for this type of separation automatically.

The problem of recognizing Iris Setosa apart from the other two species was very easy. However, we cannot immediately identify the best cut for distinguishing Iris Virginica from Iris Versicolor. We can even see that we will never achieve perfect separation with a simple rule like, if feature X is above a certain value, then A, or else B.

We can try to combine multiple rules in a **decision tree**. This is one of the simplest models for classification and was one of the first models to be proposed for machine learning. It has the further advantage that the model can be simple to interpret.

With scikit-learn, it is easy to learn a decision tree:

```
from sklearn import tree
tr = tree.DecisionTreeClassifier(min_samples_leaf=10)
tr.fit(features, labels)
```

That's it. Visualizing the tree requires that we first write it out to a file in dot format and then display it:

```
import graphviz
tree.export_graphviz(tr, feature_names=feature_names, round-ed=True,
out_file='decision.dot')

graphviz.Source(open('decision.dot').read())
```

We can see that the first split is petal width and results in two nodes, one node where all the samples are of the first class (denoted by `[50,0,0]`) and the rest of the data (`[0,50,50]`).

How good is this model? We can try it out by applying it to the data (using the `predict` method) and seeing how well it matches with the input:

```
prediction = tr.predict(features)
print("Accuracy: {:.1%}".format(np.mean(prediction == labels)))
```

This prints out the accuracy: `96.0` percent.

Evaluation – holding out data and cross-validation

The model discussed in the previous section is a simple model; it achieves `96.0` percent accuracy of the whole data. However, this evaluation is almost certainly overly optimistic. We used the data to define what the tree would look like, and then we used the same data to evaluate the model. Of course, the model will perform well on this dataset as it was optimized to perform well on it. The reasoning is circular.

What we really want to do is estimate the ability of the model to generalize to new instances. We should measure its performance in instances that the algorithm has not seen at training. Therefore, we are going to do a more rigorous evaluation and use held-out data. To do this, we are going to break up the data into two groups: in one group, we'll train the model, and in the other, we'll test the one we held out of training. The full code, which is an adaptation of the code presented earlier, is available on the online support repository. Its output is as follows:

```
Training accuracy was 96.0%.
Testing accuracy was 94.7%.
```

The result on the training data (which is a subset of the whole data) is the same as before. However, what is important to note is that the result for the testing data is lower than that of the training error. In this case, the difference is very small, but it can be much larger. When using a complex model, it is possible to get 100 percent accuracy in training and do no better than random guessing on testing! While this may surprise an inexperienced machine learner, it is expected that testing accuracy will be lower than the training accuracy.

To understand why, think about how the decision tree works: it defines a series of thresholds on different features. Sometimes it may be very clear where the threshold should be, but there are areas where even a single datapoint can change the threshold and move it up or down.

 The accuracy on the training data, the **training accuracy**, is almost always an overly optimistic estimate of how well your algorithm is doing. We should always measure and report the **testing accuracy**, which is the accuracy on a collection of examples that were not used for training.

One possible problem with what we just did is that we only used half the data for training. Perhaps it would have been better to use more training data. On the other hand, if we then leave too little data for testing, the error estimation is performed on a very small number of examples. Ideally, we would like to use all of the data for training and all of the data for testing as well, which is impossible.

We can achieve a good approximation of this impossible ideal via a method called **cross-validation**. One simple form of cross-validation is **leave-one-out cross-validation**. We will take an example out of the training data, learn a model without this example, and then test whether the model classifies this example correctly.

This process is then repeated for all the elements in the dataset:

```
predictions = []
for i in range(len(features)):
    train_features = np.delete(features, i, axis=0)
    train_labels = np.delete(labels, i, axis=0)
    tr.fit(train_features, train_labels)
    predictions.append(tr.predict([features[i]]))
predictions = np.array(predictions)
```

At the end of this loop, we will have tested a series of models on all the examples and will have obtained a final average result. When using cross-validation, there is no circularity problem because each example was tested on a model that was built without taking that datapoint into account. Therefore, the cross-validated estimate is a reliable estimate of how well the models will generalize to new data.

The major problem with leave-one-out cross-validation is that we are now forced to perform more work many times. In fact, you must learn a whole new model for each and every example and this cost will increase as our dataset grows.

We can get most of the benefits of leave-one-out at a fraction of the cost by using k-fold cross-validation, where *k* stands for a small number. For example, to perform five-fold cross-validation, we break up the data into five groups, so-called five folds.

Then you learn five models. Each time, you will leave one fold out of the training data. The resulting code will be similar to the code given earlier in this section, but we leave 20 percent of the data out instead of just one element. We test each of these models on the left-out fold and average the results:

Dataset	Fold 1	Fold 2	Fold 3	Fold 4	Fold 5
1	Test	Train	Train	Train	Train
2	Train	Test	Train	Train	Train
3	Train	Train	Test	Train	Train
4	Train	Train	Train	Test	Train
5	Train	Train	Train	Train	Test

The preceding diagram illustrates this process for five blocks: the dataset is split into five pieces. For each fold, you hold out one of the blocks for testing and train on the other four. You can use any number of folds you wish. There is a trade-off between computational efficiency (the more folds, the more computation is necessary) and accurate results (the more folds, the closer you are to using the whole of the data for training). Five folds is often a good compromise. This corresponds to training with 80 percent of your data, which should already be close to what you will get from using all the data. If you have little data, you can even consider using 10 or 20 folds. In an extreme case, if you have as many folds as datapoints, you are simply performing leave-one-out cross-validation. On the other hand, if computation time is an issue and you have more data, two or three folds may be the more appropriate choice.

When generating the folds, you need to be careful to keep them balanced. For example, if all of the examples in one fold come from the same class, then the results will not be representative. We will not go into the details of how to do this, because the scikit-learn machine learning package will handle them for you. Here is how to perform five-fold cross-validation with scikit-learn:

```
from sklearn import model_selection
predictions = model_selection.cross_val_predict(
    tr,
    features,
    labels,
    cv=model_selection.LeaveOneOut())
print(np.mean(predictions == labels))
```

We have now generated several models instead of just one. So, what final model do we return and use for new data? The simplest solution is to now train a single overall model on all your training data. The cross-validation loop gives you an estimate of how well this model should generalize.

 A cross-validation schedule allows you to use all your data to estimate whether your methods are doing well. At the end of the cross-validation loop, you can then use all your data to train a final model.

Although it was not properly recognized when machine learning was starting out as a field, nowadays, it is seen as a very bad sign to even discuss the training accuracy of a classification system. This is because the results can be very misleading and even just presenting them marks you as a newbie in machine learning. We always want to measure and compare either the error on a held-out dataset or the error estimated using a cross-validation scheme.

How to measure and compare classifiers

How do we decide which classifier is best? Rarely do we find the perfect solution, the model that never makes any mistakes, so we need to decide which one to use. We used accuracy before, but sometimes it will be better to optimize so that the model makes fewer errors of a specific kind. For example, in spam filtering, it may be worse to delete a good email than to erroneously let a bad email through. In that case, we may want to choose a model that is conservative in throwing out emails rather than the one that just makes the fewest mistakes overall. We can discuss these issues in terms of gain (which we want to maximize) or loss (which we want to minimize). They are equivalent, but sometimes one is more convenient than the other and you will read articles discussing minimizing the loss or maximizing the gain.

In a medical setting, false negatives and false positives are not equivalent. A **false negative** (when the result of a test comes back negative, but that is false) might lead to the patient not receiving treatment for a serious disease. A **false positive** (when the test comes back positive even though the patient does not actually have that disease) might lead to additional tests to confirm this or unnecessary treatment (which can still have costs, including side effects from the treatment, but are often less serious than missing a diagnostic). Therefore, depending on the exact setting, different trade-offs can make sense. In one extreme, if the disease is fatal and the treatment is cheap with very few negative side effects, then you want to minimize false negatives as much as you can.

What the gain/cost function should be is always dependent on the exact problem you are working on. When we present a general-purpose algorithm, we often focus on minimizing the number of mistakes, achieving the highest accuracy. However, if some mistakes are costlier than others, it might be better to accept a lower overall accuracy to minimize the overall costs.

A more complex dataset and the nearest-neighbor classifier

We will now look at a slightly more complex dataset. This will include the introduction of a new classification algorithm and a few other ideas.

Learning about the seeds dataset

We now look at another agricultural dataset, which is still small, but already too large to plot exhaustively on a page as we did with the Iris dataset. This dataset consists of measurements of wheat seeds. There are seven features that are present, which are as follows:

- Area A
- Perimeter P
- Compactness $C = 4\pi A/P^2$
- Length of kernel
- Width of kernel
- Asymmetry coefficient
- Length of kernel groove

There are three classes corresponding to three wheat varieties: Canadian, Koma, and Rosa. As earlier, the goal is to be able to classify the species based on these morphological measurements. Unlike the Iris dataset, which was collected in the 1930s, this is a very recent dataset and its features were automatically computed from digital images.

This is how image pattern recognition can be implemented: you can take images, in digital form, compute a few relevant features from them, and use a generic classification system. In Chapter 12, *Computer Vision*, we will work through the computer vision side of this problem and compute features in images. For the moment, we will work with the features that are given to us.

UCI Machine Learning Dataset Repository:
The **University of California at Irvine** (**UCI**) maintains an online repository of machine learning datasets (at the time of writing, they list 233 datasets). Both the Iris and the seeds datasets used in this chapter were taken from there. The repository is available online at `http://archive.ics.uci.edu/ml/`.

Features and feature engineering

One interesting aspect of these features is that the compactness feature is not actually a new measurement, but a function of the previous two features: area and perimeter. It is often very useful to derive new combined features. Trying to create new features is generally called **feature engineering**. It is sometimes seen as less glamorous than algorithms, but it often matters more for performance (a simple algorithm on well-chosen features will perform better than a fancy algorithm on not-so-good features).

In this case, the original researchers computed the **compactness**, which is a typical feature for shapes. It is also sometimes called **roundness**. This feature will have the same value for two kernels, one of which is twice as big as the other one, but with the same shape. However, it will have different values for kernels that are very round (when the feature is close to 1) when compared to kernels that are elongated (when the feature is closer to zero).

The goals of a good feature are to simultaneously vary with what matters (the desired output) and be invariant with what does not. For example, compactness does not vary in size, but varies in shape. In practice, it might be hard to achieve both objectives perfectly, but we want to approximate this ideal.

You will need to use background knowledge to design good features. Fortunately, for many problem domains, there is already a vast amount of possible features and feature types that you can build upon. In terms of images, all of the previously mentioned features are typical, and computer vision libraries will compute them for you. In text-based problems, too, there are standard solutions that you can mix and match (we will also look at this in Chapter 4, *Classification I - Detecting Poor Answers*). When possible, you should use your knowledge of the problem to design a specific feature or to select, from literature, the ones that are more applicable to the data at hand.

Even before you have data, you must decide which data is worthwhile to collect. Then, you hand all your features to the machine to evaluate and compute the best classifier.

A natural question is whether we can select good features automatically. This problem is known as **feature selection**. There are many methods that have been proposed for this problem, but in practice, very simple ideas work best. For the small problems we are currently exploring, it does not make sense to use feature selection, but if you had thousands of features, then throwing out most of them might make the rest of the process much faster.

Nearest neighbor classification

For use with this dataset, we will introduce a new classifier: the nearest neighbor classifier. The nearest neighbor classifier is very simple. When classifying a new element, this looks at the training data. For the object that is closest to it, its nearest neighbor. Then, it returns its label as the answer. Notice that this model performs perfectly on its training data! For each point, its closest neighbor is itself, and so its label matches perfectly (unless two examples with different labels have exactly the same feature values, which will indicate that the features you are using are not very descriptive). Therefore, it is essential to test the classification using a cross-validation protocol.

The nearest neighbor method can be generalized to look not at a single neighbor, but to multiple ones, and can take a vote amongst the neighbors. This makes the method more robust than outliers or mislabeled data.

To use scikit-learn's implementation of nearest neighbor classification, we start by importing the `KneighborsClassifier` object from the `sklearn.neighbors` submodule:

```
from sklearn.neighbors import KNeighborsClassifier
```

We can now instantiate a `classifier` object. In the constructor, we specify the number of `neighbors` to consider, as follows:

```
knn = KNeighborsClassifier(n_neighbors=1)
```

If we do not specify the number of neighbors, it defaults to 5, which is often a good choice for classification, but we stick with 1 as it's very easy to think about (in the online repository, you can play around with parameters such as these).

We will use cross-validation (of course) to look at our data. The scikit-learn module also makes this easy:

```
kf = model_selection.KFold(n_splits=5, shuffle=False)
means = []
for training,testing in kf.split(features):
    # We learn a model for this fold with `fit` and then apply it to the
```

```
# testing data with `predict`:
knn.fit(features[training], target[training])
prediction = knn.predict(features[testing])

# np.mean on an array of booleans returns fraction
# of correct decisions for this fold:
curmean = np.mean(prediction == target[testing])
means.append(curmean)
print('Mean accuracy: {:.1%}'.format(np.mean(means)))
```

Using five folds for cross-validation, for this dataset, with this algorithm, we obtain 83.8 percent accuracy. As we discussed in the earlier section, the cross-validation accuracy is lower than the training accuracy, but this is a more credible estimate of the performance of the model.

Looking at the decision boundaries

We will now examine the decision boundaryies. In order to plot these on paper, we will simplify and look at only two dimensions:

```
knn.fit(features[:, [0,2]], target)
```

We will call predict on a grid of feature values (1000 by 1000 points):

```
y0, y1 = features[:, 2].min() * .9, features[:, 2].max() * 1.1
x0, x1 = features[:, 0].min() * .9, features[:, 0].max() * 1.1
X = np.linspace(x0, x1, 1000)
Y = np.linspace(y0, y1, 1000)
X, Y = np.meshgrid(X, Y)
C = knn.predict(np.vstack([X.ravel(), Y.ravel()]).T).reshape(X.shape)
```

Now, we plot the decision boundaries:

```
cmap = ListedColormap([(1., 1., 1.), (.2, .2, .2), (.6, .6, .6)])

fig,ax = plt.subplots()
ax.scatter(features[:, 0], features[:, 2], c=target, cmap=cmap)
for lab, ma in zip(range(3), "Do^"):
    ax.plot(features[target == lab, 0], features[
            target == lab, 2], ma, c=(1., 1., 1.), ms=6)

ax.set_xlim(x0, x1)
ax.set_ylim(y0, y1)
ax.set_xlabel(feature_names[0])
ax.set_ylabel(feature_names[2])
ax.pcolormesh(X, Y, C, cmap=cmap)
```

This is what the results look like:

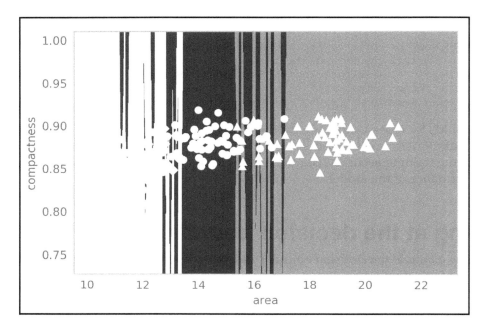

Canadian examples are shown as diamonds, Koma seeds as circles, and Rosa seeds as triangles. Their respective areas are shown as white, black, and grey. You might be wondering why the regions are so horizontal, almost weirdly so. The problem is that the x axis (area) ranges from **10** to **22**, while the y axis (compactness) ranges from **0.75** to 1.0. This means that a small change in x is actually much larger than a small change in y. So, when we compute the distance between points, we are, for the most part, only taking the x axis into account. This is also a good example of why it is a good idea to visualize our data and look for red flags or surprises.

If you studied physics (and you remember your lessons), you might have already noticed that we have been summing up lengths, areas, and dimensionless quantities, mixing up our units (which is something you never want to do in a physical system). We need to normalize all of the features to a common scale. There are many solutions to this problem; a simple one is to normalize to z-scores. The z-score of a value is how far away from the mean it is, in units of standard deviation. It comes down to this operation:

$$f' = (f - \mu)/\sigma$$

In this formula, f is the old feature value, f' is the normalized feature value, μ is the mean of the feature, and σ is the standard deviation. Both μ and σ are estimated from training data. Independent of what the original values were, after z-scoring, a value of zero corresponds to the training mean, positive values are above the mean, and negative values are below it.

The scikit-learn module makes it very easy to use this normalization as a preprocessing step. We are going to use a pipeline of transformations: the first element will do the transformation and the second element will do the classification. We start by importing both the pipeline and the feature scaling classes as follows:

```
from sklearn.pipeline import Pipeline
from sklearn.preprocessing import StandardScaler
```

Now, we can combine them:

```
clf = KNeighborsClassifier(n_neighbors=1)
clf = Pipeline([('norm', StandardScaler()), ('knn', classifier)])
```

The Pipeline constructor takes a list of pairs, (`str`, `clf`). Each pair corresponds to a step in the pipeline: the first element is a string naming the step, while the second element is the object that performs the transformation. Advanced usage of the object uses these names to refer to different steps.

After normalization, every feature is in the same units (technically, every feature is now dimensionless; it has no units) and we can more confidently mix dimensions. In fact, if we now run our nearest neighbor classifier, we obtain 86 percent accuracy, estimated with the same five-fold cross-validation code shown previously!

Look at the decision space again in two dimensions:

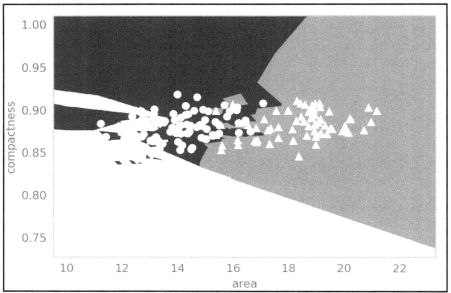

The boundaries are now different and you can see that both dimensions make a difference to the outcome. In the full dataset, everything is happening on a seven-dimensional space, which is very hard to visualize, but the same principle applies; while a few dimensions are dominant in the original data, after normalization, they are all given the same importance.

Which classifier to use

So far, we have looked at two classical classifiers, namely the decision tree and the nearest neighbor classifier. Scikit-learn supports many more, but it does not support everything that has ever been proposed in academic literature. Thus, one may be left wondering: which one should I use? Is it even important to learn about all of them?

In many cases, knowledge of your dataset may help you decide which classifier has a structure that best matches your problem. However, there is a very good study by Manuel Fernández-Delgado and his colleagues titled, *Do we Need Hundreds of Classifiers to Solve Real World Classification Problems?* This is a very readable, very practically-oriented study, where the authors conclude that there is actually one classifier which is very likely to be the best (or close to the best) for a majority of problems, namely **random forests**.

What is a random forest? As the name suggests, a forest is a collection of trees. In this case, a collection of decision trees. How do we obtain many trees from a single dataset? If you try to call the methods we used before several times, you will find that you will get the exact same tree every time. The trick is to call the method several times with different random variations of the dataset. In particular, each time, we take a fraction of the dataset and a fraction of the features. Thus, each time, there is a different tree. At classification time, all the trees vote and a final decision is reached. There are many different parameters that determine all the minor details, but only one is relevant, namely the number of trees that you use. In general, the more trees you build the more memory will be required, but your classification accuracy will also increase (up to a plateau of optimal performance). The default in scikit-learn is 10 trees. Unless your dataset is very large such that memory usage become problematic, increasing this value is often advantageous:

```
from sklearn import ensemble
rf = ensemble.RandomForestClassifier(n_estimators=100)
predict = model_selection.cross_val_predict(rf, features, target)
print("RF accuracy: {:.1%}".format(np.mean(predict == target)))
```

On this dataset, the result is about 86 percent (it may be slightly different when you run it, as they are **random** forests).

Another big advantage of random forests is that, since they are based on decision trees, ultimately they only perform binary decisions based on feature thresholds. Thus, they are invariant when features are scaled up or down.

Summary

Classification means generalizing from examples to build a model that assigns objects to a predefined class (that is, a rule that can automatically be applied to new, unclassified objects). It is one of the fundamental tools in machine learning and we will look at many more examples of this in the forthcoming chapters.

In a way, this was a very abstract and theoretical chapter, as we introduced generic concepts with simple examples. We went over a few operations with the Iris dataset. This is a small dataset. However, it has the advantage that we were able to plot all the data and see what we were doing in detail. This is something that will be lost when we move on to problems with many dimensions and many thousands of examples. The insight we gained here will still be valid.

You also learned that the training error is a misleading, over-optimistic estimate of how well the model does. We must instead evaluate it on testing data that has not been used for training. In order to not waste too many examples in testing, a cross-validation schedule can get us the best of both worlds (at the cost of more computation).

Finally, we discussed what is often the best off-the-shelf classifier, random forests. It's simple to use a classification system that is very flexible (requiring little preprocessing of the data) and achieves very high performance in a wide range of problems.

Chapter 3, *Regression*, in which we will dive deep into scikit-learn—the marvelous machine learning toolkit—give an overview of different types of learning, and show you the beauty of feature engineering.

3
Regression

You probably already learned about regression in your high school mathematics class. The specific method you learned was probably what is called **ordinary least squares** (**OLS**) regression. This 200-year-old technique is computationally fast and can be used for many real-world problems. This chapter will start by reviewing it and showing you how it is available in scikit-learn.

For some problems, however, this method is insufficient. This is particularly true when we have many features, and it completely fails when we have more features than data points. In those cases, we need more advanced methods. These methods are very modern, with major developments happening in the last 20 years. They go by names such as Lasso, Ridge, or ElasticNets. We will go into these in detail. They are also available in scikit-learn. In this chapter, we will learn the following:

- How to use different forms of linear regression with scikit-learn
- The importance of proper cross-validation, particularly when we have many features
- When and how to use two layers of cross-validation to set hyperparameters

Predicting house prices with regression

Let's start with a simple problem, namely, predicting house prices in Boston. The problem is as follows: we are given several demographic and geographical attributes, such as the crime rate or the pupil-teacher ratio in the neighborhood. The goal is to predict the median value of a house in a particular area. As in the case of classification, we have some training data and want to build a model that can be generalized to other data.

This is one of the built-in datasets that scikit-learn comes with, so it is very easy to load the data into memory:

```
from sklearn.datasets import load_boston
boston = load_boston()
```

The `boston` object contains several attributes; in particular, `boston.data` contains the input data and `boston.target` contains the price of houses in thousands of dollars.

We will start with a simple one-dimensional regression, trying to regress the price on a single attribute: the average number of rooms per dwelling in the neighborhood. We can use the standard least squares regression method you probably first saw in high school.

Our first attempt looks like this:

```
from sklearn.linear_model import LinearRegression
lr = LinearRegression()
```

We import `LinearRegression` from the `sklearn.linear_model` module and construct a `LinearRegression` object. This object will behave analogously to the classifier objects from scikit-learn that we used earlier.

The feature we will be using is stored at position 5. For now, we just use a single feature; later in the chapter, we will use all of them. You can consult `boston.DESCR` and `boston.feature_names` for detailed information on the data. The `boston.target` attribute contains the average house price (our target variable):

```
# Feature 5 is the number of rooms.
x = boston.data[:,5]
y = boston.target
x = np.transpose(np.atleast_2d(x))
lr.fit(x, y)
```

The only non-obvious line in this code block is the call to `np.atleast_2d`, which converts `x` from a one-dimensional to a two-dimensional array. This conversion is necessary as the `fit` method expects a two-dimensional array as its first argument. Finally, for the dimensions to work out correctly, we need to transpose this array.

Note that we are calling methods named `fit` and `predict` on the `LinearRegression` object, just as we did with classifier objects, even though we are now performing regression. This regularity in the API is one of the nicer features of scikit-learn.

We can easily plot the `fit`:

```
from matplotlib import pyplot as plt
fig,ax = plt.subplots()
ax.scatter(x, y)
xmin = x.min()
xmax = x.max()
ax.plot([xmin, xmax],
        [lr.predict(xmin), lr.predict(xmax)],
```

```
        '-', lw=2, color="#f9a602")
ax.set_xlabel("Average number of rooms (RM)")
ax.set_ylabel("House Price")
```

Refer to the following graph:

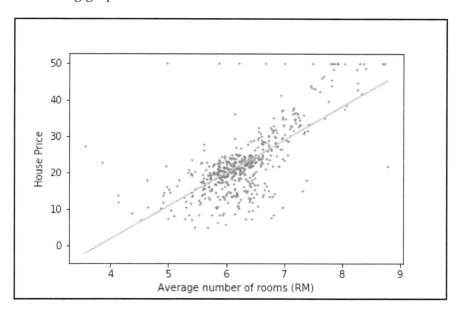

The preceding graph shows all the points (as dots) and our fit (the solid line). We can see that visually it looks good, except for a few outliers.

Ideally, though, we would like to measure how good a fit this is quantitatively. This will be critical in order to be able to compare alternative methods. To do so, we can measure how close our prediction is to the true values. For this task, we can use the `mean_squared_error` function from the `sklearn.metrics` module:

```
from sklearn.metrics import mean_squared_error
```

This function takes two arguments, the true values and the predictions, as follows:

```
mse = mean_squared_error(y, lr.predict(x))
print("Mean squared error (of training data): {:.3}".format(mse))
Mean squared error (of training data): 43.6
```

This value can sometimes be hard to interpret, and it's better to take the square root, to obtain the **root mean square error** (**RMSE**):

```
rmse = np.sqrt(mse)
print("RMSE (of training data): {:.3}".format(rmse))
RMSE (of training data): 6.6
```

One advantage of using `RMSE` is that we can quickly obtain a very rough estimate of the error by multiplying it by two. In our case, we can expect the estimated price to be different from the real price by, at most, 13,000 dollars.

Root mean squared error and prediction:
Root mean squared error corresponds approximately to an estimate of the standard deviation. Since most data is at most two standard deviations from the mean, we can double our `RMSE` to obtain a rough confident interval. This is only completely valid if the errors are normally distributed, but it is often roughly correct even if they are not.

A number such as `6.6` is still hard to immediately understand without domain knowledge. Is this a good prediction? One possible way to answer this question is to compare it with the most simple baseline, the constant model. If we knew nothing of the input, the best we could do would be to predict that the output will always be the average value of `y`. We can then compare the mean-squared error of this model with the mean-squared error of the null model. This idea is formalized in the **coefficient of determination**, which is defined as follows:

$$1 - \frac{\sum_i (y_i - \hat{y}_i)^2}{\sum_i (y_i - \bar{y})^2} \approx 1 - \frac{\text{MSE}}{\text{VAR}(y)}$$

In this formula, y_i represents the value of the element with index i, while $\overline{\hat{y}_i}$ is the estimate for the same element obtained by the regression model. Finally, $\overline{y}$ is the mean value of y, which represents the null model that always returns the same value. This is roughly the same as first computing the ratio of the mean-squared error with the variance of the output and, finally, considering one minus this ratio. This way, a perfect model obtains a score of one, while the null model obtains a score of zero. Note that it is possible to obtain a negative score, which means that the model is so poor that one is better off using the mean as a prediction.

The coefficient of determination can be obtained using the `r2_score` of the `sklearn.metrics` module:

```
from sklearn.metrics import r2_score
r2 = r2_score(y, lr.predict(x))
print("R2 (on training data): {:.2}".format(r2))
R2 (on training data): 0.48
```

This measure is also called the `r2` score. If you are using linear regression and evaluating the error on the training data, then it does correspond to the square of the correlation coefficient, R. However, this measure is more general, and, as we discussed, may even return a negative value.

An alternative way to compute the coefficient of determination is to use the `score` method of the `LinearRegression` object:

```
r2 = lr.score(x,y)
```

Multidimensional regression

So far, we have only used a single variable for prediction: the number of rooms per dwelling. This is, obviously, not the best we can do. We will now use all the data we have to fit a model, using multidimensional regression. We now try to predict a single output (the average house price) based on multiple inputs.

The code looks very much like before. In fact, it's even simpler as we can now pass the value of `boston.data` directly to the `fit` method:

```
x = boston.data
y = boston.target
lr.fit(x, y)
```

Using all the input variables, the root mean squared error is only `4.7`, which corresponds to a coefficient of determination of `0.74` (the code to compute these is the same as the previous example). This is better than what we had before, which indicates that the extra variables did help. But we can no longer easily display the regression line as we did before, because we have a 14-dimensional regression hyperplane instead of a single line!

One good solution in this situation is to plot the prediction versus the actual value. The code is as follows:

```
p = lr.predict(x)
fig,ax = plt.subplots()
ax.scatter(p, y)
ax.xlabel('Predicted price')
ax.ylabel('Actual price')
ax.plot([y.min(), y.max()], [[y.min()], [y.max()]], ':')
```

The last line plots a diagonal line that corresponds to perfect agreement; a model that made no errors would mean that all points would lie on this diagonal. This aids with visualization:

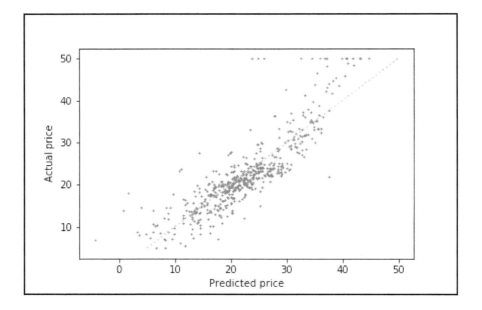

Cross-validation for regression

When we introduced classification, we stressed the importance of cross-validation for checking the quality of our predictions. When performing regression, this is not always done. In fact, we have discussed only the training errors in this chapter so far.

This is a mistake if you want to confidently infer the generalization ability. However, since ordinary least squares is a very simple model, this is often not a very serious mistake. In other words, the amount of overfitting is slight. We should still test this empirically, which we can easily do with scikit-learn.

We will use the `Kfold` class to build a five-fold cross-validation loop and test the generalization ability of linear regression:

```
from sklearn.model_selection import KFold, cross_val_predict
kf = KFold(n_splits=5)
p = cross_val_predict(lr, x, y, cv=kf)
rmse_cv = np.sqrt(mean_squared_error(p, y))
print('RMSE on 5-fold CV: {:.2}'.format(rmse_cv))
RMSE on 5-fold CV: 6.1
```

With cross-validation, we obtain a more conservative estimate (that is, the error is larger): `6.1`. As in the case of classification, the cross-validation estimate is a better estimate of how well we could generalize to predict on unseen data.

Ordinary least squares is fast at learning time and returns a simple model, which is fast at prediction time. However, we are now going to see more advanced methods and why they are sometimes preferable.

Penalized or regularized regression

This section introduces penalized regression, also called **regularized or penalized regression**, an important class of regression models.

In ordinary regression, the returned fit is the best fit on the training data. This can lead to over-fitting. Penalizing means that we add a penalty for over-confidence in the parameter values. Thus, we accept a slightly worse fit in order to have a simpler model.

Another way to think about it is to consider that the default is that there is no relationship between the input variables and the output prediction. When we have data, we change this opinion, but adding a penalty means that we require more data to convince us that this is a strong relationship.

Penalized regression is about trade-offs:
Penalized regression is another example of the bias-variance trade-off.
When using a penalty, we get a worse fit in the training data, as we are
adding bias. On the other hand, we reduce the variance and tend to avoid
over-fitting. Therefore, the overall result might generalize better to unseen
(test) data.

L1 and L2 penalties

We now explore these ideas in detail. Readers who do not care about some of the
mathematical aspects should feel free to skip directly to the next section on how to use
regularized regression in scikit-learn.

The problem, in general, is that we are given a matrix X of training data (rows are
observations, and each column is a different feature), and a vector y of output values. The
goal is to obtain a vector of weights, which we will call b^*. The ordinary least squares
regression is given by the following formula:

$$\vec{b}^* = \arg\min_{\vec{b}} \|\vec{y} - X\vec{b}\|^2$$

That is, we find vector b, which minimizes the squared distance to the target y. In these
equations, we ignore the issue of setting an intercept by assuming that the training data has
been preprocessed so that the mean of y is zero.

Adding a penalty or a regularization means that we do not simply consider the best fit on
the training data, but also how vector $\vec{b}$ is composed. There are two types of penalties that
are typically used for regression: L1 and L2 penalties. An L1 penalty means that we
penalize the regression by the sum of the absolute values of the coefficients, while an L2
penalty penalizes by the sum of squares.

When we add an L1 penalty, instead of the preceding equation, we instead optimize the
following:

$$\vec{b}^* = \arg\min_{\vec{b}} \|\vec{y} - X\vec{b}\|^2 + \alpha \sum_i |b_i|$$

Here, we are trying to simultaneously make the error small, but also make the values of the coefficients small (in absolute terms). Using an L2 penalty means that we use the following formula:

$$\vec{b}^* = \arg\min_{\vec{b}} \|\vec{y} - X\vec{b}\|^2 + \alpha \sum_i b_i^2$$

The difference is rather subtle: we now penalize by the square of the coefficient rather than their absolute value. However, the difference in the results is dramatic.

Ridge, Lasso, and ElasticNets:
These penalized models often go by rather interesting names. The L1 penalized model is often called the Lasso, while an L2 penalized one is known as Ridge regression. When using both, we call this an `ElasticNet` model.

Both the Lasso and the Ridge result in smaller coefficients than unpenalized regression (smaller in absolute value, ignoring the sign). However, the Lasso has an additional property: it results in many coefficients being set to exactly zero! This means that the final model does not even use some of its input features; the model is **sparse**. This is often a very desirable property as the model performs both feature selection and **regression** in a single step.

You will notice that whenever we add a penalty, we also add a weight α, which governs how much penalization we want. When α is close to zero, we are very close to unpenalized regression (in fact, if you set α to zero, you will simply perform OLS), and when α is large, we have a model that is very different from the unpenalized one.

The Ridge model is older as the Lasso is hard to compute with pen and paper. However, with modern computers, we can use the Lasso as easily as Ridge, or even combine them to form ElasticNets. An `ElasticNet` has two penalties, one for the absolute value and the other for the squares, and it solves the following equation:

$$\vec{b}^* = \arg\min_{\vec{b}} \|\vec{y} - X\vec{b}\|^2 + \alpha_1 \sum_i |b_i| + \alpha_2 \sum_i b_i^2$$

This formula is a combination of the two previous ones, with two parameters, α_1 and α_2. Later in this chapter, we will discuss how to choose a good value for parameters.

Using Lasso or ElasticNet in scikit-learn

Let's adapt the preceding example to use ElasticNets. Using scikit-learn, it is very easy to swap in the `ElasticNet` regressor for the least squares one that we had before:

```
from sklearn.linear_model import Lasso
las = Lasso(alpha=0.5)
```

Now we use `las`, whereas earlier we used `lr`. This is the only change that is needed. The results are exactly what we would expect. When using `Lasso`, the R2 on the training data decreases to 0.71 (it was 0.74 before), but the cross-validation fit is now 0.59 (as opposed to 0.56 with linear regression). We trade a larger error on the training data in order to gain better generalization.

Visualizing the Lasso path

Using scikit-learn, we can easily visualize what happens as the value of the regularization parameter (`alphas`) changes. We will again use the Boston data, but now we will use the `Lasso regression` object:

```
las = Lasso()
alphas = np.logspace(-5, 2, 1000)
alphas, coefs, _= las.path(x, y,
                           alphas=alphas)
```

For each value in alphas, the `path` method on the `Lasso` object returns the coefficients that solve the `Lasso` problem with that parameter value. Because the result changes smoothly with alpha, this can be computed very efficiently.

A typical way to visualize this path is to plot the value of the coefficients as alpha decreases. You can do so as follows:

```
fig,ax = plt.subplots()
ax.plot(alphas, coefs.T)
# Set log scale
ax.set_xscale('log')
# Make alpha decrease from left to right
ax.set_xlim(alphas.max(), alphas.min())
```

This results in the following plot (we left out the trivial code that adds the axis labels and the title):

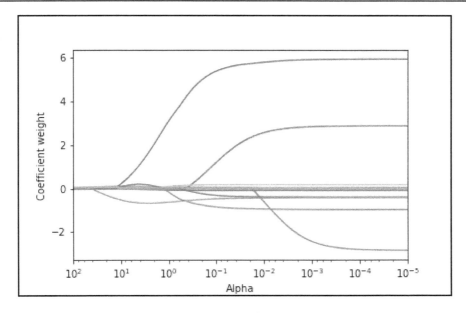

In this plot, the *x* axis shows decreasing amounts of regularization from left to right (alpha is decreasing). Each line shows how a different coefficient varies as alpha changes. The plot shows that when using very strong regularization (left side, very high alpha), the best solution is to have all values be exactly zero. As the regularization becomes weaker, one by one, the values of the different coefficients first shoot up, then stabilize. At some point, they all plateau as we are probably already close to the unpenalized solution.

P-greater-than-N scenarios

The title of this section is a bit of jargon, which you will learn now. In the 1990s, first in the biomedical domain, and then on the web, problems started to appear where P was greater than N. What this meant was that the number of features, P, was greater than the number of examples, N (these letters were the conventional statistical shorthand for these concepts).

For example, if your input is a set of written documents, a simple way to approach it is to consider each possible word in the dictionary as a feature and regress on those (we will later work on one such problem ourselves). In the English language, you have over 20,000 words (this is if you perform some stemming and only consider common words; it is more than ten times that if you skip this preprocessing step). If you only have a few hundred or a few thousand examples, you will have more features than examples.

In this case, as the number of features is greater than the number of examples, it is possible to have a perfect fit on the training data. This is a mathematical fact, which is independent of your data. You are, in effect, solving a system of linear equations with fewer equations than variables. You can find a set of regression coefficients with zero training errors (in fact, you can find more than one perfect solution).

However, and this is a major problem, zero training error does not mean that your solution will generalize well. In fact, it may generalize very poorly. In earlier examples, regularization could give you a little extra boost, but it is now absolutely required for a meaningful result.

An example based on text documents

We will now turn to an example that comes from a study performed at Carnegie Mellon University by Prof. Noah Smith's research group. The study was based on mining the so-called 10-K reports that companies file with the **Securities and Exchange Commission** (**SEC**) in the United States. This filing is mandated by law for all publicly traded companies. The goal of their study was to predict, based on this piece of public information, what the future volatility of the company's stock would be. In the training data, we are actually using historical data for which we already know the outcome.

There are 16,087 examples available. The features, which have already been preprocessed for us, correspond to different words, 150,360 in total. Thus, we have many more features than examples, almost ten times as many. In the introduction, it was stated that ordinary least regression is useful in these cases, and we will now see why by attempting to blindly apply it.

The dataset is available in SVMLight format from multiple sources, including the book's companion website. This is a format that scikit-learn can read. SVMLight is, as the name says, a support vector machine implementation, which is also available through scikit-learn; right now, we are only interested in the file format:

```
from sklearn.datasets import load_svmlight_file
data,target = load_svmlight_file('E2006.train')
```

In the preceding code, data is a sparse matrix (that is, most of its entries are zeros and, therefore, only the nonzero entries are saved in memory), while the target is a simple one-dimensional vector. We can start by looking at some attributes of the target:

```
print('Min target value: {}'.format(target.min()))
Min target value: -7.89957807347

print('Max target value: {}'.format(target.max()))
```

```
Max target value: -0.51940952694
```

```
print('Mean target value: {}'.format(target.mean()))
Mean target value: -3.51405313669
```

```
print('Std. dev. target: {}'.format(target.std()))
Std. dev. target: 0.632278353911
```

So, we can see that the data lies between -7.9 and -0.5. Now that we have a feel for the data, we can check what happens when we use OLS to predict. Note that we can use exactly the same classes and methods as we did earlier:

```
from sklearn.linear_model import LinearRegression
lr = LinearRegression()
lr.fit(data,target)
pred = lr.predict(data)
rmse_train = np.sqrt(mean_squared_error(target, pred))
print('RMSE on training: {:.2}'.format(rmse_train))
RMSE on training: 0.0024
```

```
print('R2 on training: {:.2}'.format(r2_score(target, pred)))
R2 on training: 1.0
```

The root mean squared error is not exactly zero because of rounding errors, but it is very close. The coefficient of determination is 1.0. That is, the linear model is reporting a perfect prediction on its training data. This is what we expected.

However, when we use cross-validation (the code is very similar to what we used earlier in the Boston example), we get something very different: RMSE of 0.75, which corresponds to a negative coefficient of determination of -0.42! This means that if we always predict the mean value of -3.5, we do better than when using the regression model! This is the typical P-greater-than-N situation.

Training and generalization error:
When the number of features is greater than the number of examples, you always get zero training errors with OLS, except perhaps for issues due to rounding off. However, this is rarely a sign that your model will do well in terms of generalization. In fact, you may get zero training errors and have a completely useless model.

The natural solution is to use regularization to counteract the overfitting. We can try the same cross-validation with an ElasticNet learner, having set the penalty parameter to 0.1:

```
from sklearn.linear_model import ElasticNet
```

```
met = ElasticNet(alpha=0.1)
met.fit(data, target)
pred = met.predict(data)

print('[EN 0.1] RMSE on training:
{:.2}'.format(np.sqrt(mean_squared_error(target, pred))))
```
[EN 0.1] RMSE on training: 0.4

```
print('[EN 0.1] R2 on training: {:.2}'.format(r2_score(target, pred)))
```
[EN 0.1] R2 on training: 0.61

Thus, we get worse results on the training data. However, we have a better hope that these results will generalize well:

```
kf = Kfold(n_splits=5)
pred = cross_val_predict(met, data, target, cv=kf)

rmse = np.sqrt(mean_squared_error(target, pred))
print('[EN 0.1] RMSE on testing (5 fold): {:.2}'.format(rmse))
```
[EN 0.1] RMSE on testing (5 fold): 0.4

```
print('[EN 0.1] R2 on testing (5 fold): {:.2}'.format(r2_score(target,
pred)))
```
[EN 0.1] R2 on testing (5 fold): 0.61

Indeed, they do! Unlike in the case for OLS, with ElasticNet, the result of cross-validation is the same as for the training data.

There is one problem with this solution, though, which is the choice of alpha. When using the default value (1.0), the result is very different (and worse).

In this case, we cheated as the author had previously tried a few values to see which ones would give a good result. This is not effective and can lead to overestimates of confidence (we are looking at the test data to decide which parameter values to use and which we should never use). The next section explains how to do it properly and how this is supported by scikit-learn.

Setting hyperparameters in a principled way

In the preceding example, we set the penalty parameter to 0.1. We could just as well have set it to 0.7 or 23.9. Naturally, the results will vary each time. If we pick an overly large value, we get underfitting. In an extreme case, the learning system will just return every coefficient equal to zero. If we pick a value that is too small, we are very close to OLS, which overfits and generalizes poorly (as we saw earlier).

How do we choose a good value? This is a general problem in machine learning: setting parameters for our learning methods. A generic solution is to use cross-validation. We pick a set of possible values, and then use cross-validation to choose which one is best. This performs more computation (five times more if we use five folds), but is always applicable and unbiased.

We must be careful, though. In order to obtain an unbiased estimate of generalization, we must use **two levels of cross-validation**: the top level is to estimate the generalization power of the system, while the second level is to get good parameters. That is, we split the data in, for example, five folds. We start by holding out the first fold and will learn on the other four. Now, we split these again into five folds in order to choose the parameters. Once we have set our parameters, we test on the first fold. Now we repeat this four other times:

Dataset	Fold 1	Break into 5 subfolds				
1	Test					
2	Train	Test	Train	Train	Train	Train
3	Train	Train	Test	Train	Train	Train
		Train	Train	Test	Train	Train
4	Train	Train	Train	Train	Test	Train
5	Train	Train	Train	Train	Train	Test

The preceding figure shows how you break up a single training fold into subfolds. We would need to repeat it for all the other folds. In this case, we are looking at five outer folds and five inner folds, but there is no reason to use the same number of outer and inner folds; you can use any number you want as long as you keep the folds separate.

This leads to a lot of computation, but it is necessary in order to do things correctly. The problem is that if you use any datapoint to make any decisions about your model (including which parameters to set), you can no longer use that same datapoint to test the generalization ability of your model. This is a subtle point and it may not be immediately obvious. In fact, it is still the case that many users of machine learning get this wrong and overestimate how well their systems are doing, because they do not perform cross-validation correctly!

Fortunately, scikit-learn makes it very easy to do the right thing; it provides classes named `LassoCV`, `RidgeCV`, and `ElasticNetCV`, all of which encapsulate an inner cross-validation loop to optimize the necessary parameter (hence the letters `CV` at the end of the class name). The code is almost exactly like the previous one, except that we do not need to specify any value for alpha:

```
from sklearn.linear_model import ElasticNetCV
met = ElasticNetCV()
kf = KFold(n_splits=5)
p = cross_val_predict(met, data, target, cv=kf)
r2_cv = r2_score(target, p)
print("R2 ElasticNetCV: {:.2}".format(r2_cv))
R2 ElasticNetCV: 0.65
```

This results in a lot of computation, so, depending on how fast your computer is, you may want to brew some coffee or tea while you are waiting. You can get better performance by taking advantage of multiple processors. This is a built-in feature of scikit-learn, which can be accessed quite trivially by using the `n_jobs` parameter to the `ElasticNetCV` constructor. To use four CPUs, make use of the following code:

```
met = ElasticNetCV(n_jobs=4)
```

Set the `n_jobs` parameter to -1 to use all the available CPUs:

```
met = ElasticNetCV(n_jobs=-1)
```

You may have wondered why, if ElasticNets has two penalties—the L1 and the L2 penalty—we only need to set a single value for alpha. In fact, the two values are specified by separately specifying the alpha and the `l1_ratio` variable. Then, α_1 and α_2 are set as follows (where ρ stands for `l1_ratio`):

$$\alpha_1 = \rho\alpha$$

$$\alpha_2 = (1 - \rho)\alpha$$

In an intuitive sense, alpha sets the overall amount of regularization while `l1_ratio` sets the trade-off between the different types of regularization, L1 and L2.

We can request that the `ElasticNetCV` object tests different values of `l1_ratio`, as shown in the following code:

```
l1_ratio=[.01, .05, .25, .5, .75, .95, .99]
met = ElasticNetCV(l1_ratio=l1_ratio, n_jobs=-1)
```

This set of `l1_ratio` values is recommended in the documentation. It will test models that are almost like Ridge (when `l1_ratio` is `0.01` or `0.05`) as well as models that are almost like Lasso (when `l1_ratio` is `0.95` or `0.99`). Thus, we explore a full range of different options.

Because of its flexibility and its ability to use multiple CPUs, `ElasticNetCV` is an excellent default solution for regression problems when you don't have any particular reason to prefer one type of model over the rest. In very simple problems, use ordinary least squares.

Putting all this together, we can now visualize the prediction versus real fit on this large dataset:

```
l1_ratio = [.01, .05, .25, .5, .75, .95, .99]
met = ElasticNetCV(l1_ratio=l1_ratio, n_jobs=-1)
pred = cross_val_predict(met, data, target, cv=kf)
fig, ax = plt.subplots()
ax.scatter(pred, y)
ax.plot([pred.min(), pred.max()], [pred.min(), pred.max()])
```

This results in the following plot:

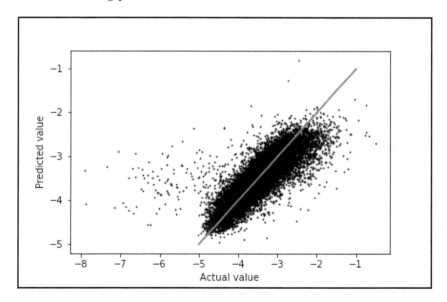

We can see that the predictions do not match very well on the bottom end of the value range. This is perhaps because there are so many fewer elements on this end of the target range (this affects only a small minority of datapoints).

Regression with TensorFlow

We will dive into TensorFlow in a future chapter, but regularized linear regression can be implemented with it, so it's good idea to get a feel for how TensorFlow works.

 Details on how TensorFlow is structured will be tackled in Chapter 8, *Artificial Neural Networks and Deep Learning*. Some of its scaffolding may seem odd, and there will be lots of magic numbers. Still, we will progressively use more of it for some small examples.

Let's try to use the Boston dataset for this experiment.

```
import tensorflow as tf
```

TensorFlow requires you to create symbols for all elements it works on. These can be variables or placeholders. The former are symbols that TensorFlow will change, whereas placeholders are externally imposed by TensorFlow.

For regression, we need two placeholders, one for the input features and one for the output we want to match. We will also require two variables, one for the slope and one for the intercept. Contrary to linear regression, we have to write far more code for the same functionality:

```
X = tf.placeholder(shape=[None, 1], dtype=tf.float32, name="X")
Y = tf.placeholder(shape=[None, 1], dtype=tf.float32, name="y")
A = tf.Variable(tf.random_normal(shape=[1, 1]), name="A")
b = tf.Variable(tf.random_normal(shape=[1, 1]), name="b")
```

The two placeholders have a shape of [None, 1]. This means that they have a dynamic size along one axis and a size of 1 on the fastest dimension (in terms of memory layout). The two variables are fully static and have a dimension of [1, 1], meaning a single element. They will both be initialized by TensorFlow following a random variable (a Gaussian with a mean of 0 and a variance of 1).

The type of symbols can be set by using dtype, or for variable it can be inferred from the type of the initial_value. In this example, it will always be a floating point value.

 All symbols can have a name and many TensorFlow functions take a name argument. It is good practice to give clear names, as TensorFlow errors will display them. If they are not set, TensorFlow will create new default names that can be difficult to decipher.

All the symbols are now created, and we can now create the `loss` function. We first create the prediction, and then we will compare it to the ground truth value:

```
model_output = tf.matmul(X, A) + b
loss = tf.reduce_mean(tf.square(Y - model_output))
```

The multiplication for the prediction seems to be transposed, and this is due to the way `X` was defined: it is indeed transposed! This allows `model_output` to have a dynamic first dimension.

We can now minimize this `cost` function with a gradient descent. First we create the TensorFlow objects:

```
grad_step = 5e-7
my_opt = tf.train.GradientDescentOptimizer(grad_step)
train_step = my_opt.minimize(loss)
```

 The gradient step is a crucial aspect of all TensorFlow objects. We will explore this further later; the important aspect is to know that this step depends on the data and the `cost` function used. There are other optimizers available in TensorFlow; gradient descent is the simplest and one of the most adapted to this case.

We also need some variables:

```
batch_size = 50
n_epochs = 20000
steps = 100
```

The batch size indicates how many elements at a time we are going to compute the loss for. This is also the dimension of the input data for the placeholders as well as the dimension of the output we predict during the optimization.

Epochs are the number of times we go through all the training data to optimize our model. Finally, steps are just how often we display the information of the `loss` function we optimize.

Now we can go to the last step and let TensorFlow loose on the function and data we have:

```
loss_vec = []
with tf.Session() as sess:
    sess.run(tf.global_variables_initializer())
    for epoch in range(n_epochs):
        permut = np.random.permutation(len(x))
        for j in range(0, len(x), batch_size):
            batch = permut[j:j+batch_size]
```

```
            Xs = x[batch]
            Ys = y[batch]

            sess.run(train_step, feed_dict={X: Xs, Y: Ys})
        temp_loss = sess.run(loss, feed_dict={X: x, Y: y})
        loss_vec.append(temp_loss)
        if epoch % steps == 0:
            (A_, b_) = sess.run([A, b])
            print('Epoch #%i A = %s b = %s' % (epoch, np.transpose(A_),
b_))
            print('Loss = %.8f' % temp_loss)
            print("")

    prediction = sess.run(model_output, feed_dict={X: trX, Y: trY})
    mse = mean_squared_error(y, prediction)
    print("Mean squared error (on training data): {:.3}".format(mse))
    rmse = np.sqrt(mse)
    print('RMSE (on training data): %f' % rmse)
    r2 = r2_score(y, prediction)
    print("R2 (on training data): %.2f" % r2)
```

We first create a TensorFlow session. This will enable us to use the symbols with calls to `sess.run`. The first argument is a function to call or a list of functions to call (and their results will be the return of this call), and we have to pass a dictionary, `feed_dict`. This dictionary maps placeholders to actual data, so dimensions must match.

The first call in the session initializes all the variables according to what we specified when they were declared. Then we have two loops, one on epochs and one on batch sizes.

For each epoch, we define a **permutation** of the training data. This randomizes the order of the data. This is important, especially for a neural network, so that they don't have bias and so they learn all the data consistently. If the batch size is equal to the size of the training data, then we don't need to randomize data, and this is usually the case when we have only a handful of data samples. For large datasets, we have to use batches. Each batch will be fed inside the `train_step` function and the variables will be optimized.

After each epoch, we save the loss over all the training data for display purposes. We also display the state of the variables every few epochs to monitor and check the state of the optimization.

Finally, we display the mean square error of the predicted outputs with our model as well as the `r2` score.

Of course, the solution for this `loss` function is analytically known, so let's modify it:

```
beta = 0.005
regularizer = tf.nn.l2_loss(A)
loss = loss + beta * regularizer
```

Then let's run the full optimization to get a Lasso result. We can see that TensorFlow doesn't really shine there. It is very slow and requires an awful number of iterations to get the result that is far from what scikit-learn can retrieve.

Let's see a fraction of the run when using just feature 5 for this dataset:

```
Epoch #9400 A = [[ 8.60801601]] b = [[-31.74242401]]
Loss = 43.75216293

Epoch #9500 A = [[ 8.57831573]] b = [[-31.81438446]]
Loss = 43.92549133

Epoch #9600 A = [[ 8.67326164]] b = [[-31.88376808]]
Loss = 43.69957733

Epoch #9700 A = [[ 8.75835037]] b = [[-31.94364548]]
Loss = 43.97978973

Epoch #9800 A = [[ 8.70185089]] b = [[-32.03764343]]
Loss = 43.69329453

Epoch #9900 A = [[ 8.66107273]] b = [[-32.10965347]]
Loss = 43.74081802

Mean squared error (on training data): 1.17e+02
RMSE (on training data): 10.8221888258
R2 (on training data): -0.39
```

Here is how the `loss` function behaves:

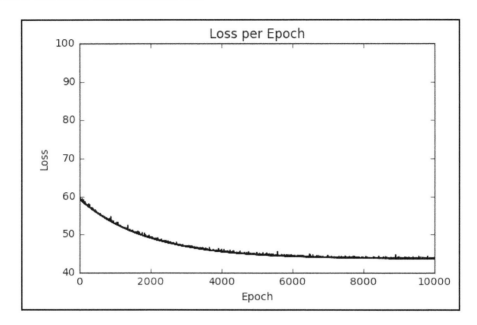

Here is the result when using only the fifth feature:

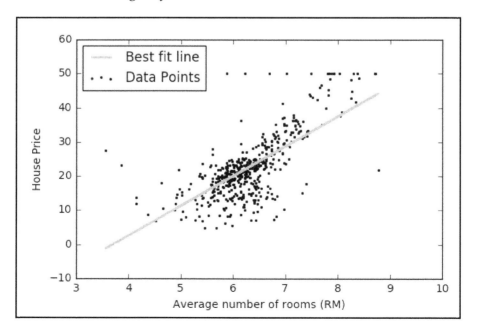

Summary

In this chapter, we started with the oldest trick in the book: ordinary least squares regression. Although centuries old, it is sometimes still the best solution for regression. However, we also saw more modern approaches that avoid overfitting and can give us better results, especially when we have a large number of features. We used Ridge, Lasso, and ElasticNets; these are state-of-the-art methods for regression.

We saw, once again, the danger of relying on training errors to estimate generalization: it can be an overly optimistic estimate to the point where our model has zero training errors, but we know that it is completely useless. When thinking through these issues, we were led on to two-level cross-validation, an important area that many in the field still have not completely internalized.

Throughout this chapter, we were able to rely on scikit-learn to support all the operations we wanted to perform, including an easy way to achieve correct cross-validation. ElasticNets with an inner cross-validation loop for parameter optimization (as implemented in scikit-learn by `ElasticNetCV`) should probably become your default method for regression. We also saw the usage of TensorFlow for regression (so the package is not restricted to neural network computations).

One reason to use an alternative is when you are interested in a sparse solution. In this case, a pure Lasso solution is more appropriate as it will set many coefficients to zero. It will also allow you to discover, from the data, a small number of variables, which are important to the output. Knowing the identity of these may be interesting in and of itself, in addition to having a good regression model.

Chapter 4, *Classification I – Detecting Poor Answers*, looks at how to proceed when your data does not have predefined classes for classification.

Classification I – Detecting Poor Answers

4

A continuous challenge for owners of Q&A sites is to maintain a decent level of quality in the posted content. Sites such as StackOverflow make considerable effort to encourage users with diverse possibilities to score content, and offer badges and bonus points to spend more energy on carving out the question or crafting a possible answer.

One particularly successful incentive is the ability for the asker to flag one answer to their question as the accepted answer (there are incentives for the asker to flag answers as such). This will result in a higher score for the author of the flagged answer.

Would it not be very useful for the user to immediately see how good their answer is while typing it in? That means the website would continuously evaluate the user's work-in-progress answer and provide feedback as to whether the answer has room for improvement. This will encourage the user to put more effort into writing the answer (such as providing a code example or even including an image), and thus improve the overall system.

Let's build such a mechanism! In this chapter, we'll cover the following topics:

- Fetching and preprocessing the raw data
- Creating a first nearest-neighbor classifier
- Looking into how to improve the classifier's performance
- Switching from nearest-neighbor to logistic regression
- Learning about precision and recall to better understand the classifier's performance
- Thinking about the necessary steps for shipping it

Sketching our roadmap

As we'll be building a system using real data that is very noisy, this chapter is not for the fainthearted, as we will not arrive at the golden solution of a classifier that achieves 100% accuracy; often, even humans disagree about whether an answer was good or not (just take a look at some of the StackOverflow comments). We will find out that some challenges, such as the one in this chapter, are so hard that we have to adjust our initial goals along the way. We will start with the nearest-neighbor approach that we learned in the previous chapters, find out why it is not very good for the task in this chapter, switch over to logistic regression, and arrive at a solution that will achieve good enough prediction quality, but on a smaller part of the answers. Finally, we will spend some time looking at how to extract the winner to deploy it on the target system.

Learning to classify classy answers

In classification, we want to find the corresponding classes, sometimes also called labels, for given data instances. To be able to achieve this, we need to answer two questions:

- How should we represent the data instances?
- Which model or structure should our classifier possess?

Tuning the instance

In its simplest form, in our case the data instance is the answer text itself and the label would be a binary value indicating whether the asker accepted this text as an answer or not. Raw text, however, is a very inconvenient representation to process for most machine learning algorithms. They want numbers. And it will be our task to extract useful features from the raw text, which the machine learning algorithm can then use to learn the right label for it.

Tuning the classifier

Once we have found or collected enough (text, label) pairs, we can train a classifier. For the underlying structure of the classifier, we have a wide range of possibilities, each of them having advantages and drawbacks. Just to name some of the more prominent choices, there are logistic regression, decision trees, SVMs, and Naïve Bayes. In this chapter, we will contrast the instance-based method from the `Chapter 2`, *Classifying with Real-world Examples*, nearest-neighbor, with model-based logistic regression.

Fetching the data

Luckily for us, the team behind StackOverflow provides most of the data behind the StackExchange universe to which StackOverflow belongs under a `cc-by-sa` license. At the time of writing this book, the latest data dump can be found at `https://archive.org/download/stackexchange`. It contains data dumps of all the Q&A sites of the StackExchange family. For StackOverflow, you will find multiple files, of which we only need the `stackoverflow.com-Posts.7z` file, which is 11.3 GB.

After downloading and extracting it, we have around 59 GB of data in the XML format, containing all questions and answers as individual row tags within the root tag posts:

```
<?xml version="1.0" encoding="utf-8"?>
<posts>
...
  <row Id="4572748" PostTypeId="2" ParentId="4568987"
CreationDate="2011-01-01T00:01:03.387" Score="4" ViewCount=""
Body="&lt;p&gt;IANAL, but &lt;a
href=&quot;http://support.apple.com/kb/HT2931&quot;
rel=&quot;nofollow&quot;&gt;this&lt;/a&gt; indicates to me that you cannot
use the loops in your
application:&lt;/p&gt;&lt;blockquote&gt;&lt;p&gt;...however, individual
audio loops may not be commercially or otherwise distributed on a
standalone basis, nor may they be repackaged in whole or in part as audio
samples, sound effects or music beds.&quot;&lt;/p&gt;&lt;p&gt;So don't
worry, you can make
 commercial music with GarageBand, you just can't distribute the loops as
loops.&lt;/p&gt; &lt;/blockquote&gt; " OwnerUserId="203568"
LastActivityDate="2011-01-01T00:01:03.387" CommentCount="1" />
...
</posts>
```

Refer to the following table:

Name	Type	Description
Id	Integer	This is a unique identifier of the post.
PostTypeId	Integer	This describes the category of the post. The values of interest to us are the following: • 1: Question • 2: Answer Other values will be ignored.
ParentId	Integer	This is a unique identifier of the question to which this answer belongs. It is missing for questions, in which case we will set it to −1.

Name	Type	Description
CreationDate	DateTime	This is the date of submission.
Score	Integer	This is the score of the post.
ViewCount	Integer or empty	This is the number of user views for this post.
Body	String	This is the complete post as encoded HTML text.
OwnerUserId	Id	This is a unique identifier of the poster. If 1, then it is a wiki question.
Title	String	This is the title of the question (missing for answers).
AcceptedAnswerId	Id	This is the ID for the accepted answer (missing for answers).
CommentCount	Integer	This is the number of comments for the post.

 Normally, we try to stick to the Python style guides for variable naming. In this chapter, we will use the names in the XML fomat so they are easier to follow. For example, we will have `ParentId` instead of `parent_id`.

Slimming the data down to chewable chunks

We will need to train many variants, until we arrive at the final classifier. Given the current data, we will be slowed down considerably by the following:

- Post-it stores attributes, which we might not need.
- It is stored as XML, which is not the fastest format to parse.
- The dump contains posts that date back to 2011. Restricting to just the year 2017, we will still end up with over 6,000,000 posts, which should be enough.

Preselecting and processing attributes

We can certainly drop attributes that we think will not help the classifier in distinguishing between good and not-so-good answers. But we have to be cautious here. Although some features do not directly impact the classification, they are still necessary to keep:

- The `PostTypeId` attribute, for example, is necessary to distinguish between questions and answers. It will not be picked to serve as a feature, but we will need it to filter the data.

- `CreationDate` could be interesting to determine the time span between posting the question and posting the individual answers. In this chapter, however, we will ignore it.
- Score is important as an indicator of the community's evaluation.
- `ViewCount`, in contrast, is most likely of no use for our task. Even if it would help the classifier to distinguish between good and bad, we would not have this information at the time when an answer is being submitted. So we ignore it.
- The `Body` attribute obviously contains the most important information. As it is encoded HTML, we will have to decode it to plain text.
- `OwnerUserId` is only useful if we take user-dependent features into account, which we won't.
- The Title attribute is also ignored here, although it could add some more information about the question.
- `CommentCount` is also ignored. Similar to `ViewCount`, it could help the classifier with posts that are out there for a while (more comments = more ambiguous post?). It will, however, not help the classifier at the time an answer is posted.
- `AcceptedAnswerId` is similar to Score in that it is an indicator of a post's quality. This is, however, a signal that may get stale over time. Imagine a user posts a question, receives a couple of answers, marks one of them as accepted and forgets about it. Years later, many more users have read the question will have read the answers, some of which didn't exist when the asker accepted the answer. So it might turn out that the highest scored answer is not the accepted one. Since we have the score already, we will ignore the acceptance information.

Suffice to say that in order to speed up processing, we will use the `lxml` module to parse the XML file and then output two files. In one file, we will store a dictionary that maps a post's Id value to its other data, except Text in the JSON format, so that we can read it easily and keep it in memory in the meta dictionary. For example, the score of a post would reside at `meta[post_id]['Score']`. We will do the same for the new features that we will create throughout this chapter.

We will then store the actual posts in another tab-separated file, where the first column is Id and the second one is Text, which we can easily read with the following method:

```
def fetch_posts(fn):
    for line in open(fn, "r"):
        post_id, text = line.split("\t")
        yield int(post_id), text.strip()
```

We call the two files as follows:

```
>>> import os
>>> fn_sample = os.path.join('data', "sample.tsv")
>>> fn_sample_meta = os.path.join('data', "sample-meta.json")
```

For the sake of brevity, please check the Jupyter notebook for the code.

Defining what a good answer is

Before we can train a classifier to distinguish between good and bad answers, we have to create the training data. So far, we only have a bunch of data. We still need to define labels.

Of course, we could simply take the best and worst-scoring answer per question as positive and negative examples. However, what do we do with questions that have only good answers, say, one with two and the other with four points? Should we really take the answer with two points as a negative example just because it happened to be the one with the lower score? Or let's say that we have only two negative answers, one with a score of -2 and the other with -4. Clearly, we cannot take the answer with -2 as a positive example.

We will therefore look for answers that have at least an answer with a score higher than 0 and at least one with a negative score and throw away those that don't fit this criterion. If we take all the remaining data, we would have to wait quite some time at every step, so we filter down further to 10,000 questions. From those, we will pick the highest-scoring answer as the positive example and the lowest-scoring answer as a negative one, which results into 20,000 answers for our training set.

As mentioned earlier, throughout this chapter (and in the Jupyter notebook), we will maintain a meta dictionary, which maps the answer IDs to the features, of which score is one (we will design more features along the way). Therefore, we can create our labels as follows:

```
>>> all_answers = [a for a,v in meta.items() if v['ParentId']!=-1]
>>> Y = np.asarray([meta[aid]['Score'] > 0 for aid in all_answers])
>>> print(np.unique(Y, return_counts=True))
(array([False, True], dtype=bool), array([10000, 10000], dtype=int64))
```

Creating our first classifier

Let's start with the simple and beautiful nearest-neighbor method from Chapter 2, *Classifying with Real-world Examples*. Although it is not as advanced as other methods, it is very powerful: as it is not model-based, it can learn nearly any data. But this beauty comes with a clear disadvantage, which we will find out very soon (because of which, we had to capitalize learn in the previous sentence).

Engineering the features

As mentioned earlier, we will use the Text and Score features to train our classifier. The problem with Text is that the classifier does not work well with strings. We will have to convert it into one or more numbers. So, what statistics could be useful to extract from a post? Let's start with the number of HTML links, assuming that good posts have a higher chance of having links in them.

We can do this with regular expressions. The following captures all HTML link tags that start with http:// (ignoring the other protocols for now):

```
import re
link_match = re.compile('<a href="http://.*?".*?>(.*?)</a>',
                        re.MULTILINE | re.DOTALL)
```

However, we do not want to count links that are part of a code block. If, for example, a post explains the usage of the requests Python module, it would most likely also contain URLs. This means that we have to iterate over all code blocks, count the links in there, and subtract them later on from the total link count. This can be done by another regular expression that matches the <pre> tag, which is used on the StackExchange sites to mark up code:

```
code_match = re.compile('<pre>(.*?)</pre>',
                        re.MULTILINE | re.DOTALL)

def extract_features_from_body(s):
    link_count_in_code = 0
    # count links in code to later subtract them
    for match_str in code_match.findall(s):
        link_count_in_code += len(link_match.findall(match_str))
    return len(link_match.findall(s)) - link_count_in_code
```

For production systems, we would not want to parse HTML content with regular expressions. Instead, we should rely on excellent libraries such as `BeautifulSoup`, which does a marvelous job of robustly handling all the weird things that typically occur in everyday HTML.

With this in place, we can generate one feature per answer and store it in meta. But before we train the classifier, let's have a look at what we will train it with. We can get a first impression with the frequency distribution of our new feature. This can be done by plotting the percentage of how often each value occurs in the data:

```python
import matplotlib.pyplot as plt

X = np.asarray([[meta[aid]['LinkCount']] for aid in all_answers])
plt.figure(figsize=(5,4), dpi=300)
plt.title('LinkCount')
plt.xlabel('Value')
plt.ylabel('Occurrence')

n, bins, patches = plt.hist(X, normed=1,
                            bins=range(max(X.ravel())-min(X.ravel())),
                            alpha=0.75)

plt.grid(True)
```

Refer to the following graph:

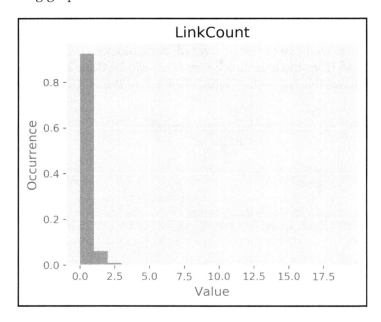

With the majority of posts having no link at all, we know now that this feature will not make a good classifier. Let's try it out anyway to get a first estimation of where we are.

Training the classifier

We have to pass the feature array together with the previously defined Y label to the kNN learner to obtain a classifier:

```
from sklearn.neighbors import KNeighborsClassifier
X = np.asarray([extract_features_from_body(text) for post_id, text in
                fetch_posts(fn_sample) if post_id in all_answers])
knn = KNeighborsClassifier()
knn.fit(X, Y)
```

Using the standard parameters, we just fitted a 5NN (meaning NN with k=5) to our data. Why 5NN? Well, at the current state of our knowledge about the data, we really have no clue what the right k should be. Once we have more insight, we will have a better idea of how to set k.

Measuring the classifier's performance

We have to be clear about what we want to measure. The naïve, but easiest, way is to simply calculate the average prediction quality over the test set. This will result in a value between 0 for predicting everything wrongly and 1 for perfect prediction.

Let's for now use the accuracy as the prediction quality, which scikit-learn conveniently calculates for us with knn.score(). But as we learned in Chapter 2, *Classifying with Real-world Examples*, we will not do it just once, but apply cross-validation here using the readymade KFold class from sklearn.model_selection. Finally, we will average the scores on the test set of each fold and see how much it varies using standard deviation:

```
from sklearn.neighbors import KNeighborsClassifier
from sklearn.model_selection import KFoldscores = []
N_FOLDS = 10
cv = KFold(n_splits=N_FOLDS, shuffle=True, random_state=0)

for train, test in cv.split(X, Y):
    X_train, y_train = X[train], Y[train]
    X_test, y_test = X[test], Y[test]
    clf =KNeighborsClassifier()
    clf.fit(X_train, Y)_train)
    scores.append(clf.score(X_test, y_test))
```

```
print("Mean(scores)=%.5f\tStddev(scores)=%.5f"\
    %(np.mean(scores), np.std(scores)))
```

Here is the output:

```
Mean(scores)=0.50170 Stddev(scores)=0.01243
```

Now, that is far from being usable. With only 50% accuracy, it is like tossing a coin. Apparently, the number of links in a post is not a very good indicator of the quality of a post. So, we can say that this feature does not have much discriminative power—at least not for kNN with `k=5`.

Designing more features

In addition to using the number of hyperlinks as a proxy for a post's quality, the number of code lines is possibly another good one, too. At least, it is a good indicator that the post's author is interested in answering the question. We can find the code embedded in the `<pre>...</pre>` tag. And once we have it extracted, we should count the number of normal words in the post:

```
# we will use regular expression to remove HTML tags
tag_match = re.compile('<[^>]*>', re.MULTILINE | re.DOTALL)
whitespace_match = re.compile(r'\s+', re.MULTILINE | re.DOTALL)

def extract_features_from_body(s):
    num_code_lines = 0
    link_count_in_code = 0

    # remove source code and count how many lines the post has
    code_free_s = s
    for match_str in code_match.findall(s):
        num_code_lines += match_str.count('\n')
        code_free_s = code_match.sub(' ', code_free_s)

        # Sometimes source code contains links, which we don't want to
        # count
        link_count_in_code += len(link_match.findall(match_str))

    links = link_match.findall(s)
    link_count = len(links) - link_count_in_code
    html_free_s = tag_match.sub(' ', code_free_s)
    text = html_free_s
    for link in links:
        if link.lower().startswith('http://'):
            text = text.replace(link, ' ')
```

```
text = whitespace_match.sub(' ', text)
num_text_tokens = text.count(' ')

return num_text_tokens, num_code_lines, link_count
```

Looking at this, we notice that at least the number of words in a post shows higher variability:

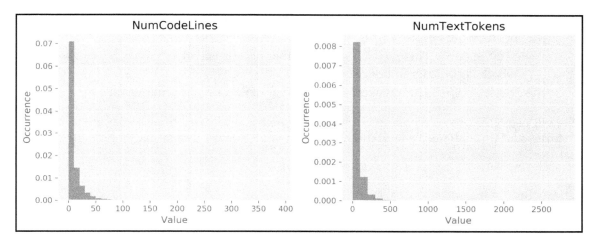

Since we have multiple features, we standardize their values:

```
scores = []
for train, test in cv.split(X, Y):
    clf = make_pipeline(StandardScaler(), KNeighborsClassifier())
    clf.fit(X[train], Y[train])
    scores.append(clf.score(X[test], Y[test]))

print("Mean(scores)=%.5f\tStddev(scores)=%.5f"%(np.mean(scores),
np.std(scores)))
```

Training on the bigger feature space improves accuracy quite a bit:

```
Mean(scores)=0.60070 Stddev(scores)=0.00759
```

But still, this would mean that we would classify roughly 4 out of 10 wrong. At least we are going in the right direction. More features lead to higher accuracy, which leads us to add more features. Therefore, let's extend the feature space by even more features:

- `AvgSentLen`: This measures the average number of words in a sentence. Maybe there is a pattern that particularly good posts don't overload the reader's brain with overly long sentences
- `AvgWordLen`: Similar to `AvgSentLen`, this feature measures the average number of characters in the words of a post
- `NumAllCaps`: This measures the number of words that are written in uppercase, which is considered poor style
- `NumExclams`: This measures the number of exclamation marks

We will use NLTK to conveniently determine sentence and word boundaries, calculate the features, and immediately attach them to the meta dictionary that already holds the other features:

```
import nltk
def add_sentence_features(m):
    for pid, text in fetch_posts(fn_sample):
        if not text:
            for feat in ['AvgSentLen', 'AvgWordLen',
                         'NumAllCaps', 'NumExclams']:
                m[pid][feat] = 0
        else:
            sent_lens = [len(nltk.word_tokenize(sent)) for sent in
                         nltk.sent_tokenize(text)]
            m[pid]['AvgSentLen'] = np.mean(sent_lens)
            text_tokens = nltk.word_tokenize(text)
            m[pid]['AvgWordLen'] = np.mean([len(w) for w in
text_tokens])
            m[pid]['NumAllCaps'] = np.sum([word.isupper() \
                                           for word in text_tokens])
            m[pid]['NumExclams'] = text.count('!')
add_sentence_features(meta)
```

The following charts show the value distributions for average sentence and word lengths, as well as the number of uppercase words and exclamation marks:

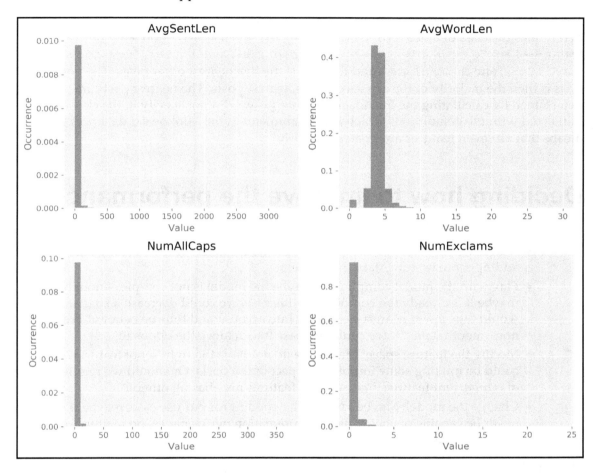

With these four additional features, we now have seven features representing the individual posts. Let's see how we progress:

```
Mean(scores)=0.60225 Stddev(scores)=0.00729
```

Now, that's interesting. We added four more features and didn't get anything in return. How can that be?

To understand this, we have to remind ourselves how `kNN` works. Our `5NN` classifier determines the class of a new post by calculating the seven aforementioned features—`LinkCount`, `NumTextTokens`, `NumCodeLines`, `AvgSentLen`, `AvgWordLen`, `NumAllCaps`, and `NumExclams`—and then finds the five nearest other posts. The new post's class is then the majority of the classes of those nearest posts. The nearest posts are determined by calculating the Euclidean distance (as we did not specify it, the classifier was initialized with the default `p=2`, which is the parameter in the Minkowski distance). That means that all seven features are treated similarly.

Deciding how to improve the performance

To improve on this, we basically have the following options:

- Add more data: Maybe there is just not enough data for the learning algorithm; adding more training data should help.
- Play with the model complexity: Maybe the model is not complex enough? Or maybe it is already too complex? In this case, we could decrease k so that it would take fewer nearest-neighbors into account and thus be better at predicting non-smooth data. Or we could increase it to achieve the opposite.
- Modify the feature space: Maybe we do not have the right set of features? We could be missing some important aspect of the posts. Or should we remove some of our current features in case some features are aliasing others?
- Change the model: Maybe kNN isn't a good fit for our use case; maybe it will never be capable of achieving good prediction performance, no matter how complex we allow it to be and how sophisticated the feature space becomes.

Stuck at this point, people often try to improve the current performance by randomly picking one of these options and trying it out in no particular order, hoping to find the golden configuration by chance. We could do the same here, but it will surely take longer than making informed decisions. Let's take the informed route, for which we need to introduce the bias-variance tradeoff.

Bias, variance and their trade-off

In Chapter 1, *Getting Started with Python Machine Learning*, we tried to fit polynomials of different complexities controlled by the d dimensionality parameter to fit the data. We realized that a two-dimensional polynomial, a straight line, does not fit the example data very well, because the data was not linear in nature. No matter how elaborate our fitting procedure was, our two-dimensional model saw everything as a straight line. We learned that it was too biased for the data at hand and called it under-fitting.

We played a bit with the dimensions and found out that the 100-dimensional polynomial fits very well to the data on which it was trained (we did not know about train-test splits at that time). However, we quickly found out that it was fitting too well. We realized that it was over-fitting so badly that with different samples of the data points, we would have gotten totally different 100-dimensional polynomials. That's why one can also say that the model has too high a variance for the given data.

These are the extremes between which most of our machine learning problems reside. Ideally, we want to have both low bias and low variance. But, we are in a bad world and have to trade off between them. If we improve on one, the other will likely get worse.

Fixing high bias

Let's now assume we suffer from high bias. In that case, adding more training data clearly does not help. Also, removing features surely will not help, as our model would have already been overly simplistic.

The only possibilities we have are to get more features, make the model more complex, or change the model itself.

Fixing high variance

If, on the contrary, we suffer from high variance, it means that our model is too complex for the data. In this case, we can only try to get more data or decrease the complexity. This would mean increasing k so that more neighbors would be taken into account, or removing some of the features.

High or low bias?

To find out what our problem is, we have to plot the train and test errors over different data sizes and then check whether the gap between train and test is closing.

High bias is typically revealed by the test error decreasing a bit at the beginning, but then settling at a very high value with the train error approaching with a growing dataset size. High variance is recognized by a big gap between both curves.

Plotting the errors for different dataset sizes for **5NN** shows a big gap between train and test errors, hinting at a high variance problem:

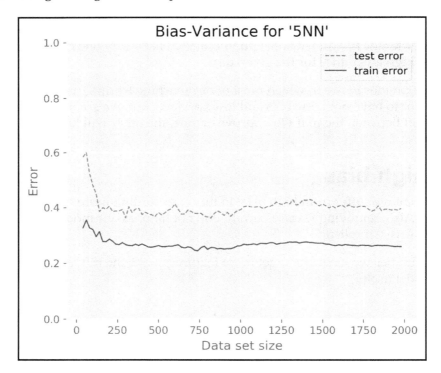

As the test error does not decrease with more data, we have to rethink the model. We certainly can decrease the model complexity, either by increasing k or by simplifying the feature space.

Reducing the feature space does not help here, as shown by the following graph, for a simplified feature space of only `LinkCount` and `NumTextTokens`:

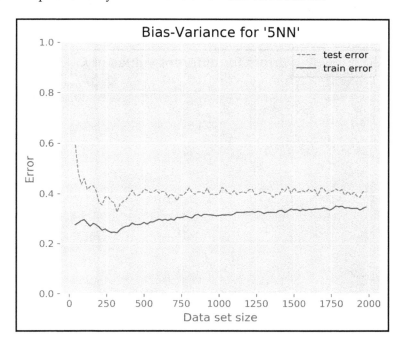

We get similar graphs for other smaller feature sets. No matter what subset of features we take, the graph would look similar.

Another way to reduce the model complexity is to increase k, which results into a smoother decision boundary. Trained again on all features, we do see a positive impact:

k	mean(scores)	stddev(scores)
5	0.6022	0.0073
10	0.6191	0.0096
40	0.6425	0.0104

But it is not enough, and also comes at the price of lower classification-runtime performance. Take, for instance, **k=40**, which has the highest average precision in the preceding table. To classify a new post, we would need to find the **40** nearest other posts to decide whether the new post is a good one or not:

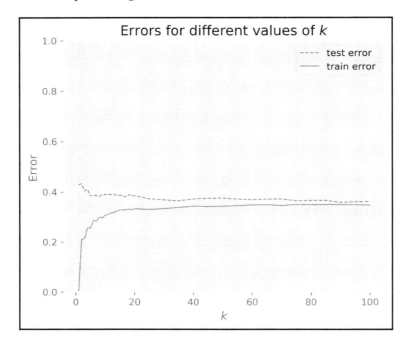

Clearly, there seems to be an issue with using nearest-neighbor for our scenario. And it has another real disadvantage. Over time, we will get more and more posts into our system. As the nearest-neighbor method is an instance-based approach, we will have to store all posts in our system. The more we get, the slower the prediction will be—this is definitely not a price we would be willing to pay given this low performance. This is different with model-based approaches, where one tries to derive a model from the data.

There we are, with enough reasons now to abandon the nearest-neighbor approach to look for better places in the classification world. Of course, we will never know whether there is that one golden feature we just didn't happen to think of. But for now, let's move on to another classification method that is known to work great in text-based classification scenarios.

Using logistic regression

Contrary to its name, logistic regression is a classification method. It is an enormously powerful one when it comes to text-based classification; it achieves this by first doing a regression on a logistic function, hence the name.

A bit of math with a small example

To get an initial understanding of the way logistic regression works, let's first take a look at the following example, where we have artificial feature values, X, plotted with the corresponding classes, 0 or 1:

```
from scipy.stats import norm
np.random.seed(3) # for reproducibility
NUM_PER_CLASS = 40
X_log = np.hstack((norm.rvs(2, size=NUM_PER_CLASS, scale=2),
                    norm.rvs(8, size=NUM_PER_CLASS, scale=3)))
y_log = np.hstack((np.zeros(NUM_PER_CLASS),
                    np.ones(NUM_PER_CLASS))).astype(int)
plt.xlim((-5, 20))
plt.scatter(X_log, y_log, c=np.array(['blue', 'red'])[y_log], s=10)
plt.xlabel("feature value")
plt.ylabel("class")
```

Refer to the following graph:

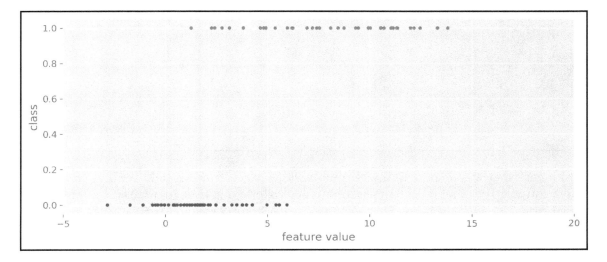

As we can see, the data so noisy that classes overlap in the feature value range between 1 and 6. Therefore, it is better to not directly model the discrete classes, but rather the probability that a feature value belongs to class 1, *P(X)*. Once we possess such a model, we could then predict class 1 if *P(X)>0.5*, and class 0 otherwise.

Mathematically, it is always difficult to model something that has a finite range, as is the case here with our discrete labels, 0 and 1. We therefore tweak the probabilities a bit so that they always stay between 0 and 1. And for that, we will need the odds ratio and the logarithm of it.

Let's say a feature has a probability of 0.9 that it belongs to class 1, *P(y=1) = 0.9*. The odds ratio is then *P(y=1)/P(y=0) = 0.9/0.1 = 9*. We could say that the chance is 9:1 that this feature maps to class 1. If *P(y=0.5)*, we would consequently have a 1:1 chance that the instance is of class 1. The odds ratio is bounded by 0 but goes to infinity (the left graph in the following set of graphs). If we now take the logarithm of it, we can map all probabilities between 0 and 1 to the full range from negative to positive-infinity (the right graph in the following set of graphs). The nice thing is that we still maintain the relationship that higher probability leads to a higher log of odds, just not limited to 0 and 1 anymore:

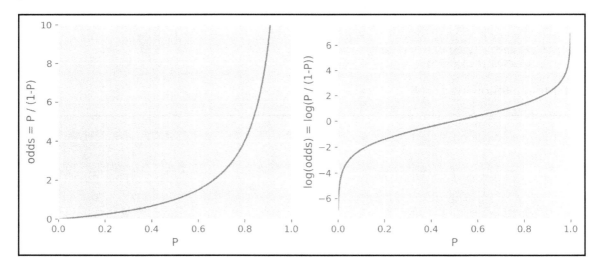

This means that we can now fit linear combinations of our features (OK, we only have one and a constant, but that will change soon) to the log(odds) values. In a sense, we replace the linear from Chapter 1, *Getting Started with Python Machine Learning*, $y_i = c_0 + c_1 x_i$ with $\log\left(\frac{p_i}{1 - p_i}\right) = c_0 + c_1 x_i$ (replacing y with log(odds)).

We can solve this for p_i, so that we have $p_i = \dfrac{1}{1+e^{-(c_0+c_1 x_i)}}$.

We simply have to find the right coefficients, such that the formula gives the lowest errors for all our (xi, pi) pairs in our dataset, but that will be done by scikit-learn.

After fitting, the formula will give the probability for every new data point, x, that belongs to class 1:

```
>>> from sklearn.linear_model import LogisticRegression
>>> clf = LogisticRegression()
>>> print(clf)
LogisticRegression(C=1.0, class_weight=None, dual=False,
fit_intercept=True, intercept_scaling=1, max_iter=100, multi_class='ovr',
n_jobs=1, penalty='12', random_state=None, solver='liblinear', tol=0.0001,
verbose=0, warm_start=False)
>>> clf.fit(X_log, y_log)
>>> print(np.exp(clf.intercept_), np.exp(clf.coef_.ravel()))
[ 0.09437188] [ 1.80094112]
>>> def lr_model(clf, X):
...        return 1 / (1 + np.exp(-(clf.intercept_ + clf.coef_* X)))
>>> print("P(x=-1)=%.2f\tP(x=7)=%.2f"%(lr_model(clf, -1),
lr_model(clf, 7)))
P(x=-1)=0.05 P(x=7)=0.85
```

You might have noticed that scikit-learn exposes the first coefficient through the `intercept_` special field.

If we plot the fitted model, we see that it makes perfect sense given the data:

```
X_range = np.arange(-5, 20, 0.1)
plt.figure(figsize=(10, 4), dpi=300)
plt.xlim((-5, 20))
plt.scatter(X_log, y_log, c=np.array(['blue', 'red'])[y_log], s=5)
# we use ravel() to get rid of the additional axis
plt.plot(X_range, lr_model(clf, X_range).ravel(), c='green')
plt.plot(X_range, np.ones(X_range.shape[0]) * 0.5, "--")
plt.xlabel("feature value")
plt.ylabel("class")
plt.grid(True)
```

Refer to the following graph:

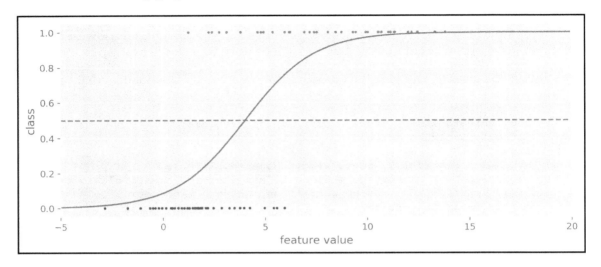

Applying logistic regression to our post-classification problem

Admittedly, the example in the previous section was created to show the beauty of logistic regression. How does it perform on the real noisy data?

Comparing it to the best nearest-neighbor classifier (k=40) as a baseline, we see that it won't change the situation a whole lot:

Method	mean(scores)	stddev(scores)
LogReg C=0.001	0.6369	0.0097
LogReg C=0.01	0.6390	0.0109
LogReg C=0.1	0.6382	0.0097
LogReg C=1.00	0.6380	0.0099
LogReg C=10.00	0.6380	0.0097
40NN	0.6425	0.0104

We have shown the accuracy for different values of the C regularization parameter. With it, we can control the model complexity, similar to the k parameter for the nearest-neighbor method. Smaller values for C result in more penalization of the model complexity.

A quick look at the bias-variance chart for one of our best candidates, `C=0.01`, shows that our model has high bias-test and train-error curves, approach closely but stay at unacceptably high values. This indicates that logistic regression with the current feature space is under-fitting and cannot learn a model that captures the data correctly:

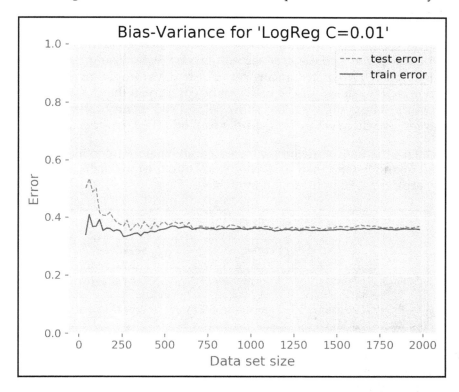

So, what now? We switched the model and tuned it as much as we could with our current state of knowledge, but we still have no acceptable classifier. The only thing we gained by switching is that we now have a model that scales with the data, since it doesn't need to store all the instances.

More and more, it seems that either the data is too noisy for this task or that our set of features is still not appropriate enough to discriminate the classes properly.

Looking behind accuracy – precision and recall

Let's step back and think again about what we are trying to achieve. Actually, we do not need a classifier that perfectly predicts good and bad answers, as we measured it until now using accuracy. If we can tune the classifier to be particularly good at predicting one class, we could adapt the feedback to the user accordingly. If we, for example, had a classifier that was always right when it predicted an answer to be bad, we would give no feedback until the classifier detected the answer to be bad. On the contrary, if the classifier exceeded in predicting answers to be good, we could show helpful comments to the user at the beginning and remove them when the classifier said that the answer is a good one.

To find out which situation we are in, we have to understand how to measure precision and recall. And to understand that, we have to look into the four distinct classification results as they are described in the following table:

		Prediction	
		Positive	Negative
Truth	Positive	True positive (TP)	False negative (FN)
	Negative	False positive (FP)	True negative (TN)

For instance, if the classifier predicts an instance to be positive and the instance is indeed positive, this is a true positive instance. If, on the other hand, the classifier misclassified that instance, saying that it is negative while in reality it was positive, that instance is said to be a false negative.

What we want is to have a high success rate when we are predicting a post as either good or bad, but not necessarily both. That is, we want as many true positives as possible. This is what precision captures:

$$\text{Precision} = \frac{TP}{TP + FP}$$

If, instead, our goal have been to detect as many good or bad answers as possible, we would be more interested in recall:

$$\text{Recall} = \frac{\text{TP}}{\text{TP} + \text{FN}}$$

Refer to the following graph:

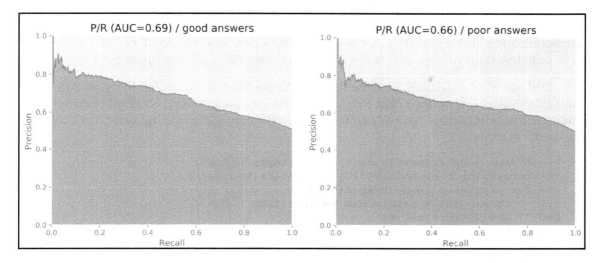

So, how can we now optimize for precision? So far, we have always used **0.5** as the threshold to decide whether an answer is good or not. What we can do now is count the number of TP, FP, and FN while we vary that threshold between **0** and **1**. With those counts, we can then plot precision over recall.

The handy `precision_recall_curve()` function from the `metrics` module does all the calculations for us:

```
>>> from sklearn.metrics import precision_recall_curve
>>> # X_test would come from KFold's train/test split
>>> precision, recall, thresholds = precision_recall_curve(y_test,
    clf.predict(X_test))
```

Predicting one class with acceptable performance does not always mean that the classifier is also acceptable at predicting the other class. This can be seen in the following two plots, where we plot the precision/recall curves for classifying bad (the left graph) and good (the right graph) answers:

In the graphs, we have also included a much better description of a classifier's performance, the **area under curve** (**AUC**). It can be understood as the average precision of the classifier and is a great way of comparing different classifiers.

Predicting good answers shows that we can get 80% precision at a recall of 20%, while we have only less than 10% recall when we want to achieve 80% prediction on poor answers.

Let's find out what threshold we need for that. As we trained many classifiers on different folds (remember, we iterated over `KFold()` a couple of pages back), we need to retrieve the classifier that was neither too bad nor too good in order to get a realistic view. Let's call it the medium clone:

```
>>> medium = np.argsort(scores)[ len(scores) // 2)]
>>> thresholds = np.hstack(([0],thresholds[medium]))
>>> for precision in np.arange(0.77, 0.8, 0.01):
...     thresh_idx = precisions >= precision
P=0.77 R=0.25 thresh=0.62
P=0.78 R=0.23 thresh=0.65
P=0.79 R=0.21 thresh=0.66
P=0.80 R=0.13 thresh=0.74
```

Setting the threshold at `0.66`, we see that we can still achieve a precision of 79% at detecting good answers when we accept a low recall of 21%. That means that we would detect only one in three good answers. But from that third of good answers we'd manage to detect, we would be reasonably sure that they are indeed good. For the rest, we could then politely display additional hints on how to improve answers in general.

Slimming the classifier

It is always worth looking at the actual contributions of the individual features. For logistic regression, we can directly take the learned coefficients (`clf.coef_`) to get an impression of the features' impact:

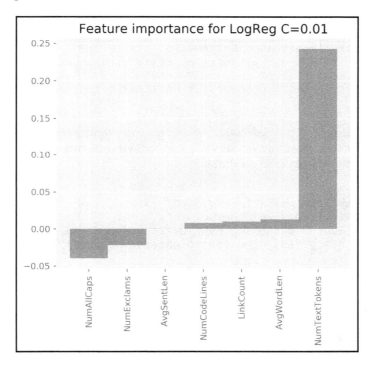

We see that `NumCodeLines`, `LinkCount`, `AvgWordLen`, and `NumTextTokens` have the highest positive impact on determining whether a post is a good one, while `AvgWordLen`, `LinkCount`, and `NumCodeLines` have a say in that as well, but much less so. This means that being more verbose will more likely result in a classification as a good answer.

On the other side, we have `NumAllCaps` and `NumExclams` have negative weights one. That means that the more an answer is shouting, the less likely it will be received well.

Then we have the `AvgSentLen` feature, which does not seem to help much in detecting a good answer. We could easily drop that feature and retain. However, just from the same classification performance magnitude of the coefficients, we cannot immediately derive the feature's importance, because we trained the classifier on the raw features, which were not normalized.

Ship it!

Let's assume we want to integrate this classifier into our site. In all of the preceding examples, we always trained on only 90% of the available data, because we used the other 10% for testing. Let's assume that the data was all we had. In that case, we should retrain the classifier on all data:

```
>>> C_best = 0.01 # determined above
>>> clf = LogisticRegression(C=C_best)
>>> clf.fit(X, Y) # now trainining an all data without cross-validation
>>> print(clf.coef_)
[[ 0.24937413 0.00777857 0.0097297 0.00061647 0.02354386 -0.03715787
 -0.03406846]]
```

Finally, we should store the trained classifier, because we definitely do not want to retrain it each time we start the classification service. Instead, we can simply serialize the classifier after training and then deserialize on that site:

```
>>> import pickle
>>> pickle.dump(clf, open("logreg.dat", "w"))
>>> clf = pickle.load(open("logreg.dat", "r"))
>>> print(clf.coef_) # showing that we indeed got the same classifier again
[[ 0.24937413 0.00777857 0.0097297 0.00061647 0.02354386 -0.03715787
 -0.03406846]]
```

Congratulations, the classifier is now ready to be used as if it had just been trained. We can now use the classifier's `predict_proba()` to calculate the probability of an answer being a good one. We will use the threshold of `0.66`, which results in 79% precision at 21% recall, as we determined earlier:

```
>>> good_thresh = 0.66
```

Let's take a look at the features of two artificial posts to show how it works:

```
>>> # Remember that the features are in this order:
>>> # LinkCount, NumCodeLines, NumTextTokens, AvgSentLen, AvgWordLen,
>>> # NumAllCaps, NumExclams
>>> good_post = (2, 1, 100, 5, 4, 1, 0)
>>> poor_post = (1, 0, 10, 5, 6, 5, 4)
>>> proba = clf.predict_proba([good_post, poor_post])
>>> print(proba) # print probabilities (poor, good) per post
array([[ 0.30127876, 0.69872124],
       [ 0.62934963, 0.37065037]])
>>> print(proba >= good_thresh)
array([[[False, True],
        [False, False]], dtype=bool)
```

As expected, we manage to detect the first post as good, but cannot say anything about the second, which is why we would show a nice, motivating message directing the writer to improve the post.

Classification using Tensorflow

Neural networks can also be designed to classify data. As with the previous classifier, they can generate a probability of belonging to a class, and as such, we can use the threshold we want for the precision we require.

This example will be our first real dive into neural networks. Just as for the previous case, we will use placeholders, but instead of explicitly setting variables, we will use standard Tensorflow functions to create them.

Just as before, we will use the same data with all our current features:

```
X = np.asarray([get_features(aid, ['LinkCount', 'NumCodeLines',
                                    'NumTextTokens', 'AvgSentLen',
                                    'AvgWordLen', 'NumAllCaps',
                                    'NumExclams']) for aid in all_answers])
Y = np.asarray([meta[aid]['Score'] > 0 for aid in all_answers])
```

Of course, an exercise here is to replicate previous results by using fewer features and see how this neural network will be able to discriminate between good and bad posts.

Neural networks are not the same as the brain. We explicitly create layers, when in reality no such thing exists (more on this later, but this is required to understand how we create a simple neural network). It is a good practice to factor out the layers we want to create, so, for instance, we will create two types of layers: one for dense layers, meaning that they connect all input to all output, and one for the output layer that has only one output unit:

```
import tensorflow as tf

def create_dense(x, n_units, name, alpha=0.2):
    # Hidden layer
    h = tf.layers.dense(x, n_units, activation=tf.nn.leaky_relu, name=name)
    return h

def create_output(x):
    # Output layer
    h = tf.layers.dense(x, 1, activation=tf.nn.sigmoid, name="Output")
    return h
```

This output unit is created with a `sigmoid` activation. This means that the inner `tf.matmult` that creates values between `-inf` and `+inf` is fed inside a function that maps these to the interval `[0, 1]`. `0` and `1` cannot be achieved for the output, so when we train our neural network, we have to keep this in memory. As such, for the target probability in our training, we change the output to accommodate this impossibility:

```
Y = Y.astype(np.float32)[:, None]
bce_ceil = 1e-5
Y = Y * (1 - 2 * bce_ceil) + bce_ceil
```

And now, we can split our data:

```
from sklearn.model_selection import train_test_split
X_train, X_test, Y_train, Y_test = train_test_split(X, Y, train_size=0.8)
```

Let's start with setting our usual hyper parameters:

```
n_epochs = 500
batch_size = 1000
steps = 10
layer1_size = 5
```

If we use all seven features, our neural network building looks like this:

```
X_tf = tf.placeholder(tf.float32, (None, 7), name="Input")
Y_ref_tf = tf.placeholder(tf.float32, (None, 1), name="Target_output")

h1 = create_dense(X_tf, layer1_size, name="Layer1")
Y_tf = create_output(h1)

loss = tf.reduce_mean(tf.square(Y_ref_tf - Y_tf))

grad_speed = .01
my_opt = tf.train.GradientDescentOptimizer(grad_speed)
train_step = my_opt.minimize(loss)
```

The gradient step is now far greater than the one from the regression example. We could use a smaller step, but this would require more steps to achieve a local minimum of our `loss` function.

We can now train our neural network, very similarly to what we did in Chapter 2, *Classifying with Real-world Examples*. The only difference is that at the end, we also run the test data inside the neural network:

```
with tf.Session() as sess:
    sess.run(tf.global_variables_initializer())
    loss_vec = []
    for epoch in range(n_epochs):
        permut = np.random.permutation(len(X_train))
        for j in range(0, len(X_train), batch_size):
            batch = permut[j:j+batch_size]
            Xs = X_train[batch]
            Ys = Y_train[batch]
            sess.run(train_step, feed_dict={X_tf: Xs, Y_ref_tf: Ys})
        temp_loss = sess.run(loss, feed_dict={X_tf: X_train, Y_ref_tf:
Y_train})
        loss_vec.append(temp_loss)
        if epoch % steps == steps - 1:
            print('Epoch #%i loss = %s' % (epoch, temp_loss))

    predict_train = sess.run(Y_tf, feed_dict={X_tf: X_train})
    predict_test = sess.run(Y_tf, feed_dict={X_tf: X_test})
```

For now, we throw away the neural network we trained, which is why we are also using the test data in the same session. We will see how to save and reuse a model in Chapter 8, *Artificial Neural Networks and Deep Learning*.

We can, of course, also display how well the optimizer behaved:

```
plt.plot(loss_vec, 'k-')
plt.title('Loss per Epoch)
plt.xlabel(Epoc')
plt.ylabel('Loss')
```

Refer to the following graph:

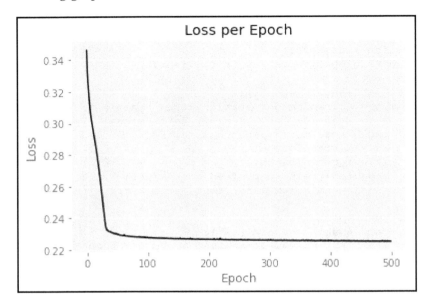

The loss per generation can be very different from one run to another. `grad_speed` is the most important parameter that changes this graph. Its value is a compromise between convergence speed and stability, and I advise you to try different values to see how this function behaves with different values and different runs.

If we look at the scores for the training and the test scores, we can see that we have results that match the best of the previous classifiers:

```
from sklearn.metrics import accuracy_score
score = accuracy_score(Y_train > .5, predict_train > .5)
print("Score (on training data): %.2f" % score)
score = accuracy_score(Y_test > .5, predict_test > .5)
print("Score (on testing data): %.2f" % score)
```

This will output:

```
Score (on training data): 0.65
Score (on testing data): 0.65
```

It is a good time to go back to the hyper parameters, especially the size of the intermediate or hidden layer and modify the number of nodes. Is lowering it degrading the classifier's behavior? Is increasing it improving it? What about adding another intermediate layer? What is the impact of its number of neurons?

A nice feature of `sklearn` is the abundance of support functions and tutorials. This is a function from a tutorial on confusion matrices that helps visualize the quality of a classifier:

```python
def plot_confusion_matrix(cm, classes,
                          normalize=False,
                          title='Confusion matrix',
                          cmap=plt.cm.Blues):
    """
    This function prints and plots the confusion matrix.
    Normalization can be applied by setting `normalize=True`.
    """
    import itertools
    if normalize:
        cm = cm.astype('float') / cm.sum(axis=1)[:, np.newaxis]
        print("Normalized confusion matrix")
    else:
        print('Confusion matrix, without normalization')

    print(cm)

    plt.imshow(cm, interpolation='nearest', cmap=cmap)
    plt.title(title)
    plt.colorbar()
    tick_marks = np.arange(len(classes))
    plt.xticks(tick_marks, classes, rotation=45)
    plt.yticks(tick_marks, classes)

    fmt = '.2f' if normalize else 'd'
    thresh = cm.max() / 2.
    for i, j in itertools.product(range(cm.shape[0]), range(cm.shape[1])):
        plt.text(j, i, format(cm[i, j], fmt),
                horizontalalignment="center",
                color="white" if cm[i, j] > thresh else "black")

    plt.tight_layout()
    plt.ylabel('True label')
    plt.xlabel('Predicted label')
```

We can now use it with a threshold at .5 to see the behavior of this classifier on trained and tested data:

```
class_names = ["Poor", "Good"]
from sklearn import metrics
print(metrics.classification_report(Y_train > .5, predict_train > .5,
target_names=class_names))
plot_confusion_matrix(metrics.confusion_matrix(Y_train > .5, pre-dict_train
> .5), classes=class_names,title='Confusion matrix, without normaliza-
tion')
plt.show()
print(metrics.classification_report(Y_test > .5, predict_test > .5,
target_names=class_names))
plot_confusion_matrix(metrics.confusion_matrix(Y_test > .5, pre-dict_test >
.5), classes=class_names,title='Confusion matrix, without normaliza-tion')
```

This will output:

```
          precision recall f1-score support

Poor         0.63   0.73     0.67     8035
Good         0.67   0.57     0.62     7965
```

Refer to the following graph:

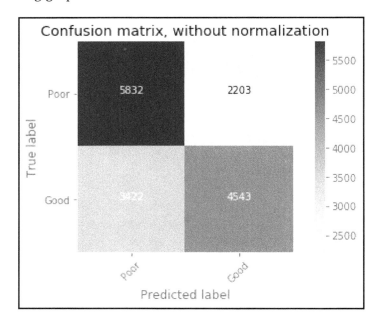

See the following data:

	precision	recall	f1-score	support
avg / total	0.65	0.65	0.65	16000
Poor	0.62	0.73	0.67	1965
Good	0.68	0.57	0.62	2035
avg / total	0.65	0.65	0.65	4000

It is very interesting to see the stability of the classifier when moving from training data to test data. In both cases, we can also see that there are still lots of misclassifications, with an emphasis on good posts that were labeled as bad posts (which is probably better than the opposite!).

Summary

We made it! From a very noisy dataset, we built two classifiers that solve part of our goal. Of course, we had to be pragmatic and adapt our initial goal to what was achievable. But on the way, we learned about the strengths and weaknesses of nearest-neighbor and logistic regression, and got an introduction to simple classification with neural networks. We learned how to extract features, such as `LinkCount`, `NumTextTokens`, `NumCodeLines`, `AvgSentLen`, `AvgWordLen`, `NumAllCaps`, and `NumExclams`, and how to analyze their impact on the classifier's performance.

But what is even more valuable is that we learned an informed way of debugging poorly performing classifiers. That will help us in the future to produce usable systems much faster.

After having looked into nearest-neighbor and logistic regression, in `Chapter 5`, *Dimensionality Reduction*, we will get familiar with yet another simple-but-powerful classification algorithm: Naïve Bayes. Along the way, we will also learn about some more convenient tools from scikit-learn.

5
Dimensionality Reduction

Garbage in, garbage out—throughout this book, we will see this pattern when applying machine learning methods to data. Looking back, we can see that the most interesting machine learning challenges always involved some sort of feature engineering, where we tried to use our insight into the problem to carefully craft additional features that the model hopefully would pick up.

In this chapter, we will go in the opposite direction with dimensionality reduction, cutting away features that are irrelevant or redundant. Removing features might seem counter-intuitive at first thought, as more information always seems to be better than less information. Also, even if we had redundant features in our dataset, wouldn't the learning algorithm be able to quickly figure it out and set their weights to 0? There are, indeed, good reasons for trimming down the dimensions as much as possible:

- Superfluous features can irritate or mislead the learner. This is not the case with all machine learning methods (for example, support vector machines love high-dimensional spaces). However, most of the models feel safer with fewer dimensions
- Another point against high-dimensional feature spaces is that more features mean more parameters to tune and a higher risk of overfitting
- The data we retrieve to solve our task might just have artificially high dimensionality, whereas the real dimension might be small
- Fewer dimensions equals to faster training equals to more parameter variations to try out in the same time frame equals to better end result
- Trimming down dimensions is better for visualization. If we want to visualize the data, we will be restricted to two or three dimensions

In this chapter, we will show you how to get rid of the garbage within our data while keeping the real valuable part of it.

Sketching our roadmap

Dimensionality reduction can be roughly grouped into feature selection and feature projection methods. We have already employed some kind of feature selection in almost every chapter so far when we invented, analyzed, and then probably dropped some features. In this chapter, we will present some ways that use statistical methods—namely correlation and mutual information—to be able to do so in vast feature spaces. Feature projection tries to transform the original feature space into a lower-dimensional feature space. This is especially useful when we cannot get rid of features using selection methods, but we still have too many features for our learner. We will demonstrate this using **principal component analysis (PCA)**, **linear discriminant analysis (LDA)**, and **multidimensional scaling (MDS)**.

Selecting features

If we want to be nice to our machine learning algorithm, we provide it with features that are not dependent on each other, but which are highly dependent on the value that is to be predicted. This means that each feature adds salient information. Removing any of the features will lead to a drop in performance.

If we only have a handful of features, we could draw a matrix of scatter plots (one scatter plot for each feature pair combination). Relationships between the features could then be easily spotted. For every feature pair showing an obvious dependence, we would then think of whether we should remove one of them or better design a newer, cleaner feature out of both.

Most of the time, however, we have more than a handful of features to choose from. Just think of the classification task where we had a bag of words to classify the quality of an answer, which would require a 1,000 x 1,000 scatter plot (using a vocabulary of 1,000 words). In this case, we need a more automated way to detect overlapping features and to resolve them. We will present two general ways to do so in the following subsections.

Detecting redundant features using filters

Filters try to clean up the feature space independent of any later-used machine learning method. They rely on statistical methods to find out which of the features are redundant or irrelevant. In the case of redundant features, a filter keeps only one per redundant feature group. Irrelevant features will simply be removed. In general, a filter works as depicted in the following workflow:

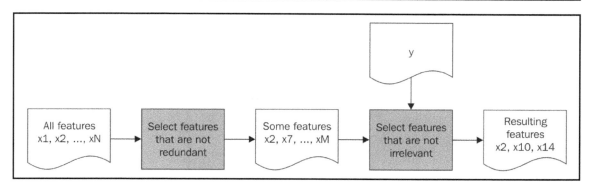

First, we filter out features that are redundant using statistics that only take into account the training data. We then check whether the remaining features are useful in classifying the label.

Correlation

Using correlation, we can easily see linear relationships between pairs of features. In the following graphs, we can see different degrees of correlation, together with a potential linear dependency plotted as a dashed line (fitted one-dimensional polynomial). The correlation coefficient $Cor (X_1, X_2)$ at the top of the individual graphs is calculated using the common Pearson correlation coefficient (pearson r value) by means of the `pearsonr()` function of `scipy.stat`.

Given two equal-sized data series, it returns a tuple of the correlation coefficient value and the *p*-value. The *p*-value describes how likely it is that the data series has been generated by an uncorrelated system. In other words, the higher the *p*-value, the less we should trust the correlation coefficient:

```
>>> from scipy.stats import pearsonr
>>> pearsonr([1,2,3], [1,2,3.1])
(0.99962228516121843, 0.017498096813278487)
>>> pearsonr([1,2,3], [1,20,6])
(0.25383654128340477, 0.83661493668227427)
```

In the first case, we have a clear indication that both series are correlated. In the second case, we still have a clearly nonzero r value.

However, the *p*-value of 0.84 tells us that the correlation coefficient is not significant, and we should not pay too much attention to it. In the first three cases that have high correlation coefficients in the following graph, we would probably want to throw out either X_1 or X_2 because they seem to convey similar, if not the same, information:

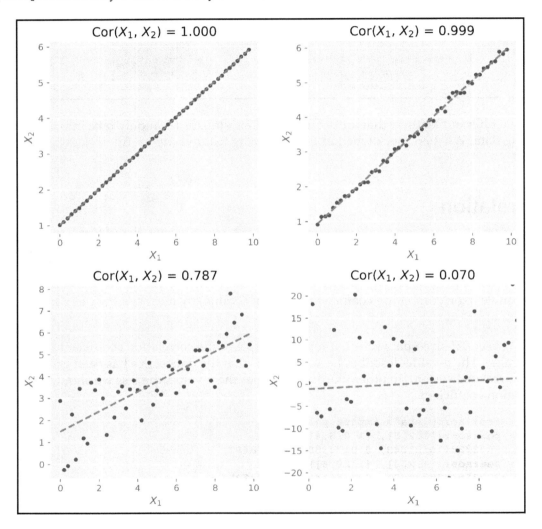

In the last case, however, we should keep both features. In our application, this decision would, of course, be driven by this *p*-value.

Although it worked nicely in the preceding example, reality is seldom nice. One big disadvantage of correlation-based feature selection is that it only detects linear relationships (a relationship that can be modeled by a straight line). We can see the problem if we use correlation on nonlinear data. In the following example, we have a quadratic relationship:

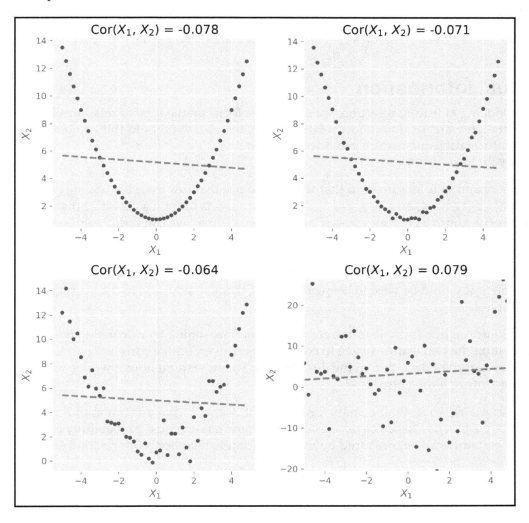

Although the human eye immediately sees the relationship between X_1 and X_2 in all but the bottom-right graph, the correlation coefficient does not. It's obvious that correlation is useful for detecting linear relationships, but fails for everything else. Sometimes, it really helps to apply simple transformations to get a linear relationship. For instance, in the preceding plot, we would have got a high correlation coefficient if we had drawn X_2 over X_1 squared. Normal data, however, seldom offers this opportunity.

Luckily, for nonlinear relationships, mutual information comes to the rescue.

Mutual information

When looking at feature selection, we should not focus on the type of relationship as we did in the previous section (linear relationships). Instead, we should think in terms of how much information one feature provides, given that
we already have another.

To understand this, let's pretend that we want to use features from the `house_size`, `number_of_levels`, and `avg_rent_price` feature sets to train a classifier that outputs whether the house has an elevator or not. In this example, we can intuitively see that, knowing `house_size`, we don't need to know `number_of_levels` anymore, as it contains, somehow, redundant information. With `avg_rent_price`, it's different because we cannot infer the value of rental space simply from the size of the house or the number of levels it has. Hence, it would be wise to keep only one of them, in addition to the average price of rental space.

Mutual information formalizes the aforementioned reasoning by calculating how much information the two features have in common. However, unlike correlation, it does not rely on the sequence of data, but on the distribution. To understand how it works, we have to dive into information entropy.

Let's assume we have a fair coin. Before we flip it, we will have maximum uncertainty as to whether it will show heads or tails, as each outcome has an equal probability of 50 percent. This uncertainty can be measured by means of Claude Shannon's information entropy:

$$H(X) = -\sum_{\{i=1\}}^{n} p(X_i) \log_2 p(X_i)$$

In our fair coin case, we have two cases: let X_0 be the case of heads and X_1 the case of tails with $p(X_0) = p(X_1) = 0.5$.

Hence, it concludes in the following:

$$H(X) = -p(X_0) \log_2 p(X_0)$$
$$- p(X_1) \log_2 p(X_1) = -0.5 \cdot \log_2(0.5) - 0.5 \cdot \log_2(0.5) = 1.0$$

> **TIP**
> For convenience, we can also use `scipy.stats.entropy([0.5, 0.5], base=2)`. We set the base parameter to 2 to get the same result as earlier. Otherwise, the function will use the natural logarithm via `np.log()`. In general, the base does not matter (as long as you use it consistently).

Now, imagine that we knew upfront that the coin is actually not that fair, with heads having a 60 percent chance of showing up after flipping:

$$H(X) = -0.6^{\log_2}(0.6) - 0.4^{\log_2}(0.4)=0.97$$

We can see that this situation is less uncertain. The uncertainty will decrease the further away we get from 0.5, reaching the extreme value of 0 for either 0 percent or 100 percent probability of heads showing up, as we can see in the following graph:

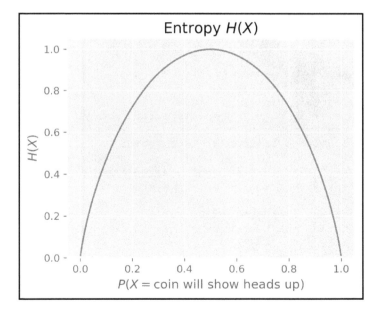

We will now modify the entropy, **H(X)**, by applying it to two features instead of one in such a way that it measures how much uncertainty is removed from X when we learn about Y. Then, we can catch how one feature reduces the uncertainty of another.

For example, without having any further information about the weather, we are totally uncertain whether or not it's raining outside. If we now learn that the grass outside is wet, the uncertainty has been reduced (we will still have to check whether the sprinkler had been turned on).

More formally, mutual information is defined as the following:

$$I(X;Y) = \sum_{\{i=1\}}^{m} \sum_{\{j=1\}}^{n} P(X_i,Y_j) \log_2 \frac{P(X_i,Y_j)}{P(X_i)P(Y_j)}$$

This looks a bit intimidating but is really nothing more than sums and products. For instance, the calculation of p() can be done by binning the feature values and then calculating the fraction of values in each bin. In the following plots, we have set the number of bins to ten.

In order to restrict mutual information to the interval of [0, 1], we have to divide it by their added individual entropy, which gives us the following normalized mutual information:

$$NI(X;Y) = \frac{I(X;Y)}{H(X) + H(Y)}$$

The code is as follows:

```
def normalized_mutual_info(x, y, bins=10):
    counts_xy, bins_x, bins_y = np.histogram2d(x, y, bins=(bins, bins))
    counts_x, bins = np.histogram(x, bins=bins)
    counts_y, bins = np.histogram(y, bins=bins)

    counts_xy += 1 # add-one smoothing as we have
    counts_x += 1 # seen in the previous chapters
    counts_y += 1
    P_xy = counts_xy / np.sum(counts_xy)
    P_x = counts_x / np.sum(counts_x)
    P_y = counts_y / np.sum(counts_y)

    I_xy = np.sum(P_xy * np.log2(P_xy / (P_x.reshape(-1, 1) * P_y)))

    return I_xy / (entropy(counts_x) + entropy(counts_y))
```

The nice thing about mutual information is that, unlike correlation, it does not only look at linear relationships, as we can see in the following graphs:

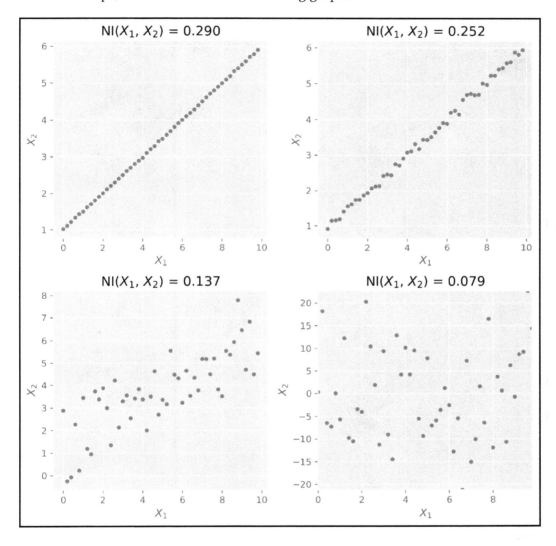

As we can see, mutual information is able to indicate the strength of a linear relationship. The following diagram shows that it also works for squared relationships:

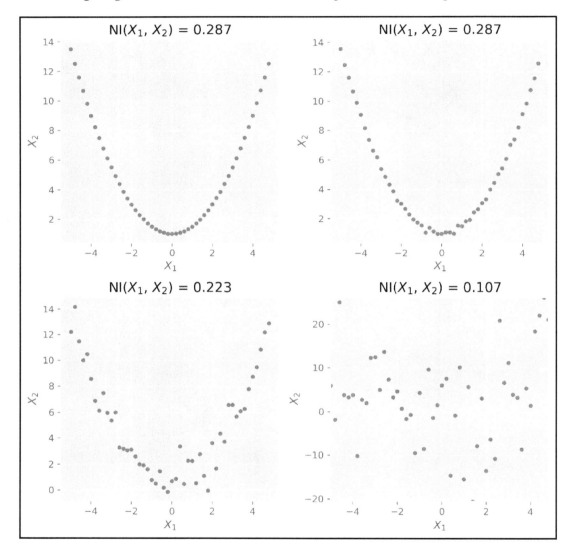

So, what we would have to do is calculate the normalized mutual information for all feature pairs. For every pair with too high a value (we would have to determine what this means), we would then drop one of them. In the case of regression, we could drop the feature that has too little mutual information with the desired result value.

This might work for a smallish set of features. At some point, however, this procedure can be really expensive, because the amount of calculation grows quadratically with the number of features.

Another huge disadvantage of filters is that they drop features that don't seem to be useful in isolation. More often than not, there are a handful of features that seem to be totally independent of the target variable, yet when combined, they rock. To keep these, we need wrappers.

Asking the model about the features using wrappers

While filters can help tremendously in getting rid of useless features, they can only go so far. After all the filtering, there might still be some features that are independent among themselves and that show some degree of dependence with the result variable, but that are totally useless from the model's point of view. Just think of the following data that describes the XOR function. Individually, neither **A** nor **B** would show any signs of dependence on **Y**, whereas together they clearly do:

A	B	Y
0	0	0
0	1	1
1	0	1
1	1	0

So, why not ask the model itself to give its vote on the individual features? This is what scikit wrappers do, as we can see in the following process chart:

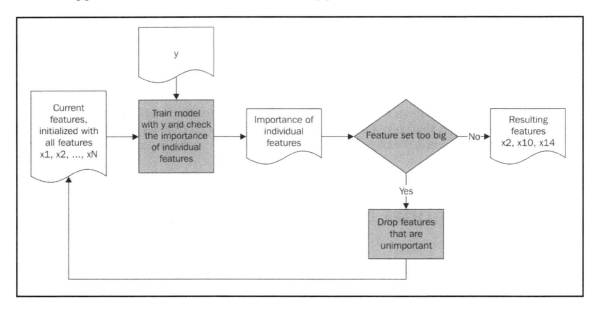

Here, we pushed the calculation of feature importance to the model training process. Unfortunately (but understandably), feature importance is not determined as a binary, but as a ranking value, so we still have to specify where to make the cut, what part of the features we are willing to take, and what part we want to drop.

Coming back to scikit-learn, we find various excellent wrapper classes in the `sklearn.feature_selection` package. A real workhorse in this field is RFE, which stands for recursive feature elimination. It takes an estimator and the desired number of features to keep as parameters and then trains the estimator with various feature sets, as long as it has found a subset of features that is small enough. The RFE instance itself pretends to be an estimator, thereby, indeed, wrapping the provided estimator.

In the following example, we will create an artificial classification problem of 100 samples using the dataset's convenient `make_classification()` function. It lets us specify the creation of 10 features, out of which only three are really valuable, to solve the classification problem:

```
>>> from sklearn.feature_selection import RFE
>>> from sklearn.linear_model import LogisticRegression
>>> from sklearn.datasets import make_classification
>>> X,y = make_classification(n_samples=100, n_features=10,
```

```
                        n_informative=3, random_state=0)
>>> clf = LogisticRegression()
>>> selector = RFE(clf, n_features_to_select=3)
>>> selector = selector.fit(X, y)
>>> print(selector.support_)
[False False True False False False True True False False]
>>> print(selector.ranking_)
[5 4 1 2 6 7 1 1 8 3]
```

The problem in real-world scenarios is, of course, how can we know the right value for n_features_to_select? The truth is, we can't. However, most of the time, we can use a sample of the data and play with it using different settings to quickly get a feeling for the right ballpark.

The good thing is that we don't have to be that exact using wrappers. Let's try different values for n_features_to_select to see how support_ and ranking_ change:

n_features_to_select	support_	ranking_
1	[False False False False False False False True False False]	[7 6 3 4 8 9 2 1 10 5]
2	[False False False False False False True True False False]	[6 5 2 3 7 8 1 1 9 4]
3	[False False True False False False True True False False]	[5 4 1 2 6 7 1 1 8 3]
4	[False False True True False False True True False False]	[4 3 1 1 5 6 1 1 7 2]
5	[False False True True False False True True False True]	[3 2 1 1 4 5 1 1 6 1]
6	[False True True True False False True True False True]	[2 1 1 1 3 4 1 1 5 1]
7	[True True True True False False True True False True]	[1 1 1 1 2 3 1 1 4 1]
8	[True True True True True False True True False True]	[1 1 1 1 1 2 1 1 3 1]
9	[True True True True True True True True False True]	[1 1 1 1 1 1 1 1 2 1]
10	[True True True True True True True True True True]	[1 1 1 1 1 1 1 1 1 1]

We can see that the result is very stable. Features that have been used when requesting smaller feature sets keep on getting selected when letting more features in. Lastly, we rely on our train/test set splitting to warn us when we go the wrong way.

Other feature selection methods

There are several other feature-selection methods that you will discover while reading through machine learning literature. Some don't even look like they are feature selection methods because they are embedded in the learning process (not to be confused with the aforementioned wrappers). Decision trees, for instance, have a feature selection mechanism implanted deep in their core. Other learning methods employ some kind of regularization that punishes model complexity, hence driving the learning process toward good performing models that are still simple. They do this by decreasing the less impactful features' importance to zero and then dropping them (L1 regularization).

Often, the power of machine learning methods has to be attributed to their implanted feature selection methods to a great degree.

Feature projection

At some point, after we have removed redundant features and dropped irrelevant ones, we will often still find that we have too many features. No matter what learning method we use, they all perform badly and, given the huge feature space, we understand that they actually cannot do better. We have to get rid of features, even though common sense tells us that they are valuable. Another situation where we need to reduce the feature dimension, and where feature selection does not help much, is when we want to visualize data. Then, we need to have, at most, three dimensions at the end to provide any meaningful graphs.

Enter feature projection methods. They restructure the feature space to make it more accessible to the model, or simply cut down the dimensions to two or three so that we can show dependencies visually.

Again, we can distinguish feature projection methods as being linear or nonlinear. Also, as seen before in the *Selecting features* section, we will present one method for each type (principal component analysis as a linear and nonlinear version of multidimensional scaling). Although they are widely known and used, they are only a selection of the more interesting and powerful feature projection methods available.

Principal component analysis

Principal component analysis (**PCA**) is often the first thing to try out if you want to cut down the number of features and do not know which feature projection method to use. PCA is limited as it's a linear method, but chances are that it already goes far enough for your model to learn well enough. Add to this the strong mathematical properties it offers, the speed at which it finds the transformed feature space, and the speed at which it is later able to transform between original and transformed features, and we can almost guarantee that it will also become one of your frequently used machine learning tools.

To summarize, given the original feature space, PCA finds a linear projection of itself in a lower dimensional space that has the following properties:

- The conserved variance is maximized
- The final reconstruction error (when trying to go back from transformed features to the original ones) is minimized

As PCA simply transforms the input data, it can be applied to both classification and regression problems. In this section, we will use a classification task to discuss the method.

Sketching PCA

PCA involves a lot of linear algebra, which we do not want to go into. Nevertheless, the basic algorithm's process can be easily described as follows:

1. Center the data by subtracting the mean from it
2. Calculate the covariance matrix
3. Calculate the eigenvectors of the covariance matrix

If we start with N features, then the algorithm will return a transformed feature space with N dimensions (we have gained nothing so far). The nice thing about this algorithm, however, is that the eigenvalues indicate how much of the variance is described by the corresponding eigenvector.

Let's assume that we start with $N = 1000$ features and that we know that our model does not work well with more than 20 features. Then, we simply pick the 20 eigenvectors with the highest eigenvalues.

Applying PCA

Let's consider the following artificial dataset, which is visualized in the following left-hand plot diagram:

```
>>> x1 = np.arange(0, 10, .2)
>>> x2 = x1+np.random.normal(loc=0, scale=1, size=len(x1))
>>> X = np.c_[(x1, x2)]
>>> good = (x1>5) | (x2>5) # some arbitrary classes
>>> bad = ~good
```

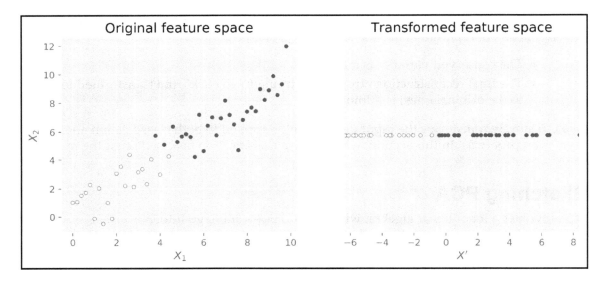

Scikit-learn provides the PCA class in its decomposition package. In this example, we can clearly see that one dimension should be enough to describe the data. We can specify this using the n_components parameter:

```
>>> from sklearn import linear_model, decomposition, datasets
>>> pca = decomposition.PCA(n_components=1)
```

Also, here, we can use the fit() and transform() methods of pca (or its fit_transform() combination) to analyze the data and project it in the transformed feature space:

```
>>> Xtrans = pca.fit_transform(X)
```

As we have specified, Xtrans contains only one dimension. You can see the result in the preceding right-hand plot diagram. The outcome is even linearly separable in this case. We would not even need a complex classifier to distinguish between both classes.

To get an understanding of the reconstruction error, we can have a look at the variance of the data that we have retained in the transformation:

```
>>> print(pca.explained_variance_ratio_)
>>> [ 0.96393127]
```

This means that, after going from two dimensions to one, we are still left with 96 percent of the variance.

Of course, it's not always this simple. Frequently, we don't know what number of dimensions is advisable upfront. In that case, we leave the n_components parameter unspecified when initializing PCA to let it calculate the full transformation. After fitting the data, explained_variance_ratio_ contains an array of ratios in decreasing order: the first value is the ratio of the basis vector describing the direction of the highest variance, the second value is the ratio of the direction of the second highest variance, and so on. After plotting this array, we quickly get a feel of how many components we would need: the number of components immediately before the chart elbow is often a good guess.

Plots displaying the explained variance over the number of components are called scree plots. A nice example of combining a scree plot with a grid search to find the best setting for the classification problem can be found at http://scikit-learn.org/stable/auto_examples/plot_digits_pipe.html.

Limitations of PCA and how LDA can help

Being a linear method, PCA has, of course, its limitations when we are faced with data that has nonlinear relationships. We won't go into details here, but it's sufficient to say that there are extensions of PCA, for example, Kernel PCA, that introduce nonlinear transformations so that we can still use the PCA approach.

Another interesting weakness of PCA is when it's being applied to special classification problems. If we replace *good = (x1 > 5) | (x2 > 5)* with *good = x1 > x2* to simulate such a special case, we can quickly see the problem, as can be seen in the following diagram:

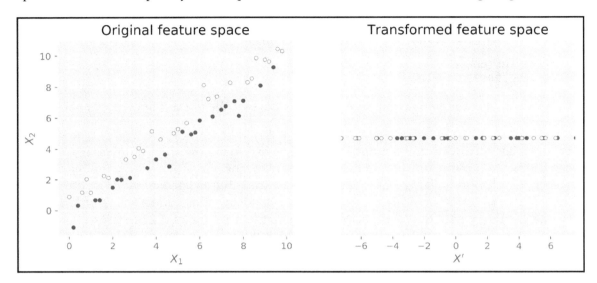

Here, the classes are not distributed according to the axis with the highest variance, but the axis with the second highest variance. Clearly, PCA falls flat on its face. As we don't provide PCA with any cues regarding class labels, it cannot do any better.

Linear discriminant analysis (**LDA**) comes to the rescue here. It's a method that tries to maximize the distance of points belonging to different classes while minimizing the distances of points of the same class. We won't give any more details regarding how exactly the underlying theory works, just a quick tutorial on how to use it, as shown in the following code:

```
>>> from sklearn import lda
>>> lda_inst = lda.LDA(n_components=1)
>>> Xtrans = lda_inst.fit_transform(X, good)
```

That's all. Note that, in contrast to the previous PCA example, we provide class labels to the `fit_transform()` method. Hence, PCA is an unsupervised feature projection method, whereas LDA is a supervised one. The result looks as expected:

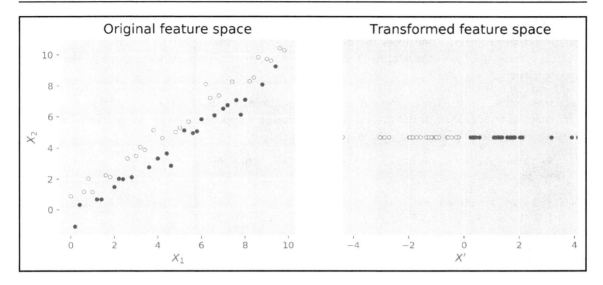

So, why consider PCA at all? Why not simply use LDA? Well, it's not that simple. With an increasing number of classes and fewer samples per class, LDA does not look that good any more. Also, PCA seems to be not as sensitive to different training sets as LDA. So, when we have to advise which method to use, we can only say it depends.

Multidimensional scaling

Whereas PCA tries to use optimization for retained variance, **multidimensional scaling** (**MDS**) tries to retain the relative distances as much as possible when reducing the dimensions. This is useful when we have a high-dimensional dataset and want to get a visual impression.

MDS does not care about the data points themselves; instead, it's interested in the dissimilarities between pairs of data points and it interprets these as distances. It takes all the N data points of dimension k and calculates a distance matrix using a distance function, d_0, which measures the (most of the time, Euclidean) distance in the original feature space:

$$\begin{pmatrix} X_{11} & \cdots & X_{N1} \\ \vdots & \ddots & \vdots \\ X_{1k} & \cdots & X_{NK} \end{pmatrix} \rightarrow \begin{pmatrix} d_o(X_1,X_1) & \cdots & d_o(X_N,X_1) \\ \vdots & \ddots & \vdots \\ d_o(X_1,X_N) & \cdots & d_o(X_N,X_N) \end{pmatrix}$$

Now, MDS tries to position the individual data points in the lower dimensional so such that the new distance there resembles the distances in the original space as much as possible. As MDS is often used for visualization, the choice of the lower dimension is, most of the time, two or three.

Let's have a look at the following simple data consisting of three data points in five-dimensional space. Two of the data points are close by and one is very distinct, and we want to visualize this in three and two dimensions:

```
>>> X = np.c_[np.ones(5), 2 * np.ones(5), 10 * np.ones(5)].T
>>> print(X)
[[ 1.  1.  1.  1.  1.]
 [ 2.  2.  2.  2.  2.]
 [ 10. 10. 10. 10. 10.]]
```

Using the MDS class in scikit-learn's manifold package, we first specify that we want to transform X into a three-dimensional Euclidean space:

```
>>> from sklearn import manifold
>>> mds = manifold.MDS(n_components=3)
>>> Xtrans = mds.fit_transform(X)
```

To visualize it in two dimensions, we would need to set n_components accordingly.

The results can be seen in the following two graphs. The triangle and circle are both close together, whereas the star is far away:

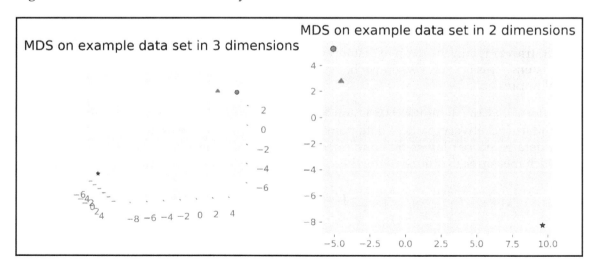

Let's have a look at the slightly more complex Iris dataset. We will use it later to contrast LDA with PCA. The Iris dataset contains four attributes per flower. With the preceding code, we would project it into three-dimensional space while keeping the relative distances between the individual flowers as much as possible. In the previous example, we did not specify any metric, so MDS will default to Euclidean. This means that flowers that were different according to their four attributes should also be far away in the MDS-scaled, three-dimensional space, and flowers that were similar should be almost together now, as shown in the following diagram:

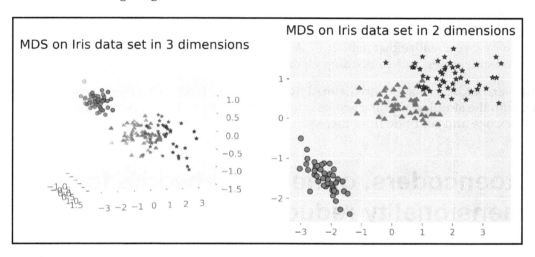

Reducing the dimensionality to three and two dimensions with PCA instead, we see the expected larger spread of flowers belonging to the same class:

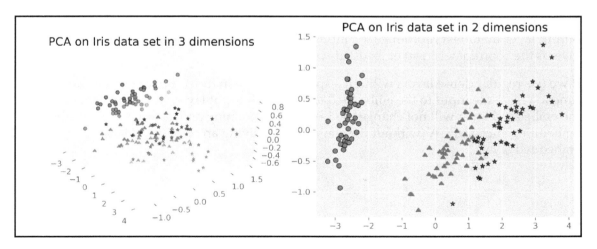

Of course, using MDS requires an understanding of the individual feature's units; maybe we are using features that cannot be compared using the Euclidean metric. For instance, a categorical variable, even when encoded as an integer (0 = circle, 1 = star, 2 = triangle, and so on), cannot be compared using a Euclidean metric (is a circle closer to a star than to triangle?).

However, once we are aware of this issue, MDS is a useful tool that reveals similarities in our data that would otherwise be difficult to see in the original feature space.

Looking a bit deeper into MDS, we realize that it's not a single algorithm, but rather a family of different algorithms, of which we have used just one. The same was true for PCA. Also, in case you realize that neither PCA nor MDS solves your problem, just look at the many other learning and embedding algorithms that are available in the scikit-learn toolkit.

However, before you get overwhelmed by the many different algorithms, it's always best to start with the simplest one and see how far you get with it. Then, take the next more complex one and continue from there.

Autoencoders, or neural networks for dimensionality reduction

A little bit more than a decade ago, the main tool for dimensionality reduction with neural networks was Kohonen maps, or **self-organizing maps** (**SOM**). They were neural networks that would map data in a discrete, 1D-embedded space. Since then, with faster computers, it is now possible to use deep learning to create embedded spaces.

The trick is to have an intermediate layer that has fewer nodes than the input layer and an output layer that must reproduce the input layer. The data on this intermediate layer will give us the coordinates in an embedded space.

If we use regular dense layers without a specific activation function, we get a linear function from the input to the embedded layer to the output layer. More than one layer to the embedded layer will not change the result of the training and, as such, we get a linear embedding such as PCA (without the constraint of having an orthogonal basis in the embedded layer).

Adding a nonlinear activation function to the dense layer is what will enable finding **manifolds** in data, instead of just hyperplans. As opposed to tools such as Isomap, which try to match distances between data (it's a variant of MDS, trying to match approximated geodesic distances instead of Euclidian distances), or Laplacian eigenmaps, which try to match similarities between data, autoencoders have no concept of what we are trying to keep—they will just attempt to reproduce whatever we provide at the input.

 Neural networks can extract features from data, as we will see in the TensorFlow chapter, but we will keep things simple here by using a dataset that is features-only.

The dataset we will be considering is the Swiss Roll. It is one of the most famous datasets used in manifold, as it's a nonlinear dataset that can be easily understood by human eyes, but that is wrapped enough to make it difficult for algorithms to properly describe it:

```python
import numpy as np
max = 4
def generate_swissroll(n):
    """
    Generates data for the swissroll
    Returns the parameter space, the swissroll
    """
    orig = np.random.random((2, n)) * max
    return (orig.T, np.array((orig[1] * np.cos(orig[1]),
                              orig[1] * np.sin(orig[1]),
                              orig[0])).T)

def color_from_parameters(params):
    """
    Defines a color scheme for the swissroll
    """
    return np.array((params[:,0], params[:,1], max - params[:,1])).T / max
```

From these functions, we can generate new data along with a color code that will allow us to check that the embedded data matches the original parameters we used, as shown in the following diagram:

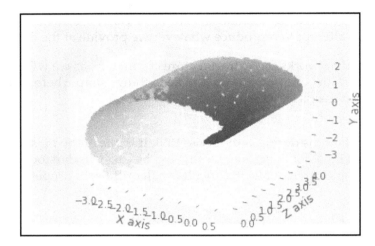

It is now time to think of the architecture we will use. We will start with the input layer that will feed the data inside the network using two layers that will do the heavy lifting of unwrapping the input data into the embedded layer with two layers. To rebuild the Swiss Roll, we will use another dense layer before ending on the three-unit output layer. To create the nonlinearities, each of the layers (except the input) will use a `leaky_relu` activation. The arrangement is shown in the following diagram:

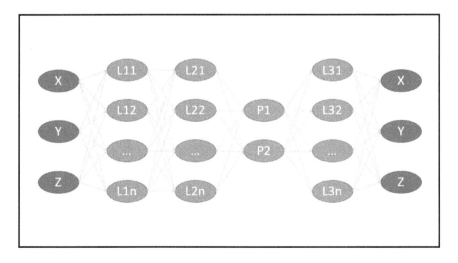

Let's create the scaffolding:

```
import tensorflow as tf

def tf_create_variables():
    swissroll_tf = tf.placeholder(tf.float32, (None, 3), name="swissroll")
    return swissroll_tf
def tf_create_dense_layer(x, size):
    return tf.layers.dense(x, size, activation=tf.nn.leaky_relu,
        kernel_initializer=tf.contrib.layers.xavier_initializer())
```

This time, the autoencoder will be encapsulated in a class. The constructor will create the variables, and the `train` method will run the optimization, as well as create a few display images.

When we build the layers, we save the embedded layer variable, as this variable is the one we want to use to get the parameters of a new sample in the embedded space:

```
class Autoencoder(object):
    def __init__(self, swissroll, swissroll_test, nb_intermediate,
                 learning_rate):
        self.swissroll = swissroll
        self.swissroll_test = swissroll_test
        self.swissroll_tf = tf_create_variables()
        intermediate_input = tf_create_dense_layer(self.swissroll_tf,
                                        nb_intermediate)
        intermediate_input = tf_create_dense_layer(intermediate_input,
                                        nb_intermediate)
        self.encoded = tf_create_dense_layer(intermediate_input, 2)
        intermediate_output = tf_create_dense_layer(self.encoded,
                                        nb_intermediate)
        self.output = tf_create_dense_layer(intermediate_output, 3)
        self.meansq = tf.reduce_mean(tf.squared_difference(
                                self.output, self.swissroll_tf))
        self.train_step = tf.train
                        .GradientDescentOptimizer(learning_rate)
                        .minimize(self.meansq)
    def train(self, display, n_epochs, batch_size, **kwargs):
        n = len(self.swissroll)
        with tf.Session() as sess:
            sess.run(tf.global_variables_initializer())
            for i in range(n_epochs):
                permut = np.random.permutation(n)
                for j in range(0, n, batch_size):
                    samples = permut[j:j+batch_size]
                    batch = self.swissroll[samples]
                    sess.run(self.train_step,
                            feed_dict={self.swissroll_tf: batch})
```

```
                         if i % step == step - 1:
                             print("Epoch :%i\n Loss %f" %\
                                 (i, sess.run(self.meansq,
                                 feed_dict={self.swissroll_tf: self.swissroll})))
                    error = sess.run(self.meansq,
                             feed_dict={self.swissroll_tf: self.swissroll})
                    error_test = sess.run(self.meansq,
                             feed_dict={self.swissroll_tf:
self.swissroll_test})
                if display:
                    pred = sess.run(self.encoded,
                             feed_dict={self.swissroll_tf : self.swissroll})
                    pred = np.asarray(pred)
                    recons = sess.run(self.output,
                             feed_dict={self.swissroll_tf : self.swissroll})
                    recons = np.asarray(recons)
                    recons_test = sess.run(self.output,
                             feed_dict={self.swissroll_tf :
self.swissroll_test})
                    recons_test = np.asarray(recons_test)
                    print("Embedded manifold")
                    plot_2d(pred, colors)
                    save_png("swissroll_embedded")
                    plt.show()
                    print("Reconstructed manifold")
                    plot_3d(recons, colors)
                    save_png("swissroll_reconstructed")
                    plt.show()
                    print("Reconstructed test manifold")
                    plot_3d(recons_test, kwargs['colors_test'])
                    save_png("swissroll_test")
                    plt.show()
            return error, error_test
```

We can run this autoencoder and check whether it also works on new data:

```
n = 5000
n_epochs = 2000
batch_size = 100
nb_intermediate = 20
learning_rate = 0.05
step = 100
params, swissroll = generate_swissroll(n)
params_test, swissroll_test = generate_swissroll(n)
colors = color_from_parameters(params)
colors_test = color_from_parameters(params_test)

model = Autoencoder(swissroll, swissroll_test,
```

```
                    nb_intermediate, learning_rate)

error, error_test = model.train(True, n_epochs, batch_size,
                                colors=colors, test=swissroll_test,
                                colors_test = colors_test)
...
Epoch :1599
   Loss 0.001498
Epoch :1699
   Loss 0.001008
Epoch :1799
   Loss 0.000870
Epoch :1899
   Loss 0.000952
Epoch :1999
   Loss 0.000830
```

The embedded space for the training data is fine, and respects the color scheme we used for generating the `swissroll`. We can see a representation of it in the following diagram:

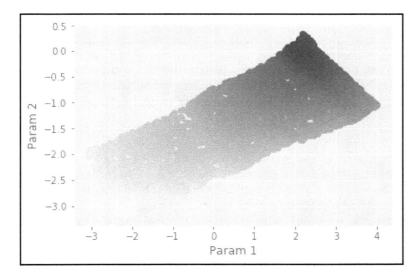

An interesting point here is that the parameter space is not directly linked to the parameters we used to create the data. The amplitude is different, and each new run will get a new embedded space. We could add a regularization in the mean square cost function, just like we did in the chapter on regression.

A crucial point is to check that the output data also matches the input data. We saw that the loss was very low. The test data also showed that the reconstruction error was low, but a visual check is sometimes a good thing to do. The following diagram shows a graphical representation:

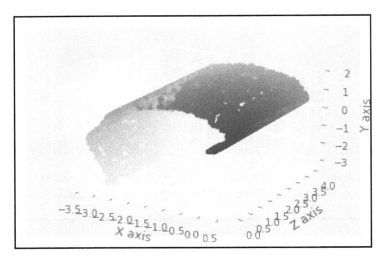

We can see that there are some bumps and discontinuities compared to the original Swiss Roll. Adding a second layer during reconstruction would help reduce this; we didn't do it here to show that we don't have to use a symmetric neural network for autoencoders.

Summary

In this chapter, you learned that, sometimes, you can get rid of complete features using feature selection methods. We also saw that, in some cases, this is not enough, and we have to employ feature projection methods that reveal the real and the lower-dimensional structure in our data, hoping that the model has an easier time with it.

For sure, we only scratched the surface of the huge body of available dimensionality reduction methods. Still, we hope that we got you interested in this whole field, as there are lots of other methods waiting for you to pick them up. In the end, feature selection and projection are an art, just like choosing the right learning method or training model.

In Chapter 6, *Clustering – Finding Related Posts*, we will introduce clustering, which is an unsupervised learning technique. We will use it to find similar news posts for a given text.

6
Clustering – Finding Related Posts

Until now, we have always considered training as learning a function that maps some data to some labels. For the tasks in this chapter, we may not possess labels that we can use to learn the classification model. This could be, for example, because they were too expensive to collect. Just imagine the cost if the only way to obtain millions of labels was to ask humans to annotate those manually. What could we do in that case?

We find some pattern within the data itself. This is what we will do in this chapter, where we again consider the challenge of a question and answer website. When a user is browsing our site, perhaps because they are searching for specific information, the search engine will most likely point them to a specific answer. If the presented answers are not what they are looking for, the website should present (at least) the related answers so that they can quickly see what other answers are available and hopefully stay on our site.

The naïve approach would be to simply take the post, calculate its similarity to all other posts, and display the top n most similar posts as links on the page. This would quickly become very costly. Instead, we need a method that quickly finds all the related posts.

We will achieve this goal in this chapter by clustering features we have extracted from text. Clustering is a method of arranging items so that similar items are in one cluster and dissimilar items are in distinct ones. The tricky thing that we must tackle first is how to turn text into something from which we can calculate similarity. With such a similarity measurement, we will then proceed to investigate how we can leverage that to quickly arrive at a cluster that contains similar posts. Once there, we will only have to check those documents that also belong to that cluster. To achieve this, we will introduce you to the marvelous `scikit` library, which comes with diverse machine learning methods that we will also use in the following chapters.

Measuring the relatedness of posts

From a machine learning point of view, raw text is useless. If we manage to transform it into meaningful numbers, we can then feed it into our machine learning algorithms, such as clustering. This is also true for more mundane operations on text, such as similarity measurement.

How not to do it

One text similarity measure is the Levenshtein distance, which also goes by the name edit distance. Let's say we have two words, machine and mchiene. The similarity between them can be expressed as the minimum set of edits that are necessary to turn one word into the other. In this case, the edit distance will be two, as we have to add an a after the m and delete the first e. This algorithm is, however, quite costly as it is bound by the length of the first word times the length of the second word.

Looking at our posts, we could cheat by treating whole words as characters and performing the edit distance calculation on the word level. Let's say we have two posts called, how to format my hard disk, and hard disk format problems (and let us assume the post consists only of the title for simplicity's sake). We will need an edit distance of five because of removing, how, to, format, my, and then adding format and problems at the end. Thus, one could express the difference between two posts as the number of words that have to be added or deleted so that one text morphs into the other. Although we could speed up the overall approach quite a bit, the time complexity remains the same.

But even if it would have been fast enough, there is another problem. In the earlier post, the word format accounts for an edit distance of two, due to deleting it first, then adding it. So, our distance seems to be not robust enough to take word reordering into account.

How to do it

More robust than edit distance is the so-called **bag of words** approach. It ignores the order of words and simply uses word counts as their basis. For each word in the post, its occurrence is counted and noted in a vector. Not surprisingly, this step is also called vectorization. The vector is typically huge as it contains as many elements as words that occur in the whole dataset. The previously mentioned two example posts would then have the following word counts:

Word	Occurrences in post 1	Occurrences in post 2
disk	1	1
format	1	1
how	1	0
hard	1	1
my	1	0
problems	0	1
to	1	0

The columns occurrences in post 2 and occurrences in post 1 can now be treated as vectors. We can simply calculate the Euclidean distance between the vectors of all posts and take the nearest one (too slow, as we have found out earlier). And as such we can use them later as our feature vectors in the clustering steps, according to the following procedure:

1. Extract salient features from each post and store them as a vector per post
2. Cluster the vectors
3. Determine the cluster for the post in question
4. From this cluster, fetch a handful of posts having a different similarity to the post in question. This will increase diversity

But there is some more work to be done before we get there. Before we can do that work, we need some data to work on.

Preprocessing – similarity measured as a similar number of common words

As we have seen earlier, the bag of words approach is both fast and robust. It is, though, not without challenges. Let's dive directly into them.

Converting raw text into a bag of words

We do not have to write custom code for counting words and representing those counts as a vector. Scikit's `CountVectorizer` method, does the job efficiently but also has a very convenient interface:

```
>>> from sklearn.feature_extraction.text import CountVectorizer
>>> vectorizer = CountVectorizer(min_df=1)
```

The `min_df` parameter determines how `CountVectorizer` treats seldom words (minimum document frequency). If it is set to an integer, all words occurring in fewer documents will be dropped. If it is a fraction, all words that occur in less than that fraction of the overall dataset will be dropped. The `max_df` parameter works in a similar manner. If we print the instance, we can see what other parameters scikit provides together with their default values:

```
>>> print(vectorizer)
```

```
CountVectorizer(analyzer='word', binary=False, decode_error='strict',
        dtype=<class 'numpy.int64'>, encoding='utf-8', input='content',
        lowercase=True, max_df=1.0, max_features=None, min_df=1,
        ngram_range=(1, 1), preprocessor=None, stop_words=None,
        strip_accents=None, token_pattern='(?u)\b\w\w+\b',
        tokenizer=None, vocabulary=None)
```

We can see that, as expected, the counting is done at the word level (`analyzer=word`) and words are determined by the regular expression pattern `token_pattern`. It will, for example, split cross-validated into cross and validated. This process is also called tokenization.

Let's ignore the other parameters for now and consider the following two example subject lines:

```
>>> content = ["How to format my hard disk",
                " Hard disk format  problems "]
```

We can now put this list of subject lines into the `fit_transform()` function of our vectorizer, which does all the hard vectorization work:

```
>>> X = vectorizer.fit_transform(content)
>>> vectorizer.get_feature_names()
['disk', 'format', 'hard', 'how', 'my', 'problems', 'to']
```

The vectorizer has detected seven words for which we can fetch the counts individually:

```
>>> print(X.toarray().transpose())
[[1 1]
 [1 1]
 [1 1]
 [1 0]
 [1 0]
 [0 1]
 [1 0]]
```

This means that the first sentence contains all the words except problems, while the second contains all but how, my, and to. In fact, these are the same columns as we have seen in the preceding table. From X, we can extract a feature vector that we will use to compare two documents with each other.

We will start with a naïve approach first, to point out some preprocessing peculiarities we have to account for. So let's pick a random post, for which we then create the count vector. We will then compare its distance to all the count vectors and fetch the post with the smallest one.

Counting words

Let's play with the toy dataset, consisting of the following posts:

Post filename	Post content
01.txt	This is a toy post about machine learning. Actually, it contains not much interesting stuff
02.txt	Imaging databases can get huge
03.txt	Most imaging databases save images permanently
04.txt	Imaging databases store images
05.txt	Imaging databases store images

In this post dataset, we want to find the most similar post for the short post imaging databases.

Assuming that the posts are located in the "data/toy" directory (please check the Jupyter notebook), we can feed CountVectorizer with it:

```
>>> from pathlib import Path # for easy path management
>>> TOY_DIR = Path('data/toy')
>>> posts = []
>>> for fn in TOY_DIR.iterdir():
```

```
...            with open(fn, 'r') as f:
...                posts.append(f.read())
...
>>> from sklearn.feature_extraction.text import CountVectorizer
>>> vectorizer = CountVectorizer(min_df=1)
```

We have to notify the vectorizer about the full dataset so that it knows upfront which words are to be expected:

```
>>> X_train = vectorizer.fit_transform(posts)
>>> num_samples, num_features = X_train.shape
>>> print("#samples: %d, #features: %d" %
...          (num_samples, num_features))
#samples: 5, #features: 25
```

Unsurprisingly, we have five posts with a total of 25 different words. The following words that have been tokenized will be counted:

```
>>> print(vectorizer.get_feature_names())
['about', 'actually', 'capabilities', 'contains', 'data', 'databases',
'images', 'imaging', 'interesting', 'is', 'it', 'learning', 'machine',
'most', 'much', 'not', 'permanently', 'post', 'provide', 'save', 'storage',
'store', 'stuff', 'this', 'toy']
```

Now we can vectorize our new post:

```
>>> new_post = "imaging databases"
>>> new_post_vec = vectorizer.transform([new_post])
```

Note that the count vectors returned by the transform method are sparse, which is the appropriate format because the data itself is also sparse. That is, each vector does not store one count value for each word, as most of those counts will be zero (the post does not contain the word). Instead, it uses the more memory-efficient implementation, coo_matrix (for coordinate). Our new post, for instance, actually contains only two elements:

```
>>> print(new_post_vec)
(0, 7)    1
(0, 5)    1
```

Via its toarray() member, we can once again access fully ndarray:

```
>>> print(new_post_vec.toarray())
[[0 0 0 0 0 1 0 1 0 0 0 0 0 0 0 0 0 0 0 0 0 0 0 0 0]]
```

We need to use the full array if we want to use it as a vector for similarity calculations. For the similarity measurement (the naïve one), we calculate the Euclidean distance between the count vectors of the new post and all the old posts:

```
import scipy
def dist_raw(v1, v2):
    delta = v1-v2
    return scipy.linalg.norm(delta.toarray())
```

The `norm()` function calculates the Euclidean norm (shortest distance). This is just one obvious first pick, and there are many more interesting ways to calculate the distance. Just take a look at the paper distance coefficients between two lists or sets in The Python papers source codes, in which Maurice Ling nicely presents 35 different ones.

With `dist_raw`, we just need to iterate over all the posts and remember the nearest one. As we will play with it throughout the book, let's define a convenience function that takes the current dataset and the new post in vectorized form as well as a distance function and prints out an analysis of how well the distance function works:

```
def best_post(X, new_vec, dist_func):
    best_doc = None
    best_dist = float('inf') # infinite value as a starting point
    best_i = None
    for i, post in enumerate(posts):
        if post == new_post:
            continue
        post_vec = X.getrow(i)
        d = dist_func(post_vec, new_vec)
        print("=== Post %i with dist=%.2f:n    '%s'" % (i, d, post))
        if d < best_dist:
            best_dist = d
            best_i = i
    print("n==> Best post is %i with dist=%.2f" % (best_i, best_dist))
```

When we execute as `best_post(X_train, new_post_vec, dist_raw)`, we can see in the output the posts with their respective distance to the new post:

```
=== Post 0 with dist=4.00:
    'This is a toy post about machine learning. Actually, it contains
not much interesting stuff.'
=== Post 1 with dist=1.73:
    'Imaging databases provide storage capabilities.'
=== Post 2 with dist=2.00:
    'Most imaging databases save images permanently.'
=== Post 3 with dist=1.41:
    'Imaging databases store data.'
=== Post 4 with dist=5.10:
```

```
'Imaging databases store data. Imaging databases store data.
Imaging databases store data.'
    ==> Best post is 3 with dist=1.41
```

Congratulations, we have our first similarity measurement. `Post 0` is most dissimilar from our new post. Quite understandably, it does not have a single word in common with the new post. We can also understand that `Post 1` is very similar to the new post, but not the winner, as it contains one word more than `Post 3`, which is not contained in the new post.

Looking at `Post 3` and `Post 4`, however, the picture is not so clear. `Post 4` is the same as `Post 3` duplicated three times. So, it should also be as similar to the new post as `Post 3`.

Printing the corresponding feature vectors explains why:

```
>>> print(X_train.getrow(3).toarray())
[[0 0 0 0 1 1 0 1 0 0 0 0 0 0 0 0 0 0 0 0 1 0 0 0]]
>>> print(X_train.getrow(4).toarray())
[[0 0 0 0 3 3 0 3 0 0 0 0 0 0 0 0 0 0 0 0 3 0 0 0]]
```

Obviously, using only the counts of the raw words is insufficient. We will have to normalize them to get vectors of unit length.

Normalizing word count vectors

We will have to extend `dist_raw` to calculate the vector distance not on the raw vectors but on the normalized ones instead:

```
def dist_norm(v1, v2):
    v1_normalized = v1 / scipy.linalg.norm(v1.toarray())
    v2_normalized = v2 / scipy.linalg.norm(v2.toarray())
    delta = v1_normalized - v2_normalized
    return scipy.linalg.norm(delta.toarray())
```

This leads to the following similarity measurement, when being executed with `best_post(X_train, new_post_vec, dist_norm)`:

```
=== Post 0 with dist=1.41:
    'This is a toy post about machine learning. Actually, it contains
not much interesting stuff.'
=== Post 1 with dist=0.86:
    'Imaging databases provide storage capabilities.'
=== Post 2 with dist=0.92:
    'Most imaging databases save images permanently.
    '
=== Post 3 with dist=0.77:
    'Imaging databases store data.'
```

```
=== Post 4 with dist=0.77:
      'Imaging databases store data. Imaging databases store data.
Imaging databases store data.'
   ==> Best post is 3 with dist=0.77
```

This looks a bit better now. Post 3 and Post 4 are calculated as being equally similar. One could argue whether that much repetition would be a delight to the reader, but in terms of counting the words in the posts this seems to be right.

Removing less important words

Let's have another look at Post 2. Of its words that are not in the new post, we have most, save, images, and permanently. They are quite different in the overall importance to the post. Words such as most appear very often in all sorts of different contexts and are called stop words. They do not carry as much information and thus should not be weighed as high as words such as images, which don't occur often in different contexts. The best option would be to remove all the words that are so frequent that they do not help us to distinguish between different texts. These words are called stop words.

As this is such a common step in text processing, there is a simple parameter in CountVectorizer to achieve that:

```
>>> vect_engl = CountVectorizer(min_df=1, stop_words='english')
```

If you have a clear picture of what kind of stop words you would want to remove, you can also pass a list of them. Setting stop_words to english will use a set of 318 English stop words. To find out which ones, you can use get_stop_words():

```
>>> sorted(vect_engl.get_stop_words())[0:20]
['a', 'about', 'above', 'across', 'after', 'afterwards', 'again',
'against', 'all', 'almost', 'alone', 'along', 'already', 'also',
'although', 'always', 'am', 'among', 'amongst', 'amoungst']
```

The new word list is seven words lighter:

```
>>> X_train_engl = vect_engl.fit_transform(posts)
>>> num_samples_engl, num_features_engl = X_train_engl.shape
>>> print(vect_engl.get_feature_names())
['actually', 'capabilities', 'contains', 'data', 'databases', 'images',
'imaging', 'interesting', 'learning', 'machine', 'permanently', 'post',
'provide', 'save', 'storage', 'store', 'stuff', 'toy']
```

After discarding stop words, we arrive at the following similarity measurement:

```
>>> best_post(X_train_engl, new_post_vec_engl, dist_norm)
=== Post 0 with dist=1.41:
    'This is a toy post about machine learning. Actually, it contains
not much interesting stuff.'
=== Post 1 with dist=0.86:
    'Imaging databases provide storage capabilities.'
=== Post 2 with dist=0.86:
    'Most imaging databases save images permanently.'
=== Post 3 with dist=0.77:
    'Imaging databases store data.'
=== Post 4 with dist=0.77:
    'Imaging databases store data. Imaging databases store data.
Imaging databases store data.'
==> Best post is 3 with dist=0.77
```

`Post 2` is now on par with `Post 1`. It has, however, not changed much overall since our posts are kept short for demonstration purposes. It will become vital when we look at real-world data.

Stemming

One thing is still missing. We count similar words in different variants as different words. Post 2, for instance, contains imaging and images. It make sense to count them together. After all, it is the same concept they are referring to.

We need a function that reduces words to their specific word stem. Scikit does not contain a stemmer by default. With the **Natural Language Toolkit** (**NLTK**), we can download a free software toolkit, which provides a stemmer that we can easily plug into `CountVectorizer`.

Installing and using NLTK

NLTK is a simple `pip install nltk` away.

To check whether your installation was successful, open a Python interpreter and type:

```
>>> import nltk
```

You will find a very nice tutorial on NLTK in the book *Python 3 Text Processing with NLTK 3 Cookbook* by Jacob Perkins, published by Packt Publishing.

To play around a little bit with a stemmer, you can visit the web page `http://text-processing.com/demo/stem/`.

NLTK comes with different stemmers. This is necessary, because every language has a different set of rules for stemming. For English, we can take `SnowballStemmer`:

```
>>> import nltk.stem
>>> s = nltk.stem.SnowballStemmer('english')
>>> s.stem("graphics")
'graphic'
>>> s.stem("imaging")
'imag'
>>> s.stem("image")
'imag'
>>> s.stem("imagination")
'imagin'
>>> s.stem("imagine")
'imagin'
```

 The stemming does not necessarily have to result in valid English words.

It also works with verbs:

```
>>> s.stem("buys")
'buy'
>>> s.stem("buying")
'buy'
```

This means it works most of the time:

```
>>> s.stem("bought")
'bought'
```

Extending the vectorizer with NLTK's stemmer

We need to stem the posts before we feed them into `CountVectorizer`. The class provides several hooks with which we can customize the stage's preprocessing and tokenization. The preprocessor and tokenizer can be set as parameters in the constructor. We do not want to place the stemmer into any of them, because we will then have to do the tokenization and normalization ourselves. Instead, we overwrite the `build_analyzer` method:

```
import nltk.stem
english_stemmer = nltk.stem.SnowballStemmer('english')
class StemmedCountVectorizer(CountVectorizer):
    def build_analyzer(self):
        analyzer = super(StemmedCountVectorizer, self).build_analyzer()
        return lambda doc: (english_stemmer.stem(w) for w in
analyzer(doc))
vect_engl_stem = StemmedCountVectorizer(min_df=1, stop_words='english')
```

This will do the following process for each post:

1. Lowercase the raw post in the preprocessing step (done in the parent class).
2. Extract all individual words in the tokenization step (done in the parent class).
3. Convert each word into its stemmed version (done in our `build_analyzer`).

As a result, we now have one less feature, because images and imaging collapsed to one:

```
['actual', 'capabl', 'contain', 'data', 'databas', 'imag', 'interest',
'learn', 'machin', 'perman', 'post', 'provid', 'save', 'storag', 'store',
'stuff', 'toy']
```

Running our new stemmed vectorizer over our posts, we see that collapsing imaging and images revealed that actually, `Post 2` is the most similar post to our new post, as it contains the concept image twice:

```
=== Post 0 with dist=1.41:
    'This is a toy post about machine learning. Actually, it contains
not much interesting stuff.'
=== Post 1 with dist=0.86:
    'Imaging databases provide storage capabilities.'
=== Post 2 with dist=0.63:
    'Most imaging databases save images permanently.'
=== Post 3 with dist=0.77:
    'Imaging databases store data.'
=== Post 4 with dist=0.77:
    'Imaging databases store data. Imaging databases store data.
Imaging databases store data.'
    ==> Best post is 2 with dist=0.63
```

Stop words on steroids

Now that we have a reasonable way to extract a compact vector from a noisy textual post, let's step back for a while to think about what the feature values actually mean.

The feature values simply count occurrences of terms in a post. We silently assumed that higher values for a term also mean that the term is of greater importance to the given post. But what about, for instance, the word subject, which naturally occurs in each and every single post (Subject: ...)? Alright, we can tell `CountVectorizer` to remove it as well by means of its `max_df` parameter. We can, for instance, set it to `0.9` so that all words that occur in more than 90 percent of all posts will always be ignored. But what about words that appear in 89 percent of all posts? How low will we be willing to set `max_df`? The problem is that however we set it, there will always be the problem that some terms are just more discriminative than others.

This can only be solved by counting term frequencies for every post and, in addition, discounting those that appear in many posts. In other words, we want a high value for a given term in a given value if that term occurs often in that particular post and very seldom anywhere else.

This is exactly what **term frequency - inverse document frequency (TF-IDF)** does. TF stands for the counting part, while IDF factors in the discounting. A naïve implementation will look like this:

```
def tfidf(term, doc, corpus):
    tf = doc.count(term) / len(doc)
    idf = np.log(float(len(corpus)) / (len([d for d in corpus if term in
d])))
    tf_idf = tf * idf
    print("term='%s'   doc=%-17s tf=%.2f   idf=%.2f   tf*idf=%.2f"%
          (term, doc, tf, idf, tf_idf))
    return tf_idf
```

You can see that we did not simply count the terms, but also normalized the counts by the document length. This way, longer documents do not have an unfair advantage over shorter ones. Of course for fast computation, we would move the IDF calculation out of the function, since it is the same value for all documents.

For the following documents, `D`, consisting of three already tokenized documents, we can see how the terms are treated differently, although all appear equally often per document:

```
>>> a, abb, abc = ["a"], ["a", "b", "b"], ["a", "b", "c"]
>>> D = [a, abb, abc]
>>> print("=> tfidf=%.2f" % tfidf("a", a, D))
term='a'   doc=['a']              tf=1.00   idf=0.00
```

```
=> tfidf=0.00

>>> print("=> tfidf=%.2f" % tfidf("a", abb, D))
term='a'    doc=['a', 'b', 'b']    tf=0.33    idf=0.00
=> tfidf=0.00

>>> print("=> tfidf=%.2f" % tfidf("a", abc, D))
term='a'    doc=['a', 'b', 'c']    tf=0.33    idf=0.00
=> tfidf=0.00

>>> print("=> tfidf=%.2f" % tfidf("b", abb, D))
term='b'    doc=['a', 'b', 'b']    tf=0.67    idf=0.41
=> tfidf=0.27

>>> print("=> tfidf=%.2f" % tfidf("b", abc, D))
term='b'    doc=['a', 'b', 'c']    tf=0.33    idf=0.41
=> tfidf=0.14

>>> print("=> tfidf=%.2f" % tfidf("c", abc, D))
term='c'    doc=['a', 'b', 'c']    tf=0.33    idf=1.10
=> tfidf=0.37
```

We see that a carries no meaning for any document since it is contained everywhere. The b term is more important for the document abb than for abc as it occurs there twice.

In reality, there are more corner cases to handle than in the preceding example. Thanks to scikit, we don't have to think of them as they are already nicely packaged in TfidfVectorizer, which inherits from CountVectorizer. We don't want to miss our stemmer:

```
from sklearn.feature_extraction.text import TfidfVectorizer
class StemmedTfidfVectorizer(TfidfVectorizer):
    def build_analyzer(self):
        analyzer = super(TfidfVectorizer, self).build_analyzer()
        return lambda doc: (english_stemmer.stem(w) for w in
analyzer(doc))
    vect_tfidf = StemmedTfidfVectorizer(stop_words='english')
```

The resulting document vectors will not contain counts any more. Instead, they will contain the individual TF-IDF values per term.

Our achievements and goals

Our current text preprocessing phase includes the following steps:

1. Firstly, tokenizing the text
2. This is followed by throwing away words that occur way too often to be of any help in detecting relevant posts
3. Throwing away words that occur so infrequently that there is little chance that they will occur in future posts
4. Counting the remaining words
5. Finally, calculating TF-IDF values from the counts, considering the whole text corpus

Again, we can congratulate ourselves. With this process, we are able to convert a bunch of noisy text into a concise representation of feature values.

But as simple and powerful the bag of words approach with its extensions is, it has some drawbacks, which we should be aware of:

- **It does not cover word relations**: With the aforementioned vectorization approach, the text, car hits wall and, wall hits car, will both have the same feature vector
- **It does not capture negations correctly**: For instance, the text, I will eat ice cream, and, I will not eat ice cream, will look very similar by means of their feature vectors although they contain quite the opposite meaning. This problem, however, can easily be mitigated by not only counting individual words, also called unigrams, but instead also considering bigrams (pairs of words) or trigrams (three words in a row)
- **It totally fails with misspelled words**: Although it is clear to us that, database, and databas convey the same meaning, our approach will treat them as totally different words

For brevity's sake, let's nevertheless stick with the current approach, which we can now use to efficiently build clusters.

Clustering

Finally, we have our vectors, which we believe capture the posts to a sufficient degree. Not surprisingly, there are many ways to group them together. One way to classify clustering algorithms is to distinguish between flat and hierarchical clustering.

Flat clustering divides the posts into a set of clusters without relating the clusters to each other. The goal is simply to come up with a partition such that all posts in one cluster are most similar to each other while being dissimilar from the posts in all other clusters. Many flat clustering algorithms require the number of clusters to be specified up front.

In hierarchical clustering, the number of clusters does not have to be specified. Instead, hierarchical clustering creates a hierarchy of clusters. While similar posts are grouped into one cluster, similar clusters are again grouped into one *uber-cluster*. In the agglomerative clustering approach, for instance, this is done recursively until only one cluster is left that contains everything. In this hierarchy, one can then choose the desired number of clusters after the fact. However, this comes at the cost of lower efficiency.

Scikit provides a wide range of clustering approaches in the `sklearn.cluster` package. You can get a quick overview of advantages and drawbacks of each of them at `http://scikit-learn.org/stable/modules/clustering.html`.

In the following sections, we will use the flat clustering method K-means.

K-means

K-means is the most widely used flat clustering algorithm. After initializing it with the desired number of clusters, `num_clusters`, it maintains that number of so-called cluster centroids. Initially, it will pick any `num_clusters` posts and set the centroids to their feature vector. Then it will go through all other posts and assign them the nearest centroid as their current cluster. Following this, it will move each centroid into the middle of all the vectors of that particular class. This changes, of course, the cluster assignment. Some posts are now nearer to another cluster. So it will update the assignments for those changed posts. This is done as long as the centroids move considerably. After some iterations, the movements will fall below a threshold and we consider clustering to be converged.

Let's play this out with a toy example of posts containing only two words. Each point in the following chart represents one document:

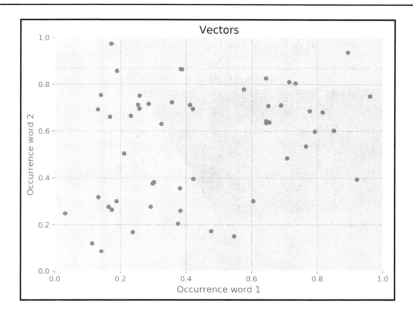

After running one iteration of K-means, that is, taking any two vectors as starting points, assigning the labels to the rest, and updating the cluster centers to be the center point of all points in that cluster, we get the following clustering:

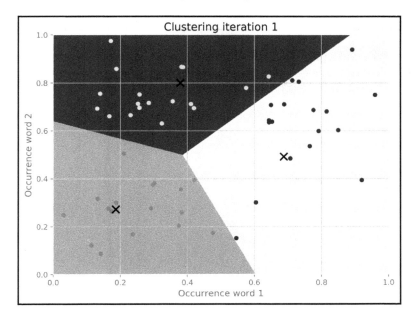

Because the cluster centers moved, we have to reassign the cluster labels and recalculate the cluster centers. After iteration 2, we get the following clustering:

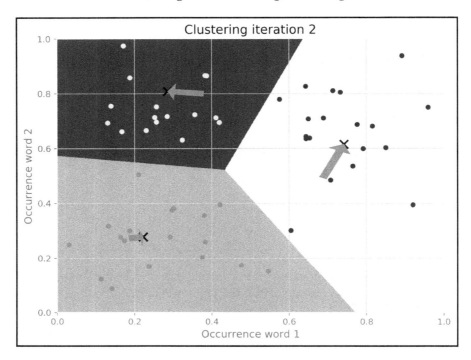

The arrows show the movements of the cluster centers. After ten iterations. as shown in the following screenshot of this example, the cluster centers don't move noticeably anymore (scikit's tolerance threshold is 0.0001 by default):

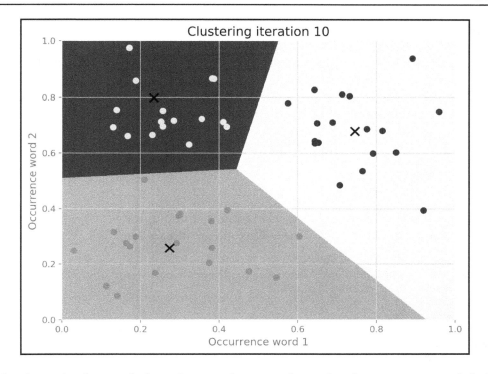

After the clustering has settled, we just need to note down the cluster centers and their cluster number. For each new document that comes in, we then have to vectorize and compare against all cluster centers. The cluster center with the smallest distance to our new post vector belongs to the cluster we will assign to the new post.

Getting test data to evaluate our ideas

In order to test clustering, let's move away from the toy text examples and find a dataset that resembles the data we are expecting in the future so that we can test our approach. For our purpose, we need documents about technical topics that are already grouped together so that we can check whether our algorithm works as expected when we apply it later to the posts we hope to receive.

One standard dataset in machine learning is the `20newsgroup` dataset, which contains 18,826 posts from 20 different newsgroups. Among the groups' topics are technical ones such as `comp.sys.mac.hardware` or `sci.crypt`, as well as more politics- and religion-related ones such as `talk.politics.guns` or `soc.religion.christian`. We will restrict ourselves to the technical groups. If we assume each newsgroup as one cluster, we can nicely test whether our approach of finding related posts works.

 The dataset can be downloaded from
`http://people.csail.mit.edu/jrennie/20Newsgroups`.

For convenience, the `sklearn.datasets` module also contains the `fetch_20newsgroups` function, which automatically downloads the data behind the scenes:

```
>>> import sklearn.datasets
>>> all_data = sklearn.datasets.fetch_20newsgroups(subset='all')
>>> print(len(all_data.filenames))
18846
>>> print(all_data.target_names)
['alt.atheism', 'comp.graphics', 'comp.os.ms-windows.misc',
 'comp.sys.ibm.pc.hardware', 'comp.sys.mac.hardware',
 'comp.windows.x', 'misc.forsale', 'rec.autos', 'rec.motorcycles',
 'rec.sport.baseball', 'rec.sport.hockey', 'sci.crypt',
 'sci.electronics', 'sci.med', 'sci.space', 'soc.religion.christian',
 'talk.politics.guns', 'talk.politics.mideast', 'talk.politics.misc',
 'talk.religion.misc']
```

We can choose between training and test sets:

```
>>> train_data = sklearn.datasets.fetch_20newsgroups(subset='train')
>>> print(len(train_data.filenames))
11314
>>> test_data = sklearn.datasets.fetch_20newsgroups(subset='test')
>>> print(len(test_data.filenames))
7532
```

For simplicity's sake, we will restrict ourselves to only some newsgroups so that the overall experimentation cycle is shorter. We can achieve this with the `categories` parameter:

```
>>> groups = ['comp.graphics', 'comp.os.ms-windows.misc',
 'comp.sys.ibm.pc.hardware', 'comp.sys.mac.hardware',
 'comp.windows.x', 'sci.space']
>>> train_data = sklearn.datasets.fetch_20newsgroups(subset='train',
                    categories=groups)
>>> print(len(train_data.filenames))
3529
>>> test_data = sklearn.datasets.fetch_20newsgroups(subset='test',
                    categories=groups)
>>> print(len(test_data.filenames))
2349
```

Clustering posts

We have already noticed one thing—real data is noisy. The newsgroup dataset is no exception. It even contains invalid characters that will result in `UnicodeDecodeError`.

We have to tell the vectorizer to ignore them:

```
>>> vectorizer = StemmedTfidfVectorizer(min_df=10, max_df=0.5,
...                 stop_words='english', decode_error='ignore')
>>> vectorized = vectorizer.fit_transform(train_data.data)
>>> num_samples, num_features = vectorized.shape
>>> print("#samples: %d, #features: %d" % (num_samples, num_features))
#samples: 3529, #features: 4712
```

We now have a pool of 3529 posts and, extracted for each of them, a feature vector of 4712 dimensions. That is what K-means takes as input. We will fix the cluster size to 50 for this chapter, and hope you are curious enough to try out different values as an exercise:

```
>>> num_clusters = 50
>>> from sklearn.cluster import KMeans
>>> km = KMeans(n_clusters=num_clusters, n_init=1, verbose=1,
random_state=3)
>>> km.fit(vectorized)
```

That's it. We provided a random state just so that you can get the same results. In real-world applications, you will not do this. After fitting, we can get the clustering information out of members of `km`. For every vectorized post that has been fit, there is a corresponding integer label in `km.labels_`:

```
>>> print("km.labels_=%s" % km.labels_)
km.labels_=[48 23 31 ..., 6 2 22]
>>> print("km.labels_.shape=%s" % km.labels_.shape)
km.labels_.shape=3529
```

The cluster centers can be accessed via `km.cluster_centers_`.

In the next section, we will see how we can assign a cluster to a newly arriving post, using `km.predict`.

Solving our initial challenge

We will now put everything together and demonstrate our system for the following new post that we assign to the `new_post` variable:

```
new_post = '''
Disk drive problems. Hi, I have a problem with my hard disk.
After 1 year it is working only sporadically now.
I tried to format it, but now it doesn't boot any more.
Any ideas? Thanks. '''
```

As you learned earlier, you will first have to vectorize this post before you predict its label:

```
>>> new_post_vec = vectorizer.transform([new_post])
>>> new_post_label = km.predict(new_post_vec)[0]
```

Now that we have the clustering, we do not need to compare `new_post_vec` to all post vectors. Instead, we can focus only on the posts of the same cluster. Let's fetch their indices in the original data set:

```
>>> similar_indices = (km.labels_ == new_post_label).nonzero()[0]
```

The comparison in the bracket results in a Boolean array, and `nonzero` converts that array into a smaller array containing the indices of the `True` elements.

Using `similar_indices`, we then simply have to build a list of posts together with their similarity scores:

```
>>> similar = []
>>> for i in similar_indices:
...     dist = scipy.linalg.norm((new_post_vec - vectorized[i]).toarray())
...     similar.append((dist, train_data.data[i]))
>>> similar = sorted(similar)
>>> print("Count similar: %i" % len(similar))
Count similar: 56
```

We found `56` posts in the cluster of our post. To give the user a quick idea of what kind of similar posts are available, we can now present the most similar post (`show_at_1`), and two less similar but still related ones, all from the same cluster:

```
>>> show_at_1 = similar[0]
>>> show_at_2 = similar[len(similar) // 10]
>>> show_at_3 = similar[len(similar) // 2]
```

The following table shows the posts together with their similarity values:

Position	Similarity	Excerpt from post
1	1.038	BOOT PROBLEM with IDE controller Hi, I've got a Multi I/O card (IDE controller + serial/parallel interface) and two floppy drives (5 1/4, 3 1/2) and a Quantum ProDrive 80AT connected to it. I was able to format the hard disk, but I could not boot from it. I can boot from drive A: (which disk drive does not matter) but if I remove the disk from drive A and press the reset switch, the LED of drive A: continues to glow, and the hard disk is not accessed at all. I guess this must be a problem of either the Multi I/O card or floppy disk drive settings (jumper configuration?) Does anyone have any idea what the reason for this could be. [...]
2	1.150	Booting from B drive I have a 5 1/4" drive as drive A. How can I make the system boot from my 3 1/2" B drive? (Optimally, the computer would be able to boot from either A or B, checking them in order for a bootable disk. But if I have to switch cables around and simply switch the drives so that it can't boot 5 1/4" disks, that's OK. Also, boot_b won't do the trick for me. [...] [...]
3	1.280	IBM PS/1 vs TEAC FD Hello, I already tried our national news group without success. I tried to replace a friend's original IBM floppy disk in his PS/1-PC with a normal TEAC drive. I already identified the power supply on pins 3 (5V) and 6 (12V), shorted pin 6 (5.25"/3.5" switch), and inserted pullup resistors (2K2) on pins 8, 26, 28, 30, and 34. The computer doesn't complain about a missing FD, but the FD's light stays on all the time. The drive spins up ok. when I insert a disk, but I can't access it. The TEAC works fine in a normal PC. Are there any points I missed? [...] [...]

It is interesting that the posts reflect the similarity measurement score. The first post contains all the salient words from our new post. The second also revolves around booting problems but is about floppy disks and not hard disks. Finally, the third is neither about hard disks nor about booting problems. Still, all the posts, we would say, belong to the same domain as the new post.

Another look at noise

We should not expect perfect clustering in the sense that posts from the same newsgroup (for example, comp.graphics) are also clustered together. An example will give us a quick impression of the noise that we have to expect. For the sake of simplicity, we will focus on one of the shorter posts:

```
>>> post_group = zip(train_data.data, train_data.target)
>>> all = [(len(post[0]), post[0], train_data.target_names[post[1]])
             for post in post_group]
>>> graphics = sorted([post for post in all if post[2]=='comp.graphics'])
>>> print(graphics[5])
(245, 'From: SITUNAYA@IBM3090.BHAM.AC.UKnSubject:
test....(sorry)nOrganization: The University of Birmingham, United
KingdomnLines: 1nNNTP-Posting-Host: ibm3090.bham.ac.uk&lt;...snip...>',
 'comp.graphics')
```

For this post, there is no real indication that it belongs to comp.graphics, considering only the wording that is left after the preprocessing step:

```
>>> noise_post = graphics[5][1]
>>> analyzer = vectorizer.build_analyzer()
>>> print(list(analyzer(noise_post)))
['situnaya', 'ibm3090', 'bham', 'ac', 'uk', 'subject', 'test',
 'sorri', 'organ', 'univers', 'birmingham', 'unit', 'kingdom', 'line',
 'nntp', 'post', 'host', 'ibm3090', 'bham', 'ac', 'uk']
```

We received these words after applying tokenization, lowercasing, and stop word removal. If we also subtract those words that will be later filtered out via min_df and max_df, which will be done later in fit_transform, it gets even worse:

```
>>> useful = set(analyzer(noise_post)).intersection
  (vectorizer.get_feature_names())
>>> print(sorted(useful))
['ac', 'birmingham', 'host', 'kingdom', 'nntp', 'sorri', 'test',
 'uk', 'unit', 'univers']
```

Most of the words occur frequently in other posts as well, as we can see from the IDF scores. Remember that the higher the TF-IDF, the more discriminative a term is for a given post. As IDF is a multiplicative factor here, a low value of it signals that it is not of great value in general:

```
>>> for term in sorted(useful):
...     print('IDF(%-10s) = %.2f' % (term,
...             vectorizer._tfidf.idf_[vectorizer.vocabulary_[term]]))
IDF(ac         ) = 3.51
IDF(birmingham) = 6.77
IDF(host       ) = 1.74
IDF(kingdom    ) = 6.68
IDF(nntp       ) = 1.77
IDF(sorri      ) = 4.14
IDF(test       ) = 3.83
IDF(uk         ) = 3.70
IDF(unit       ) = 4.42
IDF(univers    ) = 1.91
```

So, the terms with the highest discriminative power, birmingham and kingdom, are clearly not that computer graphics related, as is the case with the terms with lower IDF scores. Understandably, posts from different newsgroups will be clustered together.

For our goal, however, this is no big deal, as we are only interested in cutting down the number of posts that we have to compare a new post to. After all, the particular newsgroup that our training data came from is of no special interest.

Tweaking the parameters

What about all the other parameters? We could, for instance, tweak the number of clusters, or play with the vectorizer's max_features parameter (you should try that!). Also, we can play with different cluster center initializations. Then there are more exciting alternatives to K-means itself. There are, for example, clustering approaches that let you use different similarity measurements, such as Cosine similarity, Pearson, or Jaccard. An exciting field for you to play.

But before you go there, you will have to define what you actually mean by better. Scikit has a complete package dedicated only to this definition. The package is called sklearn.metrics and also contains a full range of different metrics to measure clustering quality. Maybe that should be the first place to go now—right into the sources of the metrics package.

Summary

That was a tough ride—we covered preprocessing over clustering and a solution that could convert noisy text into a meaningful concise vector representation, which we could cluster. If we look at what we had to do to finally be able to cluster, it was more than half of the overall task. But on the way, we learned quite a bit about text processing and how simple counting can get you very far with noisy real-world data.

This ride has been made much smoother, though, because of scikit and its powerful packages. And there is more to explore. In this chapter, we were scratching the surface of its capabilities. In Chapter 7, *Recommendations*, we will build a recommendation system, and we will see more of its power.

7
Recommendations

Recommendations have become one of the staples of online services and commerce. This type of automated system can provide each user with a personalized list of suggestions (be it a list of products to purchase, features to use, or new connections). In this chapter, we will see the basic ways in which automated recommendation generation systems work. The field of generating recommendations based on consumer input is often called collaborative filtering, as the users collaborate through the system to find the best items for each other.

In the first part of this chapter, we will see how we can use past product ratings from consumers to predict new ratings. We start with a few ideas that are helpful and then combine all of them. When combining them, we use regression to learn the best way in which they can be combined. This will also allow us to explore a generic concept in machine learning: ensemble learning.

In the second part of this chapter, we will take a look at a different way of learning recommendations: basket analysis. Unlike the cases in which we have numeric ratings, in the basket analysis setting, all we have is information about the shopping baskets—that is, what items were bought together. The goal is to learn about recommendations. You have probably already seen recommendations along the lines of, people who bought X also bought Y, in online shopping. We will develop a similar feature of our own. In summary, this chapter will cover the following:

- Different ways of building recommendation systems by predicting product ratings.
- Stacking as a way of combining multiple predictions. This is a general technique for combining machine learning methods.
- Basket analysis and association-rule mining to build predictions based solely on which items were consumed together.

Rating predictions and recommendations

If you have used any online shopping system in the last 10 years, you have probably seen recommendations. Some are like Amazon's, customers who bought X also bought Y, feature. These will be discussed in the *Basket analysis* section. Other recommendations are based on predicting the rating of a product, such as a movie.

The problem of learning recommendations based on past product ratings was made famous by the Netflix prize, a million-dollar machine-learning public challenge by Netflix. Netflix is a movie-streaming company. One of the distinguishing features of the service is that it gives users the option to rate the films they have seen. Netflix then uses these ratings to recommend other films to its customers. In this machine-learning problem, you not only have the information about which films the user saw, but also about how the user rated them.

In 2006, Netflix made a large number of customer ratings of films in its database available for a public challenge. The goal was to improve on their in-house algorithm for rating prediction. Whoever could beat it by 10 percent or more would win 1 million dollars. In 2009, an international team named BellKor's Pragmatic Chaos was able to beat this mark and take the prize. They did so just 20 minutes before another team, the ensemble, passed the 10 percent mark as well—an exciting photo finish for a competition that lasted several years.

Machine learning in the real world:
Much has been written about the Netflix Prize, and you may learn a lot by reading up on it. The techniques that won were a mixture of advanced machine learning and a lot of work put into preprocessing the data. For example, some users like to rate everything very highly, while others are always more negative; if you do not account for this in preprocessing, your model will suffer. Other normalizations were also necessary for a good result, bearing in mind factors such as the film's age and how many ratings it received. Good algorithms are a good thing, but you always need to get your hands dirty and tune your methods to the properties of the data you have in front of you. Preprocessing and normalizing the data is often the most time-consuming part of the machine-learning process. However, this is also the place where one can have the biggest impact on the final performance of the system.

The first thing to note about the Netflix Prize is how hard it was. Roughly speaking, the internal system that Netflix used was about 10 percent better than having no recommendations at all (that is, assigning each movie just the average value for all users). The goal was to obtain just another 10 percent improvement on this. In total, the winning system was roughly just 20 percent better than no personalization. Yet it took a tremendous amount of time and effort to achieve this goal, and even though 20 percent does not seem like much, the result is a system that is useful in practice.

Unfortunately, for legal reasons, this dataset is no longer available. Although the dataset was anonymous, there were concerns that it might be possible to discover who the clients were and reveal private details of movie rentals. However, we can use an academic dataset with similar characteristics. This data comes from GroupLens, a research laboratory at the University of Minnesota.

How can we solve a Netflix-style ratings prediction question? We will look at two different kinds of approach: neighborhood approaches and regression approaches. We will also see how to combine these methods to obtain a single prediction.

Splitting into training and testing

At a high level, splitting the dataset into training and testing data in order to obtain a principled estimate of the system's performance is performed in the same way that we saw in previous chapters: we take a certain fraction of our data points (we will use 10 percent) and reserve them for testing; the rest will be used for training.

However, because the data is structured differently in this context, the code is different. In some of the models we explore, setting aside 10 percent of the users would not work as we transfer the data.

The first step is to load the data from the disk, for which we use the following function:

```
def load():
    import numpy as np
    from scipy import sparse

    data = np.loadtxt('data/ml-100k/u.data')
    ij = data[:, :2]
    ij = 1  # original data is in 1-based system
    values = data[:, 2]
    reviews = sparse.csc_matrix((values, ij.T)).astype(float)
    return reviews.toarray()
```

Note that zero entries in this matrix represent missing ratings:

```
reviews = load()
U,M = np.where(reviews)
```

We now use the standard `random` module to choose the indices to test:

```
import random
test_idxs = np.array(random.sample(range(len(U)), len(U)//10))
```

Now we build the `train` matrix, which is like `reviews`, but with the testing entries set to zero:

```
train = reviews.copy()
train[U[test_idxs], M[test_idxs]] = 0
```

Finally, the `test` matrix contains just the testing values:

```
test = np.zeros_like(reviews)
test[U[test_idxs], M[test_idxs]] = reviews[U[test_idxs], M[test_idxs]]
```

From now on, we will work on taking the training data, and try to predict all the missing entries in the dataset. That is, we will write code that assigns each user–movie pair a recommendation.

Normalizing the training data

As we have seen, it is best to normalize the data to remove obvious movie- or user-specific effects. We will just use one very simple type of normalization that we used before: conversion to z-scores.

Unfortunately, we cannot simply use scikit-learn's normalization objects as we have to deal with the missing values in our data (that is, not all movies were rated by all users). Thus, we want to normalize by the mean and standard deviation of the values that are, in fact, present.

We will write our own class that will ignore missing values. This class will follow the scikit-learn preprocessing API. We can even derive from scikit-learn's `TransformerMixin` class to add a `fit_transform` method:

```
from sklearn.base import TransformerMixin
class NormalizePositive(TransformerMixin):
```

We want to choose the axis of normalization. By default, we normalize along the first axis, but sometimes it will be useful to normalize along the second one. This follows the convention of many other NumPy-related functions:

```
def __init__(self, axis=0):
    self.axis = axis
```

The most important method is the `fit` method. In our implementation, we compute the mean and standard deviation of the values that are not zero. Recall that zeros indicate missing values:

```
def fit(self, features, y=None):
```

If the axis is 1, we operate on the transposed array as follows:

```
if self.axis == 1:
    features = features.T
# count features that are greater than zero in axis 0:
binary = (features > 0)
count0 = binary.sum(axis=0)

# to avoid division by zero, set zero counts to one:
count0[count0 == 0] = 1.

# computing the mean is easy:
self.mean = features.sum(axis=0)/count0

# only consider differences where binary is True:
diff = (features - self.mean) * binary
diff **= 2
# regularize the estimate of std by adding 0.1
self.std = np.sqrt(0.1 + diff.sum(axis=0)/count0)
return self
```

We add `0.1` to the direct estimate of the standard deviation to avoid underestimating the value of the standard deviation when there are only a few samples, all of which may be exactly the same. The exact value used does not matter much for the final result, but we need to avoid division by zero.

The `transform` method needs to take care of maintaining the binary structure, as follows:

```
def transform(self, features):
    if self.axis == 1:
        features = features.T
    binary = (features > 0)
    features = features - self.mean
    features /= self.std
```

```
        features *= binary
        if self.axis == 1:
            features = features.T
        return features
```

Note how we took care of transposing the input matrix when the axis is 1 and then transformed it back so that the return value has the same shape as the input. The `inverse_transform` method performs the inverse operation to transform, as shown in the following code:

```
def inverse_transform(self, features, copy=True):
    if copy:
        features = features.copy()
    if self.axis == 1:
        features = features.T
    features *= self.std
    features += self.mean
    if self.axis == 1:
        features = features.T
    return features
```

Finally, we add the `fit_transform` method, which, as the name indicates, combines both the `fit` and `transform` operations:

```
def fit_transform(self, features):
    return self.fit(features).transform(features)
```

The methods that we defined (`fit`, `transform`, `transform_inverse`, and `fit_transform`) were the same as the objects defined in the `sklearn.preprocessing` module. In the following sections, we will first normalize the inputs, generate normalized predictions, and finally apply the inverse transformation to obtain the final predictions.

A neighborhood approach to recommendations

The neighborhood concept can be implemented in two ways: user neighbors or movie neighbors. User neighborhoods are based on a very simple concept: to know how a user will rate a movie, find the users most similar to them, and look at their ratings. We will only consider user neighbors for the moment. At the end of this section, we will discuss how the code can be adapted to compute movie neighbors.

One of the interesting techniques that we will now explore is to just see which movies each user has rated, even without taking a look at what rating was given. Even with a binary matrix where we have an entry equal to one when a user rates a movie, and zero when they do not, we can make useful predictions. In hindsight, this makes perfect sense—we do not completely randomly choose movies to watch, but instead pick those where we already have an expectation of liking them. We also do not make random choices of which movies to rate, but perhaps only rate those we feel most strongly about (naturally, there are exceptions, but on average this is probably true).

We can visualize the values of the matrix as an image, where each rating is depicted as a little square. Black represents the absence of a rating and the gray levels represent the rating value.

The code to visualize the data is very simple (you can adapt it to show a larger fraction of the matrix than is possible to show in this book), as shown in the following code:

```
from matplotlib import pyplot as plt
# Build an instance of the object we defined previously
norm = NormalizePositive(axis=1)
binary = (train > 0)
train = norm.fit_transform(train)
# plot just 200x200 area for space reasons
fix, ax = plt.subplots()
ax.imshow(binary[:200, :200], interpolation='nearest')
```

The following screenshot is the output of this code:

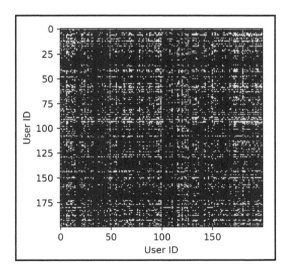

We can see that the matrix is sparse—most of the squares are black. We can also see that some users rate a lot more movies than others, and that some movies receive many more ratings than others.

We are now going to use this binary matrix to make predictions of movie ratings. The general algorithm will be calculated (in pseudocode) as follows:

- For each user, rank every other user in terms of closeness. For this step, we will use the binary matrix and use correlation as the measure of closeness (interpreting the binary matrix as zeros and ones allows us to perform this computation).
- When we need to estimate a rating for a user—movie pair, we look at all the users who have rated that movie and split them into two groups: the most similar half and the most dissimilar half. We then use the average of the most similar half as the prediction.

We can use the `scipy.spatial.distance.pdist` function to obtain the distance between all the users as a matrix. This function returns the correlation distance, which transforms the correlation value by inverting it so that larger numbers mean that they are less similar. Mathematically, the correlation distance is *1-r*, where *r* is the correlation value. The code is as follows:

```
from scipy.spatial import distance
# compute all pair-wise distances:
dists = distance.pdist(binary, 'correlation')
# Convert to square form, so that dists[i,j]
# is distance between binary[i] and binary[j]:
dists = distance.squareform(dists)
```

We can use this matrix to select the nearest `neighbors` of each user. These are the users that most resemble it. We select these `neighbors` using the following code:

```
neighbors = dists.argsort(axis=1)
```

Now, we iterate over all users to estimate predictions for all inputs:

```
# We are going to fill this matrix with results
filled = train.copy()
for u in range(filled.shape[0]):
    # n_u is neighbors of user
    n_u = neighbors[u, 1:]
    # t_u is training data

    for m in range(filled.shape[1]):
        # get relevant reviews in order!
```

```
revs = train[n_u, m]
# Only use valid entries:
revs = revs[binary[n_u, m]]

if len(revs):
    # n is the number of reviews for this movie
    n = len(revs)
    # consider half of the reviews plus one
    n //= 2
    n += 1
    revs = revs[:n]
    filled[u,m] = np.mean(revs)
```

The tricky part in the preceding snippet is indexing by the right values to select the neighbors who have rated the movie. Then, we choose the half that is closest to the user (in the `rev[:n]` line) and average those. Because some films have many reviews and others very few, it is hard to find a single number of users for all cases. Choosing half of the available data is a more generic approach than setting a fixed value.

To obtain the final result, we need to denormalize the predictions as follows:

```
predicted = norm.inverse_transform(filled)
```

We can use the same metrics we learned about when discussing regression (Chapter 2, *Classifying with Real-World Examples*). Recall that the r^2 score ranges from 0 (prediction is no better than baseline) to 1 (prediction is perfect). For convenience, we often see it in percentage terms (from 0 to 100):

```
from sklearn import metrics
r2 = metrics.r2_score(test[test > 0], predicted[test > 0])
print('R2 score (binary neighbors): {:.1%}'.format(r2))
R2 score (binary neighbors): 29.5%
```

The preceding code computes the result for user `neighbors`. That is, when attempting to make a prediction for a user—movie pair, it looks at similar users that have rated the same movie and averages them. We can use the same code to compute the movie `neighbors` by transposing the input matrix. That is, now we will look for similar movies rated by the same user and average their ratings.

In the online code repository, the recommendation code was wrapped in a function called `predict_positive_nn`, so we can call it with the transpose matrix and finally transpose the result:

```
predicted = predict_positive_nn(train.T).T
r2 = metrics.r2_score(test[test > 0], predicted[test > 0])
print('R2 score (binary movie neighbors): {:.1%}'.format(r2))
R2 score (binary movie neighbors): 29.8%
```

We can see that the results are not that different.

A regression approach to recommendations

An alternative to neighborhoods is to formulate recommendations as a regression problem and apply the methods that we learned in the `Chapter 6`, *Clustering - Finding Related Posts*.

We first consider why this problem is not a good fit for a classification formulation. We could certainly attempt to learn a five-class model, using one class for each possible movie rating. However, there are two problems with this approach:

- The different possible errors are not at all the same. For example, mistaking a 5-star movie for a 4-star one is not as serious a mistake as mistaking a 5-star movie for a 1-star one
- Intermediate values make sense. Even if our inputs are only integer values, it is perfectly meaningful to say that the prediction is 4.3. We can see that this is a different prediction than 3.5, even if they both round to 4

These two factors together mean that classification is not a good fit for the problem. The regression framework is a better fit.

For a basic approach, we again have two choices: We can build movie-specific or user-specific models. In our case, we are going to first build user-specific models. This means that, for each user, we take the movies that the user has rated as our target variable. The inputs are the ratings of other users. We hypothesize that this will give a high value to users who are similar to our user (or a negative value to users who like the same movies that our user dislikes).

Setting up the `train` and `test` matrices is the same method as before (including running the normalization steps). Therefore, we jump directly to the learning step:

1. First, we instantiate a `regression` object as follows (recall that, in Chapter 2, *Classifying with Real-World Examples,* we had reached the conclusion that an elastic net with an automatic parameter search was a good general-purpose regression method):

```
reg = ElasticNetCV(alphas=[0.0125, 0.025, 0.05, .125, .25,
.5, 1., 2., 4.])
```

2. We then build a data matrix that will contain a rating for every user–movie pair. We initialize it as a copy of the training data:

```
filled = train.copy()
```

3. Now, we iterate over all the users, and each time learn a regression model based only on the data that that user has given us:

```
for u in range(train.shape[0]):
    curtrain = np.delete(train, u, axis=0)
    # binary records whether this rating is present
    bu = binary[u]
    # fit the current user based on everybody else
    reg.fit(curtrain[:,bu].T, train[u, bu])
    # Fill in all the missing ratings
    filled[u, ~bu] = reg.predict(curtrain[:,~bu].T)
```

4. Evaluating the method can be done exactly as before:

```
predicted = norm.inverse_transform(filled)
r2 = metrics.r2_score(test[test > 0], predicted[test > 0])
print('R2 score (user regression): {:.1%}'.format(r2))
R2 score (user regression): 32.3%
```

As before, we can adapt this code to perform movie regression by using the transposed matrix (see the companion code repository for an example of this).

Combining multiple methods

We now combine the aforementioned methods into a single prediction. This seems intuitively a good idea, but how can we do this in practice? Perhaps the first thought that comes to mind is that we can average the predictions. This might give decent results, but there is no reason to think that all estimated predictions should be treated the same. It might be that one is better than the others.

We can try a weighted average, multiplying each prediction by a given weight before summing it all up. How do we find the best weights, though? We learn them from the data, of course!

Ensemble learning:

We are using a general technique in machine learning that is not just applicable in regression: ensemble learning. We learn an ensemble (that is, a set) of predictors. Then, we combine them to obtain a single output. What is interesting is that we can see each prediction as being a new feature, and we are now just combining features based on training data, which is what we have been doing all along. Note that we are doing this for regression here, but the same reasoning is applicable to classification: you learn several classifiers, then a master classifier, which takes the output of all of them and gives a final prediction. Different forms of ensemble learning differ in how you combine the base predictors.

In order to combine the methods, we will use a technique called **stacked learning**. The idea is that you learn a set of predictors, then you use the output of these predictors as features for another predictor. You can even have several layers, where each layer learns by using the output of the previous layer as features for its prediction. Have a look at the following diagram:

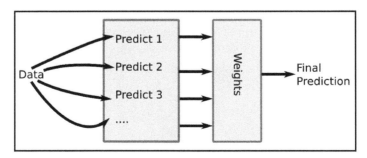

In order to fit this combination model, we will split the training data into two. Alternatively, we could have used cross-validation (the original stacked-learning model worked like this). However, in this case, we have enough data to obtain good estimates by leaving some aside.

Just as when we were fitting hyperparameters, we need two layers of training/testing splits: a first, higher-level split, and then inside the training split, a second split that can fit the stacked learner. This is analogous to how we use multiple levels of cross-validation when using an inner cross-validation loop to find hyperparameter values:

```
train,test = get_train_test(random_state=12)
# Now split the training again into two subgroups
tr_train,tr_test = load_ml100k.get_train_test(train)

tr_predicted0 = predict_positive_nn(tr_train)
tr_predicted1 = predict_positive_nn(tr_train.T).T
tr_predicted2 = predict_regression(tr_train)
tr_predicted3 = predict_regression(tr_train.T).T
# Now assemble these predictions into a single array:
stack_tr = np.array([
    tr_predicted0[tr_test > 0],
    tr_predicted1[tr_test > 0],
    tr_predicted2[tr_test > 0],
    tr_predicted3[tr_test > 0],
    ]).T

# Fit a simple linear regression
lr = linear_model.LinearRegression()
lr.fit(stack_tr, tr_test[tr_test > 0])
```

Now, we apply the whole process to the testing split and evaluate:

```
stack_te = np.array([
    tr_predicted0.ravel(),
    tr_predicted1.ravel(),
    tr_predicted2.ravel(),
    tr_predicted3.ravel(),
    ]).T
predicted = lr.predict(stack_te).reshape(train.shape)
```

Evaluation is as before:

```
r2 = metrics.r2_score(test[test > 0], predicted[test > 0])
print('R2 stacked: {:.2%}'.format(r2))
R2 stacked: 33.15%
```

The result of the stacked learning is better than any single method achieved. It is quite typical that combining methods is a simple way to obtain a small performance boost, but that the results are not earth shattering.

By having a flexible way to combine multiple methods, we can simply try any idea we wish by adding it into the mix of learners and letting the system fold it into the prediction. We can, for example, replace the neighborhood criterion in the nearest-neighbor code.

However, we do have to be careful to not overfit our dataset. In fact, if we randomly try too many things, some of them will work well on a particular dataset, but will not generalize. Even though we are splitting our data, we are not rigorously cross-validating our design decisions. In order to have a good estimate, and if data is plentiful, you should leave a portion of the data untouched until you have a final model that is about to go into production. Then, testing your model on this held-out data will give you an unbiased prediction of how well you should expect it to work in the real world.

> Of course, collaborative filtering also works with neural networks, but don't forget to keep validation data available for the testing—or, more precisely, validating—your ensemble model.

Basket analysis

The methods we have looked at so far work well when you have numeric ratings of how much a user liked a product. This type of information is not always available, as it requires active behavior on the part of consumers.

Basket analysis is an alternative mode of learning recommendations. In this mode, our data consists only of which items were bought together; it does not contain any information on whether or not individual items were enjoyed. Even if users sometimes buy items they regret, on average, knowing their purchases gives you enough information to build good recommendations. It is often easier to get this data rather than rating data, as many users will not provide ratings, while the basket data is generated as a side effect of shopping. The following screenshot shows you a snippet of Amazon.com's web page for Tolstoy's classic book *War and Peace*, demonstrating a common way to use these results:

Customers Who Bought This Item Also Bought

Anna Karenina	The Brothers Karamazov	The Idiot (Vintage Classics)
Leo Tolstoy	Fyodor Dostoevsky	Fyodor Dostoevsky
★★★★☆ (289)	★★★★☆ (248)	★★★★☆ (57)
Paperback	Paperback	Paperback
$10.35	$11.25	$10.88

This mode of learning is, of course, not only applicable to shopping baskets. It is applicable in any setting where you have groups of objects together and need to recommend another one. For example, recommending additional recipients to a user writing an email is done by Gmail, and could be implemented using similar techniques (we do not know which methods Gmail uses internally; perhaps they combine multiple techniques, as we did earlier). Or, we could use these methods to develop an app to recommend web pages to visit based on your browsing history. Even if we are handling purchases, it may make sense to group all purchases made by a customer into a single basket, independently of whether the items were bought together or in separate transactions. This depends on the business context, but keep in mind that the techniques are flexible and can be useful in many settings.

Beer and diapers:
One of the stories that is often mentioned in the context of basket analysis is the *diapers and beer* story. When supermarkets first started to look at their data, they found that diapers were often bought together with beer. Supposedly, it was the father who would go out to the supermarket to buy diapers and would then pick up some beer as well. There has been much discussion of whether this is true or just an urban myth. In this case, it seems that it is true. In the early 1990s, Osco Drug discovered that, in the early evening, beer and diapers were bought together, and it did surprise the managers who had, until then, never considered these two products to be similar. What is not true is that this led the store to move the beer display closer to the diaper section. Also, we have no idea whether it was really true that fathers were buying beer and diapers together more than mothers (or grandparents).

Obtaining useful predictions

It is not just customers who bought *X* also bought *Y*, even though that is how many online retailers phrase their recommendations (see the Amazon.com screenshot given earlier); a real system cannot work like this. Why not? Because such a system would get fooled by very frequently bought items and would simply recommend that which is popular without any personalization.

For example, at a supermarket, many customers buy bread every time they shop, or almost every time (for the sake of argument, let us say that 50 percent of visits end with the purchase of bread). So, if you focus on any particular item, say, dishwasher soap, and look at what is frequently bought with dishwasher soap, you might find that bread is frequently bought with dishwasher soap. In fact, just by random chance, let's say that 50 percent of the times when someone buys dishwasher soap, they buy bread. However, bread is frequently bought with anything else, just because people frequently buy bread.

What we are really looking for is customers who bought *X* are statistically more likely to buy *Y* than the average customer who has not bought *X*. If you buy dishwasher soap, you are likely to buy bread, but not more so than the baseline. Similarly, a bookstore that simply recommended bestsellers no matter which books you had already bought would not be doing a good job of personalizing recommendations.

Analyzing supermarket shopping baskets

As an example, we will look at `dataset` consisting of anonymous transactions at a supermarket in Belgium. This `dataset` was made available by Tom Brijs at Hasselt University. Because of privacy concerns, the data has been anonymized, so we only have a number for each product, and each basket therefore consists of a set of numbers. The data file is available from several online sources (including this book's companion website).

We begin by loading the dataset and looking at some statistics (this is always a good idea):

```
from collections import defaultdict
from itertools import chain

# File is downloaded as a compressed file
import gzip
# file format is a line per transaction
# of the form '12 34 342 5...'
dataset = [[int(tok) for tok in line.strip().split()]
        for line in gzip.open('retail.dat.gz')]
# It is more convenient to work with sets
dataset = [set(d) for d in dataset]
```

```
# count how often each product was purchased:
counts = defaultdict(int)
for elem in chain(*dataset):
    counts[elem] += 1
```

We can see the resulting counts summarized in the following table:

Number of times bought	Number of products
Just once	2,224
2 or 3	2,438
4 to 7	2,508
8 to 15	2,251
16 to 31	2,182
32 to 63	1,940
64 to 127	1,523
128 to 511	1,225
512 or more	179

There are many products that have only been bought a few times. For example, 33 percent of products were bought four or fewer times. However, this represents only 1 percent of purchases. This phenomenon, where many products are only purchased a small number of times, is sometimes labeled *the long tail*, and has only become more prominent as the internet makes it cheaper to stock and sell niche items. In order to be able to provide recommendations for these products, we would need a lot more data.

There are a few open source implementations of basket analysis algorithms out there, but none that are well integrated with scikit-learn or any of the other packages we have been using. Therefore, we are going to implement one classic algorithm ourselves. This algorithm is called the Apriori algorithm, and it is a bit old (it was published in 1994 by Rakesh Agrawal and Ramakrishnan Srikant), but it still works (algorithms, of course, never stop working; they just get superseded by better ideas).

The Apriori algorithm takes a collection of sets (that is, your shopping baskets) and returns sets that are very frequent as subsets (that is, items that together are part of many shopping baskets).

The algorithm works using a bottom-up approach: starting with the smallest candidates (those composed of a single element), it builds up, adding one element at a time. The algorithm takes a set of baskets and the minimum input that should be considered (a parameter we will call `minsupport`). The first step is to consider all baskets with just one element with minimal support. Then, these are combined in all possible ways to build up two-element baskets. These are filtered in order to keep only those that have minimal support. Then, all possible three-element baskets are considered, those with minimal support are kept, and so on. The trick of Apriori is that when building a larger basket, it only needs to consider those that are built up of smaller sets.

The following diagram presents a schematic view of the algorithm:

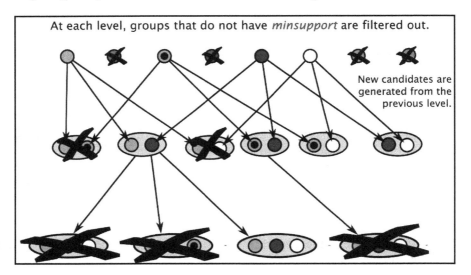

We shall now implement this algorithm in code. We need to define the minimum support we are looking for:

```
minsupport = 100
```

Support is the number of times a set of products was purchased together.

The goal of Apriori is to find item sets with high support. Logically, any item set with more than minimal support can only be composed of items that themselves have at least minimal support:

```
valid = set(k for k,v in counts.items()
            if (v >= minsupport))
```

Our initial `itemsets` are singletons (sets with a single element). In particular, all singletons that have at least minimal support are frequent `itemsets`:

```
itemsets = [frozenset([v]) for v in valid]
```

We need to set up an index to speed up computation using the following code:

```
baskets = defaultdict(set)

for i, ds in enumerate(dataset):
    for ell in ds:
        baskets[ell].add(i)
```

That is, `baskets[i]` contains the indices of all the elements in the dataset where i occurs. Now, our loop is given as follows:

```
itemsets = [frozenset([v]) for v in valid]
freqsets = []
for i in range(16):
    print(i)
    nextsets = []
    tested = set()
    for it in itemsets:
        for v in valid:
            if v not in it:
                # Create a new candidate set by adding v to it
                c = (it | frozenset([v]))
                # check if we have tested it already
                if c in tested:
                    continue
                tested.add(c)

                candidates = set()
                for elem in c:
                    candidates.update(baskets[elem])
                support_c = sum(1 for d in candidates \
                                if dataset[d].issuperset(c))
                if support_c > minsupport:
                    nextsets.append(c)
    freqsets.extend(nextsets)
    itemsets = nextsets
    if not len(itemsets):
        break
print("Finished!")
Finished!
```

The Apriori algorithm returns frequent `itemsets`—that is, baskets that are present above a certain threshold (given by the `minsupport` variable in the code).

Association rule mining

Frequent item sets are not very useful by themselves. The next step is to build **association rules**. Because of this final goal, the whole field of basket analysis is sometimes called association rule mining.

An association rule is a statement of the type, if X, then Y—for example, if a customer bought *War and Peace*, then they will buy *Anna Karenina*. Note that the rule is not deterministic (not all customers who buy X will buy Y), but it is rather cumbersome to always spell it out: if a customer bought X, they are more likely than baseline to buy Y; thus, we say if X, then Y, but we mean it in a probabilistic sense.

Interestingly, both the antecedent and the conclusion may contain multiple objects: customers who bought X, Y, and Z also bought A, B, and C. Multiple antecedents may allow you to make more specific predictions than are possible from a single item.

You can get from a frequent set to a rule by just trying all the possible combinations of X implies Y. It is easy to generate many of these rules. However, you only want to have valuable rules. Therefore, we need to measure the value of a rule. A commonly used measure is called the lift. The lift is the ratio between the probability obtained by applying the rule and the baseline, as shown in the following formula:

$$lift(X \rightarrow Y) = \frac{P(Y \vee X)}{P(Y)}$$

In the preceding formula, $P(Y)$ is the fraction of all the transactions that include Y, while $P(Y|X)$ is the fraction of transactions that include Y, given that they also include X. Using the lift helps avoid the problem of recommending bestsellers; for a bestseller, both $P(Y)$ and $P(Y|X)$ will be large. Therefore, the lift will be close to one and the rule will be deemed irrelevant. In practice, we wish to have values of lift of at least 10, perhaps even 100.

Refer to the following code:

```
minlift = 5.0
nr_transactions = float(len(dataset))
for itemset in freqsets:
    for item in itemset:
        consequent = frozenset([item])
        antecedent = itemset-consequent
```

```
base = 0.0
# acount: antecedent count
acount = 0.0
# ccount : consequent count
ccount = 0.0
for d in dataset:
    if item in d: base += 1
    if d.issuperset(itemset): ccount += 1
    if d.issuperset(antecedent): acount += 1
base /= nr_transactions
p_y_given_x = ccount/acount
lift = p_y_given_x / base
if lift > minlift:
    print('Rule {0} ->  {1} has lift {2}'
        .format(antecedent, consequent,lift))
```

Some of the results are shown in the following table. The counts are the number of transactions that include the **consequent alone** (that is, the base rate at which that product is bought), all the items in the antecedent, and all the items in the antecedent and the consequent:

Antecedent	Consequent	Consequent count	Antecedent count	Antecedent and consequent count	Lift
1378, 1379, 1380	1269	279 (0.3 percent)	80	57	225
48, 41, 976	117	1026 (1.1 percent)	122	51	35
48, 41, 1,6011	16,010	1316 (1.5 percent)	165	159	64

We can see, for example, that there were 80 transactions in which 1378, 1379, and 1380 were bought together. Of these, 57 also included 1269, so the estimated conditional probability is $57/80 \approx 71$ percent. Compared to the fact that only 0.3 percent of all transactions included 1269, this gives us a lift of 255.

The need to have a decent number of transactions in these counts in order to be able to make relatively solid inferences is why we must first select frequent itemsets. If we were to generate rules from an infrequent itemset, the counts would be very small; because of this, the relative values would be meaningless (or subject to very large error bars).

Note that there are many more association rules discovered from this dataset: the algorithm discovers 1030 rules (requiring support for the baskets of at least 80 and a minimum lift of 5). This is still a small dataset when compared to what is now possible with the web. With datasets containing millions of transactions, you can expect to generate many thousands of rules, even millions.

However, for each customer or product, only a few rules will be relevant at any given time. So each customer only receives a small number of recommendations.

More advanced basket analysis

There are now other algorithms for basket analysis that run faster than Apriori. The code we saw earlier was simple, and it was good enough for us, as we only had about 100,000 transactions. If we had many millions, it might be worth using a faster algorithm. Note, though, that learning association rules can often be done offline, where efficiency is not as great a concern.

There are also methods that you can use to work with temporal information, leading to rules that take into account the order in which you have made your purchases. Consider, as an example, that someone buying supplies for a large party may come back for trash bags. It may make sense to propose trash bags on the first visit. However, it would not make sense to propose party supplies to everyone who buys a trash bag.

Summary

In this chapter, we started by using regression for rating predictions. We saw a couple of different ways in which to do so, and then combined them all in a single prediction by learning a set of weights. This technique of ensemble learning—and in particular stacked learning—is a general technique that can be used in many situations, not just for regression. It allows you to combine different ideas, even if their internal mechanics are completely different—you can combine their final outputs.

In the second half of the chapter, we switched gears and looked at another mode of producing recommendations: shopping basket analysis, or association rule mining. In this mode, we try to discover (probabilistic) association rules of the form that customers who bought X are likely to be interested in Y. This takes advantage of the data that is generated from sales alone without requiring users to numerically rate items. This is not available in scikit-learn at the moment, so we wrote our own code.

If you are using association rule mining, then you need to be careful to not simply recommend bestsellers to every user (otherwise, what is the point of personalization?). In order to do this, we learned about measuring the value of rules in relation to the baseline, using a measure called the lift of a rule.

In Chapter 8, *Artificial Neural Networks and Deep Learning*, we will finally dive into deep learning with TensorFlow. We will learn about its API, then move on to learn about convolutional networks (and how they revolutionized image processing), and then recurrent networks.

8
Artificial Neural Networks and Deep Learning

Neural networks are leading the current machine learning trend. Whether it's Tensorflow, Keras, CNTK, PyTorch, Caffee, or any other package, they are currently achieving results that few other algorithms have achieved, especially in domains such as image processing. With the advent of fast computers and big data, the neural network algorithms designed in the 1970s are now usable. The big issue, even a decade ago, was that you needed lots of training data that was just not available, and, at the same time, even when you had enough data, the time required to train the model was just too much. This problem is now more or less solved.

The main improvement over the years has been the neural network architecture. The backpropagation algorithm used to update the neural networks is more or less the same as before, but the structure has seen numerous improvements, such as convolutional layers instead of dense layers, or, **Long Short Term Memory** (**LSTM**) for regular recurrent layers.

Here is the plan that we will follow: first a deep dive inside TensorFlow and its API, then we will apply it on convolutional neural networks for image processing, and finally we will tackle recurrent neural networks (specifically the flavor known as LSTM) for image processing and text processing.

Talks about machine learning speed are mainly about neural network speed. Why? Because neural networks are basically matrix multiplications and parallel math functions—blocks that GPUs are very good at.

Using TensorFlow

We already saw some examples of using TensorFlow, and it's now time to understand more about how it works.

First things first, the name comes of the fact that TensorFlow uses tensors (matrices with more than two dimensions) for all computations. All functions work on these objects, returning either tensors or operations that behave like tensors, with new names defined for all of them. The second part of the name comes from the graph that underlies the data flowing between tensors.

Neural networks were inspired by how the brain works, but it doesn't work as the model use for neural networks. Yes, each neuron is connected to lots of other neurons, but the output is not a product of the input times a transition matrix plus a bias fed inside an activation function. Also, neural networks have layers (deep learning refers to neural networks with more than one so-called hidden layer, meaning neither the input nor the output) with a strict progression in their architecture. A brain has connections all over the place and continuous evolution, whereas a neural network always has a stable output for a given input and a given moment in time (until we get a new tick, as we will see in recurrent networks).

Let's now dive into the TensorFlow graph API.

TensorFlow API

The best way to start is by having a look at the programming environment:

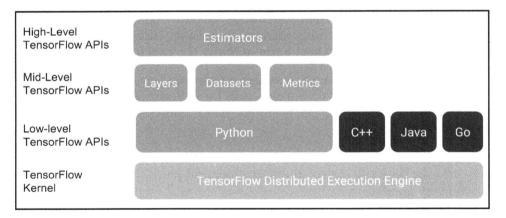

We are obviously interested in the Python stack, and we will mainly focus on layers and metrics. Datasets are interesting, but lots of them are from external contributions, and some are targeted for removal. The scikit learn API is considered as more future-proof, so we won't look at it.

Estimators are the higher-level APIs, but they are not as well developed as the one from scikit learn. As we develop new networks, being able to debug them and check what they have inside their gut is easier in the middle API than the top one, although the fact that all tensors have names makes it possible to get this information outside of the Estimator API.

Lots of online tutorials are still directly using the lower API, and we used it in our regression example by calling `tf.matmult` directly. We think it is better to use the middle- or the high-level API than the others, even if they may sometimes seem more flexible and closer to what you think you need.

Graphs

Graphs are central to TensorFlow, as we saw by the definition of TensorFlow. The default graph contains the structure between objects (placeholders, variables, or constants) as well as the type of these objects (variables are, for instance, trainable variables and all the trainable variables can be retrieved by calling `tf.trainable_variables()`).

It is possible to change the default graph by using the `with` construct:

```
g = tf.Graph()
with g.as_default():
    c = tf.constant("Node in g")
```

So each time we call a TensorFlow function, we add nodes to the default graph (whether we are in a block or not). A graph on its own doesn't do anything. No operation is actually done when we create a new layer, use a metric, or create a placeholder. The only thing we do is add nodes on the graph.

Once we have an interesting graph, we need to execute in what is called a session. This is the only place where TensorFlow will actually execute code and where values can be retrieved from the graph.

 Just as for the graph, variables, placeholders, and so on will be put on the best possible device. This device will be the CPU for all platforms, at the time of writing, that's Linux for HIP-capable AMD GPUs or nVidia GPU for Linux and Windows.

They can be pinned to a specific device with the command:

```
with tf.device("/device:CPU:0"):
```

It is sometimes interesting to have the same name for different parts of a graph. To allow this, we can use `name_scope` to prefix the name with a path. Of course, they can be used recursively:

```
var = tf.constant([0, 1, 2, 3])
with tf.name_scope("section"):
    mean = tf.reduce_mean(var)
```

Sessions

It is time to learn a little bit more about sessions. As we saw earlier, TensorFlow only executes the operations inside a session.

The simplest usage of a session is the following:

```
with tf.Session() as sess:
    sess.run(tf.global_variables_initializer())
    sess.run([mean], feed_dict={})
```

This will initialize the variables by calling their initializer inside the session. In a neural network, we cannot have all variables starting with a zero value, especially the weights in the different layers (some, such as bias, can be initialized to 0). The initializer is then of prime importance and is either set directly for explicit variables, or is implicit when calling mid-level functions (see the different initializers available with TensorFlow and play with them in all our examples).

TensorFlow uses also an external way to get reports, called summaries. They live in the `tf.summary` module, and can track tensors, and preprocess them:

```
tf.summary.histogram(var)
tf.summary.scalar('mean', tf.reduce_mean(var))
```

All these summary reports can then be written and retrieved during a session run and saved by a special object:

```
merged = tf.summary.merge_all()
writer = tf.summary.FileWriter(path/to/log-directory)
with tf.Session() as sess:
    summary, _ = sess.run([merged, train_step], feed_dict={})
    writer.add_summary(summary, i)
```

Tensorboard is a tool provided with TensorFlow that allows us to display these summaries. It can be launched with `tensorboard --logdir=path/to/log-directory`.

If we don't want to use a session directly, the **Estimator** class can be used.

From an estimator, we can call its method train, which takes as an argument a data generator and the number of steps that we want to run. For instance, this could be:

```
def input_fn():
    features = {'SepalLength': np.array([6.4, 5.0]),
        'SepalWidth': np.array([2.8, 2.3]),
        'PetalLength': np.array([5.6, 3.3]),
        'PetalWidth': np.array([2.2, 1.0])}
    labels = np.array([2, 1])
    return features, labels
estimator.train(input_fn=input_fn , steps=STEPS)
```

Similarly, we can use test to get results from the model:

```
estimator.test(input_fn=input_train)
```

If you want to use more than the simple Estimators already provided with TensorFlow, we suggest to follow the tutorial on the TensorFlow website: `https://www.tensorflow.org/get_started/custom_estimators`.

Useful operations

In all the previous TensorFlow models, we encountered functions that create layers in TensorFlow. There are a few layers that are more or less inescapable.

The first one is `tf.dense`, connecting all input to a new layer. We saw them in the auto-encoder example, and they take as an `inputs` parameter a tensor (variable, placeholder...) and then `units` the number of output units. By default, it also has bias, meaning that the layer computes `inputs * weights + bias`.

Another important layer that we will see later is `conv2d`. It computes a convolution on an image, and this times it takes the `filters` that will indicate the number of nodes in the output layer. It is what defines convolutional neural networks. Here is the usual formula for the convolution:

$$conv2d[i,j] = \sum_{k=-filters/2}^{k=filters/2} \sum_{l=-filters/2}^{l=filters/2} kernel[k,l] * input[i-k, j-l]$$

 The standard name for the tensor of coefficients in the convolution is called a kernel.

Let's have a look at a few other layers:

- `dropout` will randomly put some weights to zero during the training phase. This is very important in a complex deep-learning network to prevent it from overfitting. We will also see it later.
- `max_pooling2d` is a very important complement to the convolution layer. It selects the maximum of the input on a two-dimensional shape. There is also a one-dimensional version that works after dense layers.

All layers have an `activation` parameter. This activation transforms a linear operation to a nonlinear one. Let's have a look at the most useful ones from the `tf.nn` module:

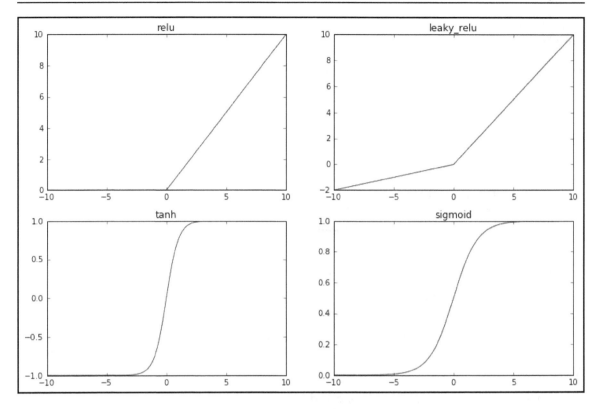

As we saw earlier, scikit learn provides lots of metrics to compute accuracy, curves, and more. TensorFlow provides similar operations in the tf.metrics module.

Saving and restoring neural networks

There are two ways of storing a trained neural network for future use and then restoring it. We will see that they enable this in the convolutional neural network example.

The first one lives in tf.train. It is created with the following statement:

```
saver = tf.train.Saver(max_to_keep=10)
```

And then each training step can be saved with:

```
saver.save(sess, './classifier', global_step=step)
```

Here the full graph is saved, but it is possible to only save part of it. We save it all here, and only keep the last 10 saves, and we postfix the name of the save with the step we are at.

Let's say that we saved the final training step with `saver.save(sess, './classifier-final')`. We know we first have to restore the graph state with:

```
new_saver = tf.train.import_meta_graph("classifier-final.meta")
```

This didn't restore the variable state, for this we have to call:

```
new_saver.restore(sess, tf.train.latest_checkpoint('./'))
```

 Be aware that only the graph is restored. If you have Python variables pointing to nodes in this graph, you need to restore them before you can use them. This is true for placeholders and operations.

We also have to restore some of our variables:

```
graph = tf.get_default_graph()
training_tf = graph.get_tensor_by_name('is_training:0')
```

This is also a good reason to use proper names for all tensors (placeholders, operations, and so on) as we need to use their name to get a reference to them again when we restore the graph.

The other mechanism builds on this one and is far more powerful, but we will present the basic usage that mimics the simple one. We first create what is usually called a `builder`:

```
builder = tf.saved_model.builder.SavedModelBuilder(export_dir)
```

 The `export_dir` folder is created by the builder here. If it already exists, you have to remove it before creating a new saved model.

Now after the training, we can call it to save the state of the network:

```
builder.add_meta_graph_and_variables(sess,
[tf.saved_model.tag_constants.TRAINING])
```

Obviously, we can save more than one network in this object, with far more attributes, but, in our case, we just need to call one function to restore the state:

```
tf.saved_model.loader.load(sess, [tf.saved_model.tag_constants.TRAINING],
export_dir)
```

Training neural networks

We haven't talked about training neural networks that much. Basically, all optimizations are a gradient descent, the questions are what step length are we going to use, and should we take the previous gradients into account or not?

When computing one gradient, there is also the question of whether we do this for just one new sample or we do it for a multitude of samples at the same time (the batch). Basically, we almost never feed only one sample at a time (as the size of a batch varies, all the placeholders have a first dimension set to None indicating that it will be dynamic).

This also imposes the creation of a special layer, batch_normalization, that scales the gradient (up or down, so that the layers can be updated in a meaningful manner, so the batch size is important here), and in some network architectures, it will be mandatory. This layer also has two learning parameters, which are the mean and the standard deviation. If they are not important, a simpler batch-normalization layer can be implemented and will be used in an example in Chapter 12, *Computer Vision*.

The optimizer we used before is GradientDescentOptimizer. It is a simple gradient descent with a fixed step. This is very fragile, as the step length is heavily dependent on the dataset and the model we are using.

Another very important one is AdamOptimizer. It is currently one of the most efficient optimizers because it scales the new gradient based on the previous one (trying to mimic the hessian scaling of the Newton approach of cost-function reduction).

Another one that is worth mentioning is RMSPropOptimizer. Here, the additional trick is the momentum. Momentum indicates that the new gradient uses a fraction of the previous gradient on top of the new gradient.

The size of the gradient step, or learning rate, is crucial. The selection of an adequate for it often requires some know-how. The rate must be small enough so that the optimizations makes the network better, but big enough to have efficient first iterations. The improvement of the training is supposed to be fast for the first iterations and then improve slowly (it is globally fitting an often requires some know-how. The rate must be small enough so that the optimizations makes the network better, but big enough to have efficient first iterations. The improvement of the training is supposed to be fast for the first iterations and then improve slowly (it is globally fitting an e^{-t} curve).

To avoid over-generalization, it is sometimes advised to stop optimization early (called early stopping), when the improvements are slow. In this context, using collaborative filtering can also achieve better results. Additional information can be found at `http://ruder.io/optimizing-gradient-descent/`.

Convolutional neural networks

Less than a decade ago, neural networks were not the best at image processing. The reason, other than data and CPU power, is that researchers were using dense layers. When stacking several layers and dense layers connecting thousands of pixels to, say, a thousand hidden units, we ended up with a non-convex cost function to optimize that had millions of parameters.

The curse of dimensionality was thus very much an issue, even the biggest databases may not have been enough. But let's go back to the introduction. Machine learning is not just training a model, it's also about feature processing. In image processing, people used lots of different tools to extract features from an image, but one common tool for all these preprocessing workflows was filtering.

So now, let's go back to neural networks. What if we could feed these filters inside a neural network? The issue then would be to know which filters would be the best ones. This is where convolutional networks come in: the convolutional layers create features and then the dense layers do their job (classification, regression, and so on).

Instead of having millions of coefficients as for a dense layer, we create an image of output pixels, with a fixed number of units for each pixel. Then there is a fixed number of weights for each of those units, and they are the same for all the pixels in the output image. When we move from one pixel to another in the output image, we also move the connections in the same way (perhaps with a stride) in the input image:

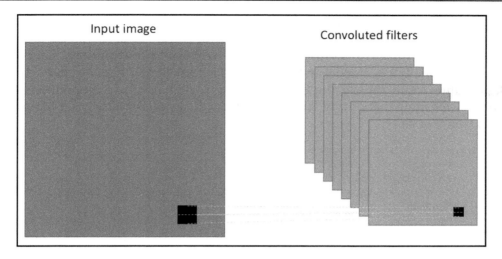

So a conv2d layer has a kernel of the of dimension `[kernel_size_1, kernel_size_2, filters]` dimension for its weight, which is very small if you consider the number of weights! That is much less than a thousand numbers, instead of over a million. This is trainable, and it's even possible to look at which features are relevant for the question we asked by looking at these weights. We should be able to see things as simple as a gradient filter, a Sobel, or perhaps a filter that looks at curves.

Now that we have all these pieces, we can put them together. We will try to use the hand-digits dataset again and classify these images into 10 classes (one for each number). We will also save the trained model and restore it with the two methods we saw earlier.

Let's start with some simple imports and some hyperparameters:

```
import tensorflow as tf
import numpy as np
from sklearn.model_selection import train_test_split
n_epochs = 10
learning_rate = 0.0002
batch_size = 128
export_dir = "data/classifier-mnist"
image_shape = [28,28,1]
step = 1000
dim_W3 = 1024
dim_W2 = 128
dim_W1 = 64
dropout_rate = 0.1
```

We will train the neural network for 10 epochs (so we will pass through the full training dataset 10 times), we will use a learning rate of 0.0002, a batch size of 128 (so we will train the model with 128 images at a time), and then we will use 64 convolutional filters, then 128 filters, and finally 1024 nodes in the last layer, before the last 10 nodes that will give us our classification result. Finally, the 1,024-nodes layer will have also a dropout section with a rate of 0.1, meaning that during the training, we will always arbitrarily set 102-node output to 0 on that layer:

```
from sklearn.datasets import fetch_mldata
mnist = fetch_mldata('MNIST original')
mnist.data.shape = (-1, 28, 28)
mnist.data = mnist.data.astype(np.float32).reshape( [-1, 28, 28, 1]) / 255.
mnist.num_examples = len(mnist.data)
mnist.labels = mnist.target.astype(np.int64)
X_train, X_test, y_train, y_test = train_test_split(mnist.data,
mnist.labels, test_size=(1. / 7.))
```

We now get the data, reshape it, change its type, and keep 60,000 images for training and 10,000 for testing purposes. The labels will be int64 because that's what we will use for our custom-check function. We don't have to transform the labels in a one-hot array, because TensorFlow already has a function that tackles that. No need to add more processing than required!

 Why a four-dimension matrix? The first dimension, -1, is our batch size, and it will be dynamic. The second two dimensions are for the width and height of our image. The final one is the number of input channels, here just 1.

Let's create our Convolutional Neural Network class:

```
class CNN():
    def __init__(
            self,
            image_shape=(28,28,1)
            dim_W3=1024,
            dim_W2=128,
            dim_W1=64,
            classes=10
            ):

        self.image_shape = image_shape

        self.dim_W3 = dim_W3
        self.dim_W2 = dim_W2
        self.dim_W1 = dim_W1
        self.classes = classes
```

We create a class for our CNN, and we save locally a few of the parameters we set earlier:

```
def create_conv2d(self, input, filters, kernel_size, name):
    layer = tf.layers.conv2d(
            inputs=input,
            filters=filters,
            kernel_size=kernel_size,
            activation=tf.nn.leaky_relu,
            name="Conv2d_" + name,
            padding="same")
    return layer
```

This method creates a convolutional layer with the parameters we saw earlier, and with `filters` and `kernel_size`. We set the output activation to be a leaky `relu`, because it gives nice results for these cases.

 The `padding` parameter can be `same` or `precise`. The second option relates to the convolution equation. When we don't want to have partial convolutions (on the edges of the image), this is the option we want to use.

```
def create_maxpool(self, input, name):
    layer = tf.layers.max_pooling2d(
            inputs=input,
            pool_size=[2,2],
            strides=2,
            name="MaxPool_" + name)
    return layer
```

The maximum pool layer is also very straightforward. We want to get the maximum on a 2x2 pixel range, and the output size will be the original image divided by 2 in all directions (hence the stride equal to 2):

```
def create_dropout(self, input, name, is_training):
    layer = tf.layers.dropout(
            inputs=input,
            rate=dropout_rate,
            name="DropOut_" + name,
            training=is_training)
    return layer
```

The dropout layer that we are introducing in this example has an additional parameter, a placeholder named `is_training`. It will be important to deactivate this layer when we test the data (or when we use the model after training):

```
def create_dense(self, input, units, name, is_training):
    layer = tf.layers.dense(
            inputs=input,
            units=units,
            name="Dense" + name,
            )
    layer = tf.layers.batch_normalization(
            inputs=layer,
            momentum=0,
            epsilon=1e-8,
            training=is_training,
            name="BatchNorm_" + name,
    )
    layer = tf.nn.leaky_relu(layer, name="LRELU_" + name)
    return layer
```

Our dense layer is more complicated than a regular one. We added a `batch_normalization` step before the activation, which will scale our gradient with respect to the batch size. There is also an option there to use momentum, which makes the optimization similar to RMSProp:

```
def discriminate(self, image, training):
    h1 = self.create_conv2d(image, self.dim_W3, 5, "Layer1")
    h1 = self.create_maxpool(h1, "Layer1")
    h2 = self.create_conv2d(h1, self.dim_W2, 5, "Layer2")
    h2 = self.create_maxpool(h2, "Layer2")
    h2 = tf.reshape(h2, (-1, self.dim_W2 * 7 * 7))
    h3 = self.create_dense(h2, self.dim_W1, "Layer3", train-ing)
    h3 = self.create_dropout(h3, "Layer3", training)
    h4 = self.create_dense(h3, self.classes, "Layer4", train-ing)
    return h4
```

Now that we have all the individual blocks for our network, we can put it together. So it's going to be:

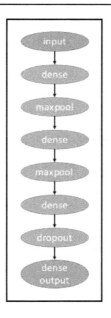

Let's start creating our model:

```
def build_model(self):
    image = tf.placeholder(tf.float32,
        [None]+self.image_shape, name="image")
    Y = tf.placeholder(tf.int64, [None], name="label")
    training = tf.placeholder(tf.bool, name="is_training")

    probabilities = self.discriminate(image, training)
    cost = tf.reduce_mean(
        tf.nn.sparse_softmax_cross_entropy_with_logits(labels=Y,
            logits=probabilities))
    accuracy = tf.reduce_mean(
        tf.cast(tf.equal(tf.argmax(probabilities, axis=1), Y),
            tf.float32), name=" accuracy")

    return image, Y, cost, accuracy, probabilities, training
```

Adding the scaffolding with a placeholder for the input image, and another one for the labels and the training, we now use the `sparse_softmax_cross_entropy_with_logits` cost function, which takes as arguments a single valued `labels` array and a tensor (output of a dense layer) named `logits`. This function is very good when we only have one active label at a time (so it's very good for classification, but not for image-annotation, for instance).

It is now time to use this new class:

```
cnn_model = CNN(
        image_shape=image_shape,
        dim_W1=dim_W1,
        dim_W2=dim_W2,
        dim_W3=dim_W3,
        )
image_tf, Y_tf, cost_tf, accuracy_tf, output_tf, training_tf =
    cnn_model.build_model()
train_step = tf.train.AdamOptimizer(learning_rate,
    beta1=0.5).minimize(cost_tf)

saver = tf.train.Saver(max_to_keep=10)
builder = tf.saved_model.builder.SavedModelBuilder(export_dir)
```

We use it to also instantiate our optimizer (here Adam), and we take the opportunity to build our model serializers:

```
accuracy_vec = []
with tf.Session() as sess:
    sess.run(tf.global_variables_initializer())
    for epoch in range(n_epochs):
        permut = np.random.permutation(len(X_train))

        print("epoch: %i" % epoch)
        for j in range(0, len(X_train), batch_size):
            if j % step == 0:
                print(" batch: %i" % j)

            batch = permut[j:j+batch_size]
            Xs = X_train[batch]
            Ys = y_train[batch]

            sess.run(train_step,
                    feed_dict={
                        training_tf: True,
                        Y_tf: Ys,
                        image_tf: Xs
                        })
            if j % step == 0:
                temp_cost, temp_prec = sess.run([cost_tf, accura-cy_tf],
                        feed_dict={
                            training_tf: False,
                            Y_tf: Ys,
                            image_tf: Xs
                            })
                print(" cost: %f\n prec: %f" % (temp_cost, temp_prec))
```

```
        saver.save(sess, './classifier', global_step=epoch)
      saver.save(sess, './classifier-final')
      builder.add_meta_graph_and_variables(sess,
                          [tf.saved_model.tag_constants.TRAINING])
builder.save()
Epoch #-1
  train accuracy = 0.068963
  test accuracy = 0.071796
Result for the 10 first training images: [0 8 9 9 7 6 3 5 1 3]
Reference for the 10 first training images: [9 8 4 4 9 8 1 8 2 5]
epoch: 0
  batch: 0
    cost: 1.319493
    prec: 0.687500
  batch: 16000
    cost: 0.452003
    prec: 1.000000
  batch: 32000
    cost: 0.383446
    prec: 1.000000
  batch: 48000
    cost: 0.392471
    prec: 0.992188
Epoch #0
  train accuracy = 0.991166
  test accuracy = 0.986650
#...
Epoch #9
  train accuracy = 0.999833
  test accuracy = 0.991693
Result for the 10 first training images: [9 8 4 4 9 3 1 8 2 5]
Reference for the 10 first training images: [9 8 4 4 9 8 1 8 2 5]
```

This is the usual pattern we followed for our previous examples; we just added the savers for intermediate layers. Note that the builder required a final `save()` call after the end of the session.

Without any training, the accuracy of the algorithm is around 1 in 10, which is what a random network will achieve. After 10 epochs, we get an accuracy close to 1 for training and testing. Let's see how the training and the test errors evolve with them:

```
from matplotlib import pyplot as plt

accuracy = np.array(accuracy_vec)
plt.semilogy(1 - accuracy[:,0], 'k-', label="train")
plt.semilogy(1 - accuracy[:,1], 'r-', label="test")
plt.title('Classification error per Epoch')
plt.xlabel('Epoch')
plt.ylabel('Classification error')
plt.legend()
plt.show()
```

Refer to the following graph:

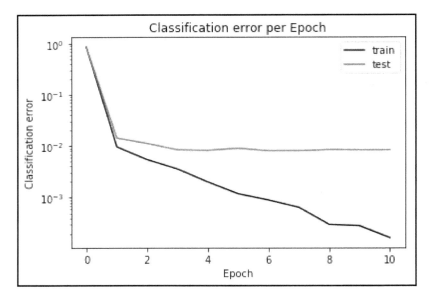

Obviously, more training epochs lower the training error, but after a handful of epochs, the test error (the generalization power) doesn't evolve. This means that there is no point in trying to throw more time at it. But perhaps changing a few parameters may help? Or a different activation function?

As we saved the trained network, we can restore it with our two methods:

```
tf.reset_default_graph()
new_saver = tf.train.import_meta_graph("classifier-final.meta")
```

```
with tf.Session() as sess:
    new_saver.restore(sess, tf.train.latest_checkpoint('./'))

    graph = tf.get_default_graph()
    training_tf = graph.get_tensor_by_name('is_training:0')
    Y_tf = graph.get_tensor_by_name('label:0')
    image_tf = graph.get_tensor_by_name('image:0')
    accuracy_tf = graph.get_tensor_by_name('accuracy:0')
    output_tf = graph.get_tensor_by_name('LeakyRELU_Layer4/Maximum:0')
    show_train(sess, 0) # Function defined in the support notebook
INFO:tensorflow:Restoring parameters from ./classifier-final
Epoch #0
  train accuracy = 0.999833
  test accuracy = 0.991693
Result for the 10 first training images: [9 8 4 4 9 3 1 8 2 5]
Reference for the 10 first training images: [9 8 4 4 9 8 1 8 2 5]
```

And the second method:

```
tf.reset_default_graph()
with tf.Session() as sess:
    tf.saved_model.loader.load(sess,
[tf.saved_model.tag_constants.TRAINING], export_dir)
    graph = tf.get_default_graph()
    training_tf = graph.get_tensor_by_name('is_training:0')
    Y_tf = graph.get_tensor_by_name('label:0')
    image_tf = graph.get_tensor_by_name('image:0')
    accuracy_tf = graph.get_tensor_by_name('accuracy:0')
    output_tf = graph.get_tensor_by_name('LeakyRELU_Layer4/Maximum:0')
    show_train(sess, 0)
INFO:tensorflow:Restoring parameters from b'data/classifier-
mnist/variables/variables'
    Epoch #0
    train accuracy = 0.999833
    test accuracy = 0.991693
    Result for the 10 first training images: [9 8 4 4 9 3 1 8 2 5]
    Reference for the 10 first training images: [9 8 4 4 9 8 1 8 2 5]
```

They both return the same training and testing error as the one we got after our training, so we are good to reuse it for additional classifications.

It is now time to tackle another type of network, the recurrent neural networks.

Recurrent neural networks

All the networks we saw earlier have one layer feeding data to another layer, and there was no loop. Recurrent networks loop on themselves, so what happens is that the new value of an output also depends on the past internal state of a node as well as its input. This can be summed up in the following picture:

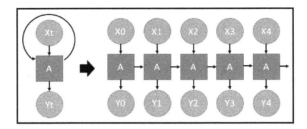

Theoretically, these networks can be trained, but it is a hard task, especially in text prediction when a new word may depend on other words that are long gone (think of clouds up in the sky where the predicted word sky depends on cloud that is three words in the past).

 More information on this problem can be found by looking up "vanishing gradient in recurrent neural networks" on your favorite search engine.

As such, other architectures were developed that don't have these problems. The main one is called LSTM. The paradoxical name reflects how it works. First, it has two internal states, as can be seen in the following schema:

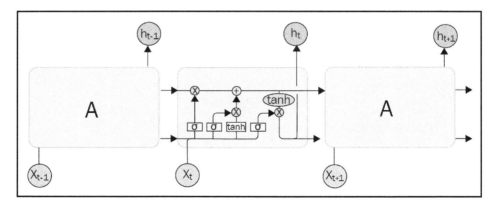

Image adapted from: http://colah.github.io/posts/2015-08-Understanding-LSTMs/

The internal state is a mix of the input we set and nonlinearity of the internal state. There are evolutions of this, but it is good enough for our applications here.

If we compare this to hidden Markov models, filters that are used in finance (AR(n) or more complex), this one is nonlinear. Just as for the convolution layers, the LSTM layers will extract features from the input signal, and then the dense layers will make the final decision (classification, in our examples).

LSTM for predicting text

Our first test for LSTM will be text prediction. Our network will learn the next word in a phrase, just like we had to do when we memorized a poem at school. Here, we just train it on a small poem, but if such a network was trained on a writer's full texts, with more capacity (so with more layers and probably larger ones), it could learn their style and write like the writer.

Let's store our fable:

```
text="""A slave named Androcles once escaped from his master and fled to
the forest. As he was wandering about there he came upon a Lion lying down
moaning and groaning. At first he turned to flee, but finding that the Lion
did not pursue him, he turned back and went up to him.

As he came near, the Lion put out his paw, which was all swollen and
bleeding, and Androcles found that a huge thorn had got into it, and was
causing all the pain. He pulled out the thorn and bound up the paw of the
Lion, who was soon able to rise and lick the hand of Androcles like a dog.
Then the Lion took Androcles to his cave, and every day used to bring him
meat from which to live.

But shortly afterwards both Androcles and the Lion were captured, and the
slave was sentenced to be thrown to the Lion, after the latter had been
kept without food for several days. The Emperor and all his Court came to
see the spectacle, and Androcles was led out into the middle of the arena.
Soon the Lion was let loose from his den, and rushed bounding and roaring
towards his victim.

But as soon as he came near to Androcles he recognised his friend, and
fawned upon him, and licked his hands like a friendly dog. The Emperor,
surprised at this, summoned Androcles to him, who told him the whole story.
Whereupon the slave was pardoned and freed, and the Lion let loose to his
native forest."""
```

We can get rid of the punctuation and tokenize it:

```
training_data = text.lower().replace(",", "").replace(".", "").split()
```

We can now convert the tokens (or words) to integers by indexing the words and then creating a mapping between words and integers and vice versa (also referred to as the Bag of Words). We can also gain some time by transforming our token array, representing the text to an array of integers, the integers being the index for the mapping to words:

```
def build_dataset(words):
    count = list(set(words))
    dictionary = dict()
    for word, _ in count:
        dictionary[word] = len(dictionary)
    reverse_dictionary = dict(zip(dictionary.values(), diction-ary.keys()))
    return dictionary, reverse_dictionary

dictionary, reverse_dictionary = build_dataset(training_data)
training_data_args = [dictionary[word] for word in training_data]
```

Our main layer for RNN is not part of TensorFlow but part of the `contrib` package. Creating it requires more than one line, but it is self-explanatory. We end up with a dense layer with as many output nodes as we have tokens:

```
import tensorflow as tf
tf.reset_default_graph()
from tensorflow.contrib import rnn

def RNN(x):
    # Generate a n_input-element sequence of inputs
    # (eg. [had] [a] [general] -> [20] [6] [33])
    x = tf.split(x,n_input,1)

    # 1-layer LSTM with n_hidden units.
    rnn_cell = rnn.BasicLSTMCell(n_hidden)

    # generate prediction
    outputs, states = rnn.static_rnn(rnn_cell, x, dtype=tf.float32)

    # there are n_input outputs but we only want the last output
    return tf.layers.dense(inputs = outputs[-1], units = vocab_size)
x = tf.placeholder(tf.float32, [None, n_input])
y = tf.placeholder(tf.int64, [None])
```

Let's add our hyper parameters:

```
import random
import numpy as np

vocab_size = len(dictionary)

# Parameters
learning_rate = 0.001
training_iters = 50000
display_step = 1000
# number of inputs (past words that we use)
n_input = 3
# number of units in the RNN cell
n_hidden = 512
```

We are ready to create the network and our optimization cost function:

```
pred = RNN(x)

cost = tf.reduce_mean(
    tf.nn.sparse_softmax_cross_entropy_with_logits(logits=pred,
        labels=y))
optimizer = tf.train.RMSPropOptimizer(
    learning_rate=learning_rate).minimize(cost)

correct_pred = tf.equal(tf.argmax(pred,1), y)
accuracy = tf.reduce_mean(tf.cast(correct_pred, tf.float32))
```

Let's got for the training:

```
with tf.Session() as session:
    session.run(tf.global_variables_initializer())
    step = 0
    offset = random.randint(0,n_input+1)
    end_offset = n_input + 1
    acc_total = 0
    loss_total = 0

    while step < training_iters:
        # Batch with just one sample. Add some randomness on se-lection
process.
        if offset > (len(training_data)-end_offset):
            offset = random.randint(0, n_input+1)

        symbols_in_keys = [ [training_data_args[i]]
            for i in range(offset, offset+n_input) ]
        symbols_in_keys = np.reshape(np.array(symbols_in_keys),
```

```
                [1, n_input])

        symbols_out_onehot = [training_data_args[offset+n_input]]

        _, acc, loss, onehot_pred = session.run(
            [optimizer, accu-racy, cost, pred],
            feed_dict={x: sym-bols_in_keys, y: symbols_out_onehot})
        loss_total += loss
        acc_total += acc
        if (step+1) % display_step == 0:
            print(("Iter= %i , Average Loss= %.6f," +
                " Average Accuracy= %.2f%%") %
                (step+1, loss_total/display_step,
                100*acc_total/display_step))
            acc_total = 0
            loss_total = 0
            symbols_in = [training_data[i]
                for i in range(offset, offset + n_input)]
            symbols_out = training_data[offset + n_input]
            symbols_out_pred = reverse_dictionary[
                np.argmax(onehot_pred, axis=1)[0]]
            print("%s - [%s] vs [%s]" %
                (symbols_in, symbols_out, symbols_out_pred))
        step += 1
        offset += (n_input+1)
Iter= 1000 , Average Loss= 4.034577, Average Accuracy= 11.50%
['shortly', 'afterwards', 'both'] - [androcles] vs [to]
Iter= 2000 , Average Loss= 3.143990, Average Accuracy= 21.10%
['he', 'came', 'upon'] - [a] vs [he]
Iter= 3000 , Average Loss= 2.145266, Average Accuracy= 44.10%
['and', 'the', 'slave'] - [was] vs [was]
...
Iter= 48000 , Average Loss= 0.442764, Average Accuracy= 87.90%
['causing', 'all', 'the'] - [pain] vs [pain]
Iter= 49000 , Average Loss= 0.507615, Average Accuracy= 85.20%
['recognised', 'his', 'friend'] - [and] vs [and]
Iter= 50000 , Average Loss= 0.427877, Average Accuracy= 87.10%
['of', 'androcles', 'like'] - [a] vs [a]
```

The accuracy is far from good, but for a small trial, it's already quite interesting. By using the pred function, we can ask the network to generate a new word based on three input words inside the previous session:

```
symbols_in_keys = [ ['causing'], ['all'], ['the']]
symbols_in_keys =
    np.reshape(np.array(symbols_in_keys), [1, n_input])

onehot_pred = session.run(pred, feed_dict={x: sym-bols_in_keys})
```

```
print("Estimate is: %s" %
    reverse_dictionary[np.argmax(onehot_pred, axis=1)[0]])
Estimate is: pain
```

An interesting question is what would happen with more training time? And what would happen if we changed the intermediate layer to use multiple LSTM layers?

Recurrent neural networks are not just for text or finance. They can also be used for image recognition.

LSTM for image processing

Let's imagine we want to perform handwriting recognition. From time to time, we get a new column of data. Is it the end of a letter? If yes, which one? Is it the end of a word? Is it punctuation? All these questions can be answered with a recurrent network.

For our test example, we will go back to our 10-digit dataset and use LSTMs instead of convolution layers.

We use similar hyperparameters:

```
import tensorflow as tf
from tensorflow.contrib import rnn

# rows of 28 pixels
n_input=28
# unrolled through 28 time steps (our images are (28,28))
time_steps=28

# hidden LSTM units
num_units=128

# learning rate for adam
learning_rate=0.001
n_classes=10
batch_size=128

n_epochs = 10
step = 100
```

Setting up training and testing data is almost similar to our CNN example, except for the way we reshape the images:

```
import os
import numpy as np

from sklearn.datasets import fetch_mldata
from sklearn.model_selection import train_test_split
mnist = fetch_mldata('MNIST original')
mnist.data = mnist.data.astype(np.float32).reshape(
    [-1, time_steps, n_input]) / 255.
mnist.num_examples = len(mnist.data)
mnist.labels = mnist.target.astype(np.int8)

X_train, X_test, y_train, y_test = train_test_split(
    mnist.data, mnist.labels, test_size=(1. / 7.))
```

Let's quickly set up our network and its scaffolding:

```
x = tf.placeholder(tf.float32, [None,time_steps, n_input])
y = tf.placeholder(tf.int64, [None])

# processing the input tensor from [batch_size, n_steps,n_input]
# to "time_steps" number of [batch_size, n_input] tensors
input = tf.unstack(x, time_steps,1)

lstm_layer = rnn.BasicLSTMCell(num_units, forget_bias=True)
outputs, _ = rnn.static_rnn(lstm_layer, input,dtype=tf.float32)

prediction = tf.layers.dense(inputs=outputs[-1], units = n_classes)

loss = tf.reduce_mean(tf.nn.sparse_softmax_cross_entropy_with_logits(
    logits=prediction, labels=y))
opt = tf.train.AdamOptimizer(learning_rate=learning_rate).minimize(loss)

correct_prediction = tf.equal(tf.argmax(prediction,1), y)
accuracy = tf.reduce_mean(tf.cast(correct_prediction, tf.float32))
```

We are now ready to train:

```
with tf.Session() as sess:
    sess.run(tf.global_variables_initializer())
    for epoch in range(n_epochs):
        permut = np.random.permutation(len(X_train))
        print("epoch: %i" % epoch)
        for j in range(0, len(X_train), batch_size):
            if j % step == 0:
                print(" batch: %i" % j)
```

```
        batch = permut[j:j+batch_size]
        Xs = X_train[batch]
        Ys = y_train[batch]

        sess.run(opt, feed_dict={x: Xs, y: Ys})

        if j % step == 0:
            acc=sess.run(accuracy,feed_dict={x:Xs,y:Ys})
            los=sess.run(loss,feed_dict={x:Xs,y:Ys})
            print(" accuracy %f" % acc)
            print(" loss %f" % los)
            print("")
epoch: 0
 batch: 0
 accuracy 0.195312
 loss 2.275624

 batch: 3200
 accuracy 0.484375
 loss 1.514501
...
 batch: 54400
 accuracy 0.992188
 loss 0.022468

 batch: 57600
 accuracy 1.000000
 loss 0.007411
```

We get quite high accuracy here as well, but we will leave it to the reader to check the accuracy over the test samples.

Summary

Using TensorFlow always follows a similar pattern. Set up your input, your graph, and the functions you want to optimize. Train your model, save it, and reuse it for your applications. As it comes with lots of functionalities, there are very few things TensorFlow cannot do. We will also explore some other types of networks in future chapters.

At this point in the book, we have seen the major mode of machine learning: classification. In the cuming two chapters, we will look at techniques used for two specific kinds of data: music and images. Our first goal will be to build a music-genre classifier.

Classification II – Sentiment Analysis

9

For companies, it is vital to closely monitor the public reception of key events, such as product launches or press releases. With real-time access and easy accessibility of user-generated content on Twitter, it is now possible to do sentiment classification of tweets. Sometimes also called opinion mining, it is an active field of research in which several companies are already selling such services. As this shows that there obviously exists a market, we are motivated to use our classification muscles built in the last chapter to build our own home-grown sentiment classifier.

Sketching our roadmap

Sentiment analysis of tweets is particularly hard, because of Twitter's size limitation per message. This leads to a special syntax, creative abbreviations, and seldom-well-formed sentences. The typical approach of analyzing sentences, aggregating their sentiment information per paragraph, and then calculating the overall sentiment of a document does not work here.

Clearly, we will not try to build a state-of-the-art sentiment classifier. Instead, we want to do the following:

- Use this scenario as a vehicle to introduce yet another classification algorithm, **Naïve Bayes**
- Explain how **Part Of Speech** (**POS**) tagging works and how it can help us
- Show some more tricks from the scikit-learn toolbox that can come in handy

Fetching the Twitter data

Naturally, we need tweets and their corresponding labels that describe sentiments. In this chapter, we will use the corpus from Niek Sanders, who has done an awesome job of manually labeling more than 5,000 tweets as positive, negative, or neutral and has granted us permission to use it in this chapter.

To comply with Twitter terms of services, we will not provide any data from Twitter nor show any real tweets in this chapter. Instead, we can use Sander's hand-labeled data, which contains the tweet IDs and their hand-labeled sentiments. We will use Twitter's API to fetch the corresponding tweets one by one. To not bore you too much, just execute the first part of the corresponding Jupyter notebook, which will start the downloading process. In order to play nicely with Twitter's servers, it will take quite some time to download all the data for more than 5,000 tweets, which means it is a good idea to start it right away.

The data comes with four sentiment labels, which are returned by `load_sanders_data()`:

```
>>> X_orig, Y_orig = load_sanders_data()
>>> classes = np.unique(Y_orig)
>>> for c in classes: print("#%s: %i" % (c, sum(Y_orig == c)))
#irrelevant: 437
#negative: 448
#neutral: 1801
#positive: 391
```

Inside `load_sanders_data()`, we are treating irrelevant and neutral labels together as neutral, and dropping all non-English tweets, resulting in 3,077 tweets.

In case you get different counts here, it is because, in the meantime, tweets might have been deleted or set to be private. In that case, you might also get slightly different numbers and graphs than the ones shown in the upcoming sections.

Introducing the Naïve Bayes classifier

Naïve Bayes is probably one of the most elegant machine learning algorithms out there that is of practical use. And despite its name, it is not that naïve when you look at its classification performance. It proves to be quite robust to irrelevant features, which it kindly ignores. It learns fast and predicts equally so. It does not require lots of storage. So, why is it called naïve?

The *Naïve* was added to account for one assumption that is required for Naïve Bayes to work optimally. The assumption is that the features are uncorrelated. This, however, is rarely the case for real-world applications. Nevertheless, it still returns very good accuracy in practice, even when the independence assumption does not hold.

Getting to know the Bayes theorem

At its core, the Naïve Bayes classification is nothing more than keeping track of which feature gives evidence to which class. The way the features are designed determines the model that is used to learn. The so-called Bernoulli model only cares about Boolean features; whether a word occurs only once or multiple times in a tweet does not matter. In contrast, the Multinomial model uses word counts as features. For the sake of simplicity, we will use the Bernoulli model to explain how to use Naïve Bayes for sentiment analysis. We will then use the Multinomial model later to set up and tune our real-world classifiers.

Let's assume the following meanings for the variables that we will use to explain Naïve Bayes:

Variable	Meaning
c	This is the class of a tweet (positive or negative–for this explanation, we ignore the neutral label)
F_1	The word awesome occurs at least once in the tweet
F_2	The word crazy occurs at least once in the tweet

During training, we learned the Naïve Bayes model, which is the probability for a C class when we already know features F_1 and F_2. This probability is written as $P(C|F_1, F_2)$.

Since we cannot estimate $P(C|F_1, F_2)$ directly, we apply a trick, which was found out by Bayes:

$$P(A) P(B|A) = P(B) P(A|B)$$

If we substitute A with the probability of both awesome and crazy, and think of B as being our C class, we arrive at the relationship that helps us to later retrieve the probability for the data instance belonging to the specified class:

$$P(F_1, F_2) P(C | F_1, F_2) = P(C) P(F_1, F_2 | C)$$

This allows us to express $P(C \mid F_1, F_2)$ by means of the other probabilities:

$$P(C \mid F_1, F_2) = \frac{P(C)\, P(F_1, F_2 \mid C)}{P(F_1, F_2)}$$

We could also describe this as follows:

$$posterior = \frac{prior \cdot likelihood}{evidence}$$

The *prior* and the *evidence* are easily determined:

- $P(C)$ is the prior probability of the C class without knowing about the data. We can estimate this quantity by simply calculating the fraction of all training data instances belonging to that particular class.
- $P(F_1, F_2)$ is the evidence or the probability of features F_1 and F_2

The tricky part is the calculation of the likelihood $P(F_1, F_2 \mid C)$. It is the value describing how likely it is to see the F_1 and F_2 feature values if we know that the class of the data instance is C. To estimate this, we need to do some thinking.

Being naïve

From probability theory, we also know the following relationship:

$$P(F_1, F_2 \mid C) = P(F_1 \mid C) P(F_2 \mid C, F_1)$$

This alone, however, does not help much, since we treat one difficult problem (estimating $P(F_1, F_2 \mid C)$) with another one (estimating $P(F_2 \mid C, F_1)$).

However, if we naïvely assume that F_1 and F_2 are independent from each other, $P(F_2 \mid C, F_1)$ simplifies to $P(F_2 \mid C)$ and we can write it as follows:

$$P(F_1, F_2 \mid C) = P(F_1 \mid C) P(F_2 \mid C)$$

Putting everything together, we get the following, quite manageable, formula:

$$P(C \mid F_1, F_2) = \frac{P(C)\, P(F_1 \mid C)\, P(F_2 \mid C)}{P(F_1, F_2)}$$

The interesting thing is that although it is not theoretically correct to simply tweak our assumptions when we are in the mood to do so, in this case, it proves to work astonishingly well in real-world applications.

Using Naïve Bayes to classify

Given a new tweet, the only part left is to calculate the probabilities:

$$P(C = "neg" \mid F_1, F_2) = \frac{P(C = neg)P(F_1 \mid C = "neg")\,P(F_2 \mid C = "neg")}{P(F_1, F_2)}$$

Then choose the C_{best} class as having the higher probability.

As for both classes, the denominator, $P(F_1, F_2)$, is the same, we can simply ignore it without changing the winner class.

Note, however, that we don't calculate any real probabilities any more. Instead, we are estimating which class is more likely given the evidence. This is another reason why Naïve Bayes is so robust: it is not interested in the real probabilities, but only in the information, which class is more likely. In short, we can write:

$$C_{best} = \underset{c \in C}{\mathrm{argmax}} P(C = c)\, P(F_1 \mid C = c) P(F_2 \mid C = c)$$

This simply says that we are calculating the part after *argmax* for all classes of C (*pos* and *neg* in our case) and returning the class that results in the highest value.

But, for the following example, let's stick to real probabilities and do some calculations to see how Naïve Bayes works. For the sake of simplicity, we will assume that Twitter allows only for the two aforementioned words, awesome and crazy, and that we have already manually classified a handful of tweets:

Tweet	Class
awesome	Positive tweet
awesome	Positive tweet
awesome crazy	Positive tweet
crazy	Positive tweet
crazy	Negative tweet
crazy	Negative tweet

In this example, we have the crazy tweet in both a positive and negative tweet to emulate some ambiguities you will often find in the real world (for example, being crazy about soccer versus a crazy idiot).

In this case, we have six total tweets, out of which four are positive and two negative, which results in the following priors:

$$P(C = "pos") = \frac{4}{6} \cong 0.67$$

$$P(C = "neg") = \frac{2}{6} \cong 0.33$$

This means, without knowing anything about the tweet itself, that it would be wise to assume the tweet to be positive.

We're still missing the calculation of $P(F_1|C)$ and $P(F_2|C)$, which are the probabilities for the two features, F_1 and F_2, conditioned in the C class.

This is calculated as the number of tweets in which we have seen the concrete feature divided by the number of tweets that have been labeled with the class of C. Let's say we want to know the probability of seeing awesome occurring in a tweet, knowing that its class is positive, we will have:

$$P(F_1|C = "pos") = \frac{number\ of\ positive\ tweets\ containing\ "awesome"}{number\ of\ all\ positive\ tweets} = \frac{3}{4}$$

This is because out of the four positive tweets, three contained the word awesome. Obviously, the probability for not having awesome in a positive tweet is its inverse:

$$P(F_1 = 0|C = "pos") = 1 - P(F_1 = 1|C = "pos") = 0.25$$

Similarly, for the rest (omitting the case that a word does not occur in a tweet):

$$P(F_2 = 1|C = "pos") = \frac{2}{4} = 0.5$$

$$P(F_1 = 1|C = "neg") = \frac{0}{2} = 0$$

$$P(F_2 = 1|C = "neg") = \frac{2}{2} = 1$$

For the sake of completeness, we will also compute the evidence so that we can see real probabilities in the following example tweets. For two concrete values of F_1 and F_2, we can calculate the evidence as follows:

$$P(F_1, F_2) = P(F_1, F_2 | C = "pos") P(C = "pos") + P(F_1, F_2 | C = "neg") P(C = "neg")$$

This leads to the following values:

$$P(F_1 = 1, F_2 = 1) = \frac{3}{4} \cdot \frac{2}{4} \cdot \frac{4}{6} + 0 \cdot 1 \cdot \frac{2}{6} = \frac{1}{4}$$

$$P(F_1 = 1, F_2 = 0) = \frac{3}{4} \cdot \frac{2}{4} \cdot \frac{4}{6} + 0 \cdot 0 \cdot \frac{2}{6} = \frac{1}{4}$$

$$P(F_1 = 0, F_2 = 1) = \frac{1}{4} \cdot \frac{2}{4} \cdot \frac{4}{6} + \frac{2}{2} \cdot \frac{2}{2} \cdot \frac{2}{6} = \frac{5}{12}$$

Now we have all the data to classify new tweets. The only work left is to parse the tweet and analyze it's features it:

Tweet	F_1	F_2	Class probabilities	Classification
awesome	1	0	$P(C = "pos"\|F_1 = 1, F_2 = 0) = \dfrac{\frac{3}{4} \cdot \frac{2}{4} \cdot \frac{4}{6}}{\frac{1}{4}} = 1$ $P(C = "neg"\|F_1 = 1, F_2 = 0) = \dfrac{0 \cdot \frac{2}{2} \cdot \frac{2}{6}}{\frac{1}{4}} = 0$	Positive
crazy	0	1	$P(C = "pos"\|F_1 = 0, F_2 = 1) = \dfrac{\frac{1}{4} \cdot \frac{2}{4} \cdot \frac{4}{6}}{\frac{5}{12}} = \frac{1}{5}$ $P(C = "neg"\|F_1 = 0, F_2 = 1) = \dfrac{\frac{2}{2} \cdot \frac{2}{2} \cdot \frac{2}{6}}{\frac{5}{12}} = \frac{4}{5}$	Negative
awesome crazy	1	1	$P(C = "pos"\|F_1 = 1, F_2 = 1) = \dfrac{\frac{3}{4} \cdot \frac{2}{4} \cdot \frac{4}{6}}{\frac{1}{4}} = 1$ $P(C = "neg"\|F_1 = 1, F_2 = 1) = \dfrac{0 \cdot \frac{2}{2} \cdot \frac{2}{6}}{\frac{1}{4}} = 0$	Positive

So far, so good. The classification of trivial tweets seems to assign correct labels to the tweets. The question remains, however, how we should treat words that did not occur in our training corpus. After all, with the preceding formula, new words will always be assigned a probability of zero.

Accounting for unseen words and other oddities

When we calculated the probabilities earlier, we actually cheated ourselves. We were not calculating the real probabilities, but only rough approximations by means of the fractions. We assumed that the training corpus would tell us the whole truth about the real probabilities. It did not. A corpus of only six tweets obviously cannot give us all the information about every tweet that has ever been written. For example, there certainly are tweets containing the word text in them. It is only that we have never seen them. Apparently, our approximation is very rough, and we should account for that. This is often done in practice with the so-called **add-one smoothing**.

 Add-one smoothing is sometimes also referred to as **additive smoothing** or **Laplace smoothing**. Note that Laplace smoothing has nothing to do with Laplacian smoothing, which is related to the smoothing of polygon meshes. If we do not smooth by 1 but by an adjustable parameter, `alpha>0`, it is called Lidstone smoothing.

It is a very simple technique that adds one to all feature occurrences. It has the underlying assumption that even if we have not seen a given word in the whole corpus, there is still a chance that our sample of tweets happened not to include that word. So, with add-one smoothing, we pretend that we have seen every occurrence once more than we actually did. That means that instead of calculating $P(F_1 = 1|C = "pos") = \frac{3}{4} = 0.75$, we now do $P(F_1 = 1|C = "pos") = \frac{3+1}{4+2} = 0.67$.

Why do we add 2 in the denominator? Because we have two features: the occurrence of awesome and crazy. Since we add 1 for each feature, we have to make sure that the end result is again a probability. And, indeed we get 1 as the total probability:

$$P(F_1 = 1|C = "pos") + P(F_1 = 0|C = "pos") = \frac{3+1}{4+2} + \frac{1+1}{4+2} = 1$$

Accounting for arithmetic underflows

There is yet another roadblock. In reality, we work with probabilities much smaller than the ones we have dealt with in the toy example. Typically, we also have many more than only two features, which we multiply with each other. This will quickly lead to the point where the floating-point accuracy provided by NumPy does not suffice any more:

```
>>> import numpy as np
>>> # tell numpy to print out more digits (default is 8)
>>> np.set_printoptions(precision=20)
```

```
>>> np.array([2.48E-324])
  array([ 4.94065645841246544177e-324])
>>> np.array([2.47E-324])
  array([ 0.])
```

So, how probable is it that we will ever hit a number such as `2.47E-324`? To answer this, we just need to imagine a likelihood for the conditional probabilities of `0.0001`, and then multiply 65 of them together (meaning that we have 65 low-probable feature values), and you've been hit by the arithmetic underflow:

```
>>> x = 0.00001
>>> x**64 # still fine
  1e-320
>>> x**65 # ouch
  0.0
```

A float in Python is typically implemented using double in C. To find out whether this is the case for your platform, you can check it as follows:

```
>>> import sys
>>> sys.float_info
  sys.float_info(max=1.7976931348623157e+308, max_exp=1024,
  max_10_exp=308, min=2.2250738585072014e-308, min_exp=-1021,
  min_10_exp=-307, dig=15, mant_dig=53, epsilon=2.220446049250313e-16,
  radix=2, rounds=1)
```

To mitigate this, one could switch to math libraries, such as mpmath (http://mpmath.org), that allow for arbitrary accuracy. However, they are not fast enough to work as a NumPy replacement.

Fortunately, there is a better way to take care of this, and it has to do with a nice relationship that we might still remember from school (also known as the logsum-trick):

$$\log(x \cdot y) = \log(x) + \log(y)$$

If we apply this formula to our case, we get the following:

$$\log P(C) P(F_1|C) P(F_2|C) = \log P(C) + \log P(F_1|C) + \log P(F_2|C)$$

As the probabilities are in the interval between **0** and **1**, the log of the probabilities lies in the interval between -∞ and 0. Don't be bothered by that. Higher numbers are still a stronger indicator for the correct class—it is only that they are negative now:

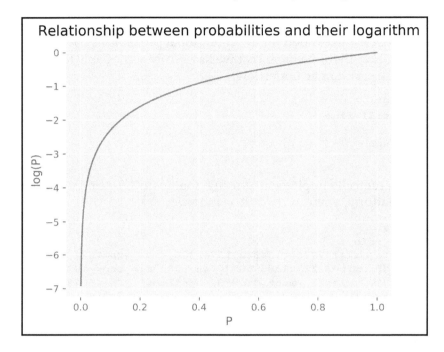

There is one caveat though: we actually don't have the log in the formula's nominator (the top part of the fraction). We only have the product of the probabilities. In our case, luckily, we are not interested in the actual value of the probabilities. We simply want to know which class has the highest posterior probability. We are lucky, because if we find the following:

$$P(C = "pos"|F_1, F_2) > P(C = "neg"|F_1, F_2)$$

Then we will always also have:

$$\log P(C = "pos"|F_1, F_2) > \log P(C = "neg"|F_1, F_2).$$

A quick look at the preceding graph shows that the curve is strictly monotonically increasing, that is, it always goes up, when we go from left to right. Let's stick this into the aforementioned formula:

$$C_{best} = \underset{c \in C}{\operatorname{argmax}} P(C = c) \, P(F_1 | C = c) \, P(F_2 | C = c)$$

This will finally retrieve the formula for two features that will give us the best class, also for the real-world data that we will see in practice:

$$C_{best} = \underset{c \in C}{\operatorname{argmax}} (\log P(C = c) + \log P(F_1 | C = c) + \log P(F_2 | C = c))$$

Of course, we will not be very successful with only two features, so let's rewrite it to allow for an arbitrary number of features:

$$C_{best} = \underset{c \in C}{\operatorname{argmax}} \left(\log P(C = c) + \sum_k \log P(F_k | C = c) \right)$$

There we are, ready to use our first classifier from the scikit-learn toolkit.

As mentioned earlier, we just learned the Bernoulli model of Naïve Bayes. Instead of having Boolean features, we can also use the number of word occurrences, also known as the Multinomial model. As this provides more information, and often also results in better performance, we will use this for our real-world data. Note, however, that the underlying formulas change a bit. However, no worries, as the general idea of how Naïve Bayes works is still the same.

Creating our first classifier and tuning it

The Naïve Bayes classifiers reside in the `sklearn.naive_bayes` package. There are different kinds of Naïve Bayes classifiers:

- `GaussianNB`: This classifier assumes the features to be normally distributed (Gaussian). One use case for it could be the classification of sex given the height and weight of a person. In our case, we are given tweet texts from which we extract word counts. These are clearly not Gaussian-distributed.

- `MultinomialNB`: This classifier assumes the features to be occurrence counts, which is our case going forward, since we will be using word counts in the tweets as features. In practice, this classifier also works well with TF-IDF vectors.
- `BernoulliNB`: This classifier is similar to `MultinomialNB`, but more suited when using binary word occurrences and not word counts.

As we will mainly look at the word occurrences, the `MultinomialNB` classifier is best suited for our purpose.

Solving an easy problem first

As we have seen, when we looked at our tweet data, the tweets are not only positive or negative. The majority of the tweets actually do not contain any sentiments, but are neutral or irrelevant, containing, for instance, raw information (for example, New book: Building Machine Learning … http://link). This leads to four classes. To not complicate the task too much, let's only focus on the positive and negative tweets for now:

```
>>> # first create a Boolean list having true for tweets
>>> # that are either positive or negative
>>> pos_neg_idx = np.logical_or(Y_orig=="positive", Y_orig =="negative")
>>> # now use that index to filter the data and the labels
>>> X = X_orig [pos_neg_idx]
>>> Y = Y_orig [pos_neg_idx]
>>> # finally convert the labels themselves into Boolean
>>> Y = Y=="positive"
```

Now, we have the raw tweet text in `X` and the binary classification in `Y`, `0` for negative and `1` for positive tweets.

We just said that we will use word-occurrence counts as features. We will not use them in their raw form, though. Instead, we will use `TfidfVectorizer` to convert the raw tweet text into TF-IDF feature values, which we then use together with the labels to train our first classifier. For convenience, we will use the `Pipeline` class, which allows us to hook the vectorizer and the classifier together and provides the same interface:

```
from sklearn.feature_extraction.text import TfidfVectorizer
from sklearn.naive_bayes import MultinomialNB
from sklearn.pipeline import Pipeline
def create_ngram_model(params=None):
    tfidf_ngrams = TfidfVectorizer(ngram_range=(1, 3),
                                   analyzer="word", binary=False)
    clf = MultinomialNB()
    pipeline = Pipeline([('tfidf', tfidf_ngrams), ('clf', clf)])
    if params:
```

```
        pipeline.set_params(**params)
    return pipeline
```

The `Pipeline` instance returned by `create_ngram_model()` can now be used to fit and predict as if we had a normal classifier. Later, we will pass a dictionary of parameters as `params`, which will help us to create custom pipelines.

Since we do not have that much data, we should do cross-validation. This time, however, we will not use `KFold`, which partitions the data in consecutive folds; instead, we'll use `ShuffleSplit`. It shuffles the data for us but does not prevent the same data instance from being in multiple folds. For each fold, then, we keep track of the area under the Precision-Recall curve and for accuracy.

To keep our experimentation agile, let's wrap everything together in a `train_model()` function, which takes a function as a parameter that creates the classifier:

```
from sklearn.metrics import precision_recall_curve, auc
from sklearn. model_selection import ShuffleSplit
def train_model(clf_factory, X, Y):
    # setting random_state to get deterministic behavior
    cv = ShuffleSplit(n_splits=10, test_size=0.3,
                      random_state=0)
    scores = []
    pr_scores = []
    for train, test in cv.split(X, Y):
        X_train, y_train = X[train], Y[train]
        X_test, y_test = X[test], Y[test]

        clf = clf_factory()
        clf.fit(X_train, y_train)
        train_score = clf.score(X_train, y_train)
        test_score = clf.score(X_test, y_test)
        scores.append(test_score)
        proba = clf.predict_proba(X_test)
        precision, recall, pr_thresholds = precision_recall_curve(y_test,
proba[:,1])
        pr_scores.append(auc(recall, precision))
        summary = (np.mean(scores), np.mean(pr_scores))
        print("Mean acc=%.3ftMean P/R AUC=%.3f" % summary)
```

Putting everything together, we can train our first model:

```
>>> X_orig, Y_orig = load_sanders_data()
>>> pos_neg_idx = np.logical_or(Y_orig =="positive", Y_orig =="negative")
>>> X = X_orig[pos_neg_idx]
>>> Y = Y_orig [pos_neg_idx]
>>> Y = Y_orig =="positive"
>>> train_model(create_ngram_model, X, Y)
Mean acc=0.777    Mean P/R AUC=0.885
```

With our first try using Naïve Bayes on vectorized TF-IDF trigram features, we get an accuracy of 77.7% and an average P/R AUC of 88.5%. Looking at the P/R chart of the median (the train/test split that is performing most similarly to the average), it shows a much more encouraging behavior than the plots we've seen in the previous chapter. Please note that the AUC of the plot of 0.90 is slightly different than the mean P/R of 0.885, since the plot is taken from the median training run, whereas the mean P/R AUC averages over all AUC scores. The same principle applies for subsequent images:

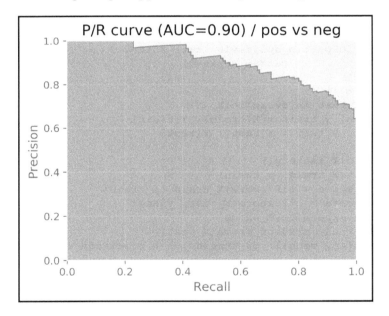

For a start, the results are quite encouraging. They get even more impressive when we realize that 100% accuracy is probably never achievable in a sentiment-classification task. For some tweets, even humans often do not really agree on the same classification label.

Using all classes

Once again, we simplified our task a bit, since we used only positive or negative tweets. That means, we assumed a perfect classifier that classified upfront whether the tweet contains a sentiment and forwarded that to our Naïve Bayes classifier.

So, how well do we perform if we also classify whether a tweet contains any sentiments at all? To find that out, let's first write a convenience function that returns a modified class array that provides a list of sentiments that we would like to interpret as positive:

```
def tweak_labels(Y, pos_sent_list):
    pos = Y==pos_sent_list[0]
    for sent_label in pos_sent_list[1:]:
        pos |= Y==sent_label
    Y = np.zeros(Y.shape[0])
    Y[pos] = 1
    return Y.astype(int)
```

Note that we are talking about two different positives now. The sentiment of a tweet can be positive, which is to be distinguished from the class of the training data. If, for example, we want to find out how well we can separate tweets having a sentiment from neutral ones, we could do:

```
>>> X = X_orig
>>> Y = tweak_labels(Y_orig, ["positive", "negative"])
```

In Y we now have 1 (positive class) for all tweets that are either positive or negative and 0 (negative class) for neutral and irrelevant ones:

```
>>> train_model(create_ngram_model, X, Y)
Mean acc=0.734    Mean P/R AUC=0.661
```

Have a look at the following plot:

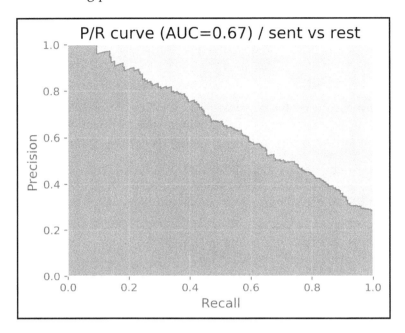

As expected, P/R AUC drops considerably, being only 66% now. The accuracy is still high, but that is only due to the fact that we have a highly imbalanced dataset. Out of 3,077 total tweets, only 839 are either positive or negative, which is about 27%. This means, if we create a classifier that always classifies a tweet as not containing any sentiments, we will already have an accuracy of 73%. This is another reason to always look at precision and recall if the training and test data is unbalanced.

So, how will the Naïve Bayes classifier perform on classifying positive tweets versus the rest, and negative tweets versus the rest? One word: poorly:

```
== Pos vs. rest ==
Mean acc=0.87   Mean P/R AUC=0.305
== Neg vs. rest ==
Mean acc=0.852 Mean P/R AUC=0.49
```

Pretty unusable if you ask me. Looking at the P/R curves in the following plots, we will also find no usable precision/recall trade-off, as we were able to do in the last chapter:

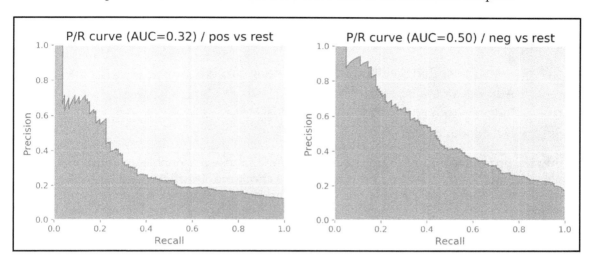

Tuning the classifier's parameters

Certainly, we have not explored the current setup enough and should investigate more. There are roughly two areas where we can play with the knobs: `TfidfVectorizer` and `MultinomialNB`. As we have no real intuition in which area we should explore, let's try to sweep the hyperparameters.

We will see the `TfidfVectorizer` parameter first:

- Using different settings for ngrams:
  - unigrams (1,1)
  - unigrams and bigrams (1,2)
  - unigrams, bigrams, and trigrams (1,3)
- Playing with `min_df`: 1 or 2
- Exploring the impact of IDF within TF-IDF using `use_idf` and `smooth_idf`: `False` or `True`
- Whether to remove stop words or not, by setting `stop_words` to `english` or `None`

- Whether to use the logarithm of the word counts (`sublinear_tf`)
- Whether to track word counts or simply track whether words occur or not, by setting `binary` to `True` or `False`

Now we will see the `MultinomialNB` classifier:

- Which smoothing method to use by setting `alpha`
- Add-one or Laplace smoothing: `1`
- Lidstone smoothing: `0.01, 0.05, 0.1, or 0.5`
- No smoothing: `0`

A simple approach could be to train a classifier for all those reasonable exploration values, while keeping the other parameters constant and check the classifier's results. As we do not know whether those parameters affect each other, doing it right will require that we train a classifier for every possible combination of all parameter values. Obviously, this is too tedious for us.

Because this kind of parameter exploration occurs frequently in machine learning tasks, scikit-learn has a dedicated class for it, called `GridSearchCV`. It takes an estimator (instance with a classifier-like interface), which will be the `Pipeline` instance in our case, and a dictionary of parameters with their potential values.

`GridSearchCV` expects the dictionary's keys to obey a certain format so that it is able to set the parameters of the correct estimator. The format is as follows:

```
<estimator>__<subestimator>__...__<param_name>
```

For example, if we want to specify the desired values to explore for the `ngram_range` parameter of `TfidfVectorizer` (named `tfidf` in the `Pipeline` description), we would have to say:

```
param_grid={"tfidf__ngram_range"=[(1, 1), (1, 2), (1, 3)]}
```

This will tell `GridSearchCV` to try out unigrams to trigrams as parameter values for the `ngram_range` parameter of `TfidfVectorizer`.

Then, it trains the estimator with all possible parameter-value combinations. We make sure that it trains on random samples of the training data using ShuffleSplit, which generates an iterator of random train/test splits. Finally, it provides the best estimator in the form of the member variable, best_estimator_.

As we want to compare the returned best classifier with our current best one, we need to evaluate it in the same way. Therefore, we can pass the ShuffleSplit instance using the cv parameter (therefore, CV in GridSearchCV).

The last missing piece is to define how GridSearchCV should determine the best estimator. This can be done by providing the desired score function to the scoring parameter, using the make_scorer helper function. We can either write one ourselves, or pick one from the sklearn.metrics package. We should certainly not take metric.accuracy because of our class imbalance (we have a lot fewer tweets containing sentiments than neutral ones). Instead, we want to have good precision and recall on both classes, tweets with sentiment and tweets without positive or negative opinions. One metric that combines both precision and recall is the **F-measure**, which is implemented as metrics.f1_score:

$$F_1 = \frac{2 \cdot precision \cdot recall}{precision + recall}$$

After putting everything together, we get the following code:

```
from sklearn. model_selection import GridSearchCV
from sklearn.metrics import make_scorer, f1_score
def grid_search_model(clf_factory, X, Y):
    cv = ShuffleSplit(n_splits=10, test_size=0.3, random_state=0)
    param_grid = dict(tfidf__ngram_range=[(1, 1), (1, 2), (1, 3)],
            tfidf__min_df=[1, 2],
            tfidf__stop_words=[None, "english"],
            tfidf__smooth_idf=[False, True],
            tfidf__use_idf=[False, True],
            tfidf__sublinear_tf=[False, True],
            tfidf__binary=[False, True],
            clf__alpha=[0, 0.01, 0.05, 0.1, 0.5, 1],
            )
    grid_search = GridSearchCV(clf_factory(),
            param_grid=param_grid, cv=cv,
            scoring=make_scorer(f1_score), verbose=10)
    grid_search.fit(X, Y)
    return grid_search.best_estimator_
```

We have to be patient while executing this:

```
print("== Pos/neg vs. irrelevant/neutral ==")
X = X_orig
Y = tweak_labels(Y_orig, ["positive", "negative"])
clf = grid_search_model(create_ngram_model, X, Y)
print(clf)
```

Since we have just requested a parameter, sweep over $3 \cdot 2 \cdot 2 \cdot 2 \cdot 2 \cdot 2 \cdot 2 \cdot 6 = 1152$ parameter combinations, each being trained on 10 folds:

```
... waiting some 20 minutes   ...
Pipeline(memory=None,
     steps=[('tfidf', TfidfVectorizer(analyzer='word', binary=True,
         decode_error='strict',
         dtype=<class 'numpy.int64'>, encoding='utf-8', input='content',
         lowercase=True, max_df=1.0, max_features=None, min_df=1,
         ngram_range=(1, 2), norm='l2', preprocessor=None,
     smooth_idf=False, vocabulary=None)),
     ('clf', MultinomialNB(alpha=0.01, class_prior=None, fit_prior=True))])
```

To be able to compare the numbers with our previous approach, we will create a best_params dictionary, which we will then pass to the classifier factory, and then run the same code as before that trains on 10-fold CV splits and outputs the mean scores:

```
best_params = dict(all__tfidf__ngram_range=(1, 2),
                   all__tfidf__min_df=1,
                   all__tfidf__stop_words=None,
                   all__tfidf__smooth_idf=False,
                   all__tfidf__use_idf=False,
                   all__tfidf__sublinear_tf=True,
                   all__tfidf__binary=False,
                   clf__alpha=0.01,
                 )
print("== Pos/neg vs. irrelevant/neutral ==")
X = X_orig
Y = tweak_labels(Y_orig, ["positive", "negative"])
train_model(lambda: create_ngram_model(best_params), X, Y)
```

Here are the results:

```
== Pos/neg vs. irrelevant/neutral ==
Mean acc=0.791    Mean P/R AUC=0.681
```

The best estimator indeed improves the P/R AUC from 65.8% to 68.1%, with the settings shown in the previous code.

Also, the devastating results for positive tweets against the rest and negative tweets against the rest improve if we configure the vectorizer and classifier with those parameters we have just found out. Only the positive versus negative classification shows slightly inferior performance:

	First try		GridCV	
	Acc	P/R AUC	Acc	P/R AUC
Pos vs neg	0.777	0.887	0.798	0.885
Sent vs rest	0.734	0.661	0.790	0.683
Pos vs rest	0.870	0.305	0.885	0.491
Neg vs rest	0.852	0.49	0.882	0.621

Have a look at the following plots:

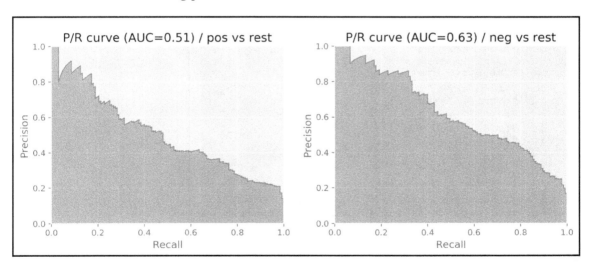

Indeed, the P/R curves look much better (note that the plots are from the medium of the fold classifiers, thus, the slightly-diverging AUC values). Nevertheless, we probably still wouldn't use those classifiers. Time for something completely different...

Cleaning tweets

New constraints lead to new forms. Twitter is no exception in this regard. Because the text has to fit into 280 characters, people naturally develop new language shortcuts to say the same in fewer characters. So far, we have ignored all the diverse emoticons and abbreviations. Let's see how much we can improve by taking that into account. For this endeavor, we will have to provide our own `preprocessor()` to `TfidfVectorizer`.

First, we define a range of frequent emoticons and their replacements in a dictionary. Although we can find more distinct replacements, we go with obvious positive or negative words to help the classifier:

```
emo_repl = {
  # positive emoticons
  "&lt;3": " good ",
  ":d": " good ", # :D in lower case
  ":dd": " good ", # :DD in lower case
  "8)": " good ",
  ":-)": " good ",
  ":)": " good ",
  ";)": " good ",
  "(-:": " good ",
  "(:": " good ",

  # negative emoticons:
  ":/": " bad ",
  ":&gt;": " sad ",
  ":')": " sad ",
  ":-(": " bad ",
  ":(": " bad ",
  ":S": " bad ",
  ":-S": " bad ",
  }
# make sure that e.g. :dd is replaced before :d
emo_repl_order = [k for (k_len,k) in reversed(sorted([(len(k),k)
                    for k in emo_repl.keys()]))]
```

Then, we define abbreviations as regular expressions together with their expansions (b marks the word boundary):

```
re_repl = {
  r"brb": "are",
  r"bub": "you",
  r"bhahab": "ha",
  r"bhahahab": "ha",
  r"bdon'tb": "do not",
```

```
        r"bdoesn'tb": "does not",
        r"bdidn'tb": "did not",
        r"bhasn'tb": "has not",
        r"bhaven'tb": "have not",
        r"bhadn'tb": "had not",
        r"bwon'tb": "will not",
        r"bwouldn'tb": "would not",
        r"bcan'tb": "can not",
        r"bcannotb": "can not",
    }
def create_ngram_model_emoji(params=None):
    def preprocessor(tweet):
        tweet = tweet.lower()
        for k in emo_repl_order:
            tweet = tweet.replace(k, emo_repl[k])
        for r, repl in re_repl.items():
            tweet = re.sub(r, repl, tweet)

        return tweet
    tfidf_ngrams = TfidfVectorizer(preprocessor=preprocessor,
                                   analyzer="word")
    clf = MultinomialNB()
    pipeline = Pipeline([('tfidf', tfidf_ngrams), ('clf', clf)])
    if params:
        pipeline.set_params(**params)

    return pipeline
```

Remember that we created a dictionary of the parameters that we found to be best using `GridSearchCV`. We will pass it to `create_ngram_model_emoji` so that our new model improves on what we already have figured out. As `train_model` requires a classifier factory, because it will be instantiated over and over again, we create the factory using Python's `lambda`:

```
print("== Pos/neg vs. irrelevant/neutral ==")
X = X_orig
Y = tweak_labels(Y_orig, ["positive", "negative"])
train_model(lambda: create_ngram_model_emoji(best_params), X, Y)
```

Certainly, there are many more abbreviations that can be used here. But already with this limited set, we get an improvement of roughly half a point for positive versus negative, as well as a sentiment versus no sentiment. Copying over the preceding table and filling in the numbers for the new approach, we see that it approves a bit for every classifier:

	First try		GridCV		GridCV+Cleaning	
	Acc	P/R AUC	Acc	P/R AUC	Acc	P/R AUC
Pos vs neg	0.777	0.887	0.798	0.885	0.808	0.889
Sent vs rest	0.734	0.661	0.790	0.683	0.791	0.689
Pos vs rest	0.870	0.305	0.885	0.491	0.886	0.498
Neg vs rest	0.852	0.49	0.882	0.621	0.883	0.632

Taking the word types into account

So far, our hope was that simply using the words independent of each other with the bag-of-words approach would suffice. Just from our intuition, however, we know that neutral tweets probably contain a higher fraction of nouns, while positive or negative tweets are more colorful, requiring more adjectives and verbs. What if we use this linguistic information of the tweets as well? If we could find out how many words in a tweet were nouns, verbs, adjectives, and so on, the classifier could probably take that into account too.

Determining the word types

This is what part-of-speech tagging, or POS tagging, is all about. A POS tagger analyzes a sentence and tags each word with its part of speech, for example, whether the word book is a noun (this is a good book) or a verb (could you please book the flight?).

You might have already guessed that NLTK will play its role in this area as well. And indeed, it comes readily packaged with all sorts of parsers and taggers. The POS tagger we will use, `nltk.pos_tag()`, is actually a full-blown classifier trained using manuallyannotated sentences from the Penn Treebank Project. It takes as input a list of word tokens and outputs a list of tuples, where each element contains the part of the original sentence and its part-of-speech tag:

```
>>> import nltk
>>> nltk.pos_tag(nltk.word_tokenize("This is a good book."))
[('This', 'DT'), ('is', 'VBZ'), ('a', 'DT'), ('good', 'JJ'), ('book',
'NN'), ('.', '.')]
>>> nltk.pos_tag(nltk.word_tokenize("Could you please book the flight?"))
[('Could', 'MD'), ('you', 'PRP'), ('please', 'VB'), ('book', 'NN'),
('the', 'DT'), ('flight', 'NN'), ('?', '.')]
```

The POS tag abbreviations are taken from the Penn Treebank (adapted from `http://www.anc.org/OANC/penn.html`):

POS tag	Description	Example
CC	coordinating conjunction	or
CD	cardinal number	2, second
DT	Determiner	the
EX	existential there	*there* are
FW	foreign word	kindergarten
IN	preposition/subordinating conjunction	on, of, like
JJ	Adjective	cool
JJR	adjective, comparative	cooler
JJS	adjective, superlative	coolest
LS	list marker	1)
MD	Modal	could, will
NN	noun, singular or mass	book
NNS	noun plural	books
NNP	proper noun, singular	Sean
NNPS	proper noun, plural	Vikings
PDT	Predeterminer	both the boys
POS	possessive ending	friend's
PRP	personal pronoun	I, he, it
PRP$	possessive pronoun	my, his
RB	Adverb	however, usually, naturally, here, good

POS tag	Description	Example
RBR	adverb, comparative	better
RBS	adverb, superlative	best
RP	Particle	give *up*
TO	To	*to* go, *to* him
UH	Interjection	uhhuhhuhh
VB	verb, base form	take
VBD	verb, past tense	took
VBG	verb, gerund/present participle	taking
VBN	verb, past participle	taken
VBP	verb, sing. present, non-3d	take
VBZ	verb, 3rd person sing. present	takes
WDT	wh-determiner	which
WP	wh-pronoun	who, what
WP$	possessive wh-pronoun	whose
WRB	wh-abverb	where, when

With these tags, it is pretty easy to filter the desired tags from the output of `pos_tag()`. We simply have to count all words whose tags start with NN for nouns, VB for verbs, JJ for adjectives, and RB for adverbs.

Successfully cheating using SentiWordNet

While linguistic information, as mentioned in the preceding section, will most likely help us, there is something better we can use to harvest it: SentiWordNet (`http://sentiwordnet.isti.cnr.it`). Simply put, it is a 13 MB file, which we have to download from the site, unzipped, and put it into the data directory of the Jupyter notebook; it assigns most of the English words a positive and negative value. That means that for every synonym set, it records both the positive and negative sentiment values. Some examples are as follows:

POS	ID	PosScore	NegScore	SynsetTerms	Description
a	00311354	0.25	0.125	studious#1	Marked by care and effort; made a studious attempt to fix the television set
a	00311663	0	0.5	careless#1	Marked by lack of attention or consideration or forethought or thoroughness; not careful...

POS	ID	PosScore	NegScore	SynsetTerms	Description
n	03563710	0	0	implant#1	A prosthesis placed permanently in tissue
v	00362128	0	0	kink#2 curve#5 curl#1	Form a curl, curve, or kink; the cigar smoke curled up at the ceiling

With the information in the **POS** column, we will be able to distinguish between the noun book and the verb book. `PosScore` and `NegScore` together will help us to determine the neutrality of the word, which is 1-PosScore-NegScore. `SynsetTerms` lists all words in the set that are synonyms. We can safely ignore the `ID` and `Description` columns.

The synset terms have a number appended, because some occur multiple times in different synsets. For example, fantasize conveys two different meanings, which also leads to different scores:

POS	ID	PosScore	NegScore	SynsetTerms	Description
v	01636859	0.375	0	fantasize#2 fantasise#2	Portray in the mind; he is fantasizing the ideal wife
v	01637368	0	0.125	fantasy#1 fantasize#1 fantasise#1	Indulge in fantasies; he is fantasizing when he says he plans to start his own company

To find out which of the synsets to take, we will need to really understand the meaning of the tweets, which is beyond the scope of this chapter. The field of research that focuses on this challenge is called word-sense disambiguation.

For our task, we take the easy route and simply average the scores over all the synsets in which a term is found. For fantasize, `PosScore` will be `0.1875` and `NegScore` will be `0.0625`.

The following function, `load_sent_word_net()`, does all that for us and returns a dictionary where the keys are strings of the word type/word form, for example, n/implant, and the values are the positive and negative scores:

```
import csv, collections
def load_sent_word_net():
    # making our life easier by using a dictionary that
    # automatically creates an empty list whenever we access
    # a not yet existing key
    sent_scores = collections.defaultdict(list)

    with open(os.path.join(DATA_DIR, "SentiWordNet_3.0.0_20130122.txt"),
              "r") as csvfile:
```

```
reader = csv.reader(csvfile, delimiter='t',
                    quotechar='"')
for line in reader:
    if line[0].startswith("#"):
        continue
    if len(line)==1:
        continue

    POS, ID, PosScore, NegScore, SynsetTerms, Gloss = line
    if len(POS)==0 or len(ID)==0:
        continue
    for term in SynsetTerms.split(" "):
        # drop number at the end of every term
        term = term.split("#")[0]
        term = term.replace("-", " ").replace("_", " ")
        key = "%s/%s"%(POS, term.split("#")[0])
        sent_scores[key].append((float(PosScore),
                                 float(NegScore)))
for key, value in sent_scores.items():
    sent_scores[key] = np.mean(value, axis=0)


return sent_scores
```

Our first estimator

Now, we have everything in place to create our own first vectorizer. The most convenient way to do it is to inherit it from `BaseEstimator`. It requires us to implement the following three methods:

- `get_feature_names()`: This returns a list of strings of the features that we will return in `transform()`.

- `fit(document, y=None)`: As we are not implementing a classifier, we can ignore this one and simply return self.

- `transform(documents)`: This returns `numpy.array()`, containing an array of a shape (`len(documents)`, `len(get_feature_names)`). This means, for every document in `documents`, it has to return a value for every feature name in `get_feature_names()`.

Here is the implementation:

```
sent_word_net = load_sent_word_net()
 class LinguisticVectorizer(BaseEstimator):
     def get_feature_names(self):
         return np.array(['sent_neut', 'sent_pos', 'sent_neg',
                          'nouns', 'adjectives', 'verbs', 'adverbs',
                          'allcaps', 'exclamation', 'question', 'hashtag',
                          'mentioning'])
     # we don't fit here but need to return the reference
     # so that it can be used like fit(d).transform(d)
     def fit(self, documents, y=None):
         return self


     def _get_sentiments(self, d):
         sent = tuple(d.split())
         tagged = nltk.pos_tag(sent)

         pos_vals = []
         neg_vals = []

         nouns = 0.
         adjectives = 0.
         verbs = 0.
         adverbs = 0.


         for w,t in tagged:
             p, n = 0, 0
             sent_pos_type = None
             if t.startswith("NN"):
                 sent_pos_type = "n"
                 nouns += 1
             elif t.startswith("JJ"):
                 sent_pos_type = "a"
                 adjectives += 1
             elif t.startswith("VB"):
                 sent_pos_type = "v"
                 verbs += 1
             elif t.startswith("RB"):
                 sent_pos_type = "r"
                 adverbs += 1

             if sent_pos_type is not None:
                 sent_word = "%s/%s" % (sent_pos_type, w)

                 if sent_word in sent_word_net:
```

```
                        p,n = sent_word_net[sent_word]

            pos_vals.append(p)
            neg_vals.append(n)

        l = len(sent)
        avg_pos_val = np.mean(pos_vals)
        avg_neg_val = np.mean(neg_vals)
        return [1-avg_pos_val-avg_neg_val, avg_pos_val, avg_neg_val,
                nouns/l, adjectives/l, verbs/l, adverbs/l]


    def transform(self, documents):
        obj_val, pos_val, neg_val, nouns, adjectives,
           verbs, adverbs = np.array([self._get_sentiments(d)
           for d in documents]).T


        allcaps = []
        exclamation = []
        question = []
        hashtag = []
        mentioning = []

        for d in documents:
            allcaps.append(np.sum([t.isupper()
                for t in d.split() if len(t)>2]))

            exclamation.append(d.count("!"))
            question.append(d.count("?"))
            hashtag.append(d.count("#"))
            mentioning.append(d.count("@"))

        result = np.array([obj_val, pos_val, neg_val, nouns, adjectives,
                          verbs, adverbs, allcaps, exclamation,
                          question, hashtag, mentioning]).T

        return result
```

Putting everything together

Nevertheless, using these linguistic features in isolation without the words themselves will not take us very far. Therefore, we have to combine the `TfidfVectorizer` parameter with the linguistic features. This can be done with scikit-learn's `FeatureUnion` class. It is initialized in the same manner as `Pipeline`; however, instead of evaluating the estimators in a sequence, each passing the output of the previous one to the next one, `FeatureUnion` does it in parallel and joins the output vectors afterward:

```python
def create_union_model(params=None):
    def preprocessor(tweet):
        tweet = tweet.lower()
        for k in emo_repl_order:
            tweet = tweet.replace(k, emo_repl[k])
        for r, repl in re_repl.items():
            tweet = re.sub(r, repl, tweet)


        return tweet.replace("-", " ").replace("_", " ")


    tfidf_ngrams = TfidfVectorizer(preprocessor=preprocessor,
                                   analyzer="word")
    ling_stats = LinguisticVectorizer()
    all_features = FeatureUnion([('ling', ling_stats),
                                 ('tfidf', tfidf_ngrams)])
    clf = MultinomialNB()
    pipeline = Pipeline([('all', all_features), ('clf', clf)])

    if params:
        pipeline.set_params(**params)

    return pipeline
```

Training and testing on the combined featurizers, however, is a bit disappointing. We improve by 1% in the positive versus rest part but lose everywhere else:

	First try		GridCV		GridCV + Cleaning		GridCV + Cleaning + SentiWord	
	Acc	P/R AUC	Acc	P/R AUC	Acc	P/R AUC	Acc	P/R AUC
Pos vs neg	0.777	0.887	0.798	0.885	0.808	0.889	0.793	0.882

With these results, we probably do not want to pay the price of the much costlier SentiWord approach, if we don't get a significant post in P/R AUC. Instead, we'll probably choose the GridCV + Cleaning approach, and first use the classifier that determines whether the tweet contains a sentiment at all (pos/neg versus irrelevant/neutral), and then in case it does, use the positive-versus-negative classifier to determine the actual sentiment.

Summary

Congratulations for sticking with us until the end! Together we have learned how Naïve Bayes works and why it is not that naïve at all. Especially for training sets, where we don't have enough data to learn all the niches in the class-probability space, Naïve Bayes does a great job of generalizing. We learned how to apply it to tweets and that cleaning the rough tweets' texts helps a lot. Finally, we realized that a bit of cheating (only after we have done our fair share of work) is okay. However, since we realized that the much costlier classifier did not reward us with a much-improved classifier, we went back to the cheaper classifier.

In `Chapter 10`, *Topic Modeling*, we will learn how we can extract topics from a document using Latent Dirichlet allocation, also called topic modeling. This will help us to compare documents by analyzing how similar the covered topics are.

10
Topic Modeling

In Chapter 6, *Clustering - Finding Related Posts*, we grouped text documents using clustering. This is a very useful tool, but it is not always the best. Clustering results in each text belonging to exactly one cluster. This book is about machine learning and Python. Should it be grouped with other Python-related works or with machine-related works? In a physical bookstore, we need to choose a single place to stock the book. In an internet store, however, the answer is that this book is about both machine learning *and* Python, and the book should be listed in both sections. This does not mean that the book will be listed in all sections, of course. We will not list this book with other baking books.

In this chapter, we will learn methods that do not cluster documents into completely separate groups but that allow each document to refer to several **topics**. These topics will be identified automatically from a collection of text documents. These documents may be whole books or shorter pieces of text, such as a blog post, a news story, or an email.

We would also like to be able to infer the fact that these documents may have topics that are central to them, while referring to other topics only in passing. This book mentions plotting every so often, but it is not a central topic like machine learning. This means that documents have topics that are central to them and others that are more peripheral. The subfield of machine learning that deals with these problems is called **topic modeling** and is the subject of this chapter. In particular, we will learn about the following:

- What topic models are and, in particular, about **latent Dirichlet allocation (LDA)**
- How to use the `gensim` package to build topic models
- How topic models can be useful as an intermediate representation for different applications
- How we can build a topic model of the whole of the English-language Wikipedia

Latent Dirichlet allocation

Unfortunately, there are two methods in machine learning with the initials LDA: latent Dirichlet allocation, which is a topic modeling method, and linear discriminant analysis, which is a classification method. They are completely unrelated, except for the fact that the initials LDA can refer to either. In certain situations, this can be confusing. The scikit-learn tool has a submodule, `sklearn.lda`, which implements linear discriminant analysis. At the moment, scikit-learn does not implement latent Dirichlet allocation.

The first topic `model` we will look at is latent Dirichlet allocation. The mathematical ideas behind LDA are fairly complex, and we will not go into the details here.

For those who are interested, and adventurous enough, Wikipedia provides all the equations behind these algorithms:
`http://en.wikipedia.org/wiki/Latent_Dirichlet_allocation`.

However, we can understand the ideas behind LDA intuitively at a high level. LDA belongs to a class of models that are called generative models as they have a sort of fable explains how the data was generated. This generative story is a simplification of reality, of course, to make machine learning easier. In the LDA fable, we first create topics by assigning probability weights to words. Each topic will assign different weights to different words. For example, a Python topic will assign high probability to the word variable and a low probability to the word inebriated. When we wish to generate a new document, we first choose the topics it will use and then mix words from these topics.

For example, let's say we have only three topics that books discuss:

- Machine learning
- Python
- Baking

For each topic, we have a list of words associated with it. This book will be a mixture of the first two topics, perhaps 50 percent each. The mixture does not need to be equal; it can also be a 70/30 split. When we are generating the actual text, we generate word by word; first we decide which topic this word will come from. This is a random decision based on the topic weights. Once a topic is chosen, we generate a word from that topic's list of words. To be precise, we choose a word in English with the probability given by the topic. The same word can be generated from multiple topics. For example, weight is a common word in both machine learning and baking (albeit with different meanings).

In this model, the order of words does not matter. This is a **bag of words** model, as we have already seen in the previous chapter. It is a crude simplification of language, but it often works well enough, because just knowing which words were used in a document and their frequencies is enough to make machine learning decisions.

In the real world, we do not know what the topics are. Our task is to take a collection of text and to reverse engineer this fable in order to discover what topics are out there and simultaneously figure out which topics each document uses.

Building a topic model

Unfortunately, scikit-learn does not implement latent Dirichlet allocation. Therefore, we are going to use the `gensim` package from Python. Gensim was developed by Radim Řehůřek who is a machine learning researcher and consultant in the United Kingdom.

As input data, we are going to use a collection of news reports from the **Associated Press** (**AP**). This is a standard dataset for text modeling research, which was used in some of the initial works on topic models. After downloading the data, we can load it by running the following code:

```
import gensim
from gensim import corpora, models
corpus = corpora.BleiCorpus('./data/ap/ap.dat', './data/ap/vocab.txt')
```

The `corpus` variable holds all of the text documents and has loaded them in a format that makes for easy processing. We can now build a topic `model`, using this object as input:

```
model = models.ldamodel.LdaModel(
            corpus,
            num_topics=100,
            id2word=corpus.id2word)
```

This single constructor call will statistically infer which topics are present in `corpus`. We can explore the resulting model in many ways. We can see the list of `topics` a document refers to using the `model[doc]` syntax, as shown in the following example:

```
doc = corpus.docbyoffset(0)
topics = model[doc]
print(topics)
[(3, 0.023607255776894751),
 (13, 0.11679936618551275),
 (19, 0.075935855202707139),
 ....
 (92, 0.10781541687001292)]
```

The result will almost surely look different on our computer! The learning algorithm uses some random numbers, and every time you learn a new topic `model` on the same input data, the result is different. What is important is that some of the qualitative properties of the model will be stable across different runs if your data is well behaved. For example, if you are using the topics to compare documents, as we do here, then the similarities should be robust and change only slightly. On the other hand, the order of the different topics will be completely different.

The format of the result is a list of pairs: `(topic_index, topic_weight)`. We can see that only a few topics are used for each document (in the preceding example, there is no weight for topics 0, 1, and 2; the weight for those topics is 0). The topic `model` is a sparse model, as although there are many possible topics, for each document, only a few of them are used. This is not strictly true as all the topics have a non-zero probability in the LDA model, but some of them have such a small probability that we can round it to zero as a good approximation.

We can explore this further by plotting a histogram of the number of topics that each document refers to:

```
num_topics_used = [len(model[doc]) for doc in corpus]
fig,ax = plt.subplots()
ax.hist(num_topics_used)
```

You will get the following plot:

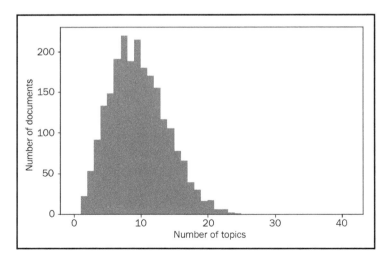

Sparsity means that while you may have large matrices and vectors, in principle, most of the values are zero (or so small that we can round them to zero as a good approximation). Therefore, only a few things are relevant at any given time.

Often problems that seem too big to solve are actually feasible because the data is sparse. For example, even though any web page can link to any other web page, the graph of links is actually very sparse as each web page will link to a very tiny fraction of all other web pages.

In the preceding graph, we can see more or less about the majority of documents deals with around 10 topics.

To a large extent, this is due to the value of the parameters that were used, namely, the `alpha` parameter. The exact meaning of alpha is a bit abstract, but bigger values for alpha will result in more topics per document.

Alpha needs to be a value greater than zero, but is typically set to a lesser value, usually, less than one. The smaller the value of `alpha`, the fewer topics each document will be expected to discuss. By default, gensim will set `alpha` to `1/num_topics`, but you can set it explicitly by passing it as an argument in the `LdaModel` constructor as follows:

```
model = models.ldamodel.LdaModel(
            corpus,
            num_topics=100,
            id2word=corpus.id2word,
            alpha=1)
```

In this case, this is a larger alpha than the default, which should lead to more topics per document. As we can see in the combined histogram given next, gensim behaves as we expected and assigns more topics to each document:

Now, we can see in the preceding histogram that many documents touch upon **20** to **25** different topics. If you set the value lower, you will observe the opposite (downloading the code from the online repository will allow you to play around with these values).

What are these topics? Technically, as we discussed earlier, they are multinomial distributions over words, which means that they assign a probability to each word in the vocabulary. Words with a high probability are more associated with that topic than words with a lower probability:

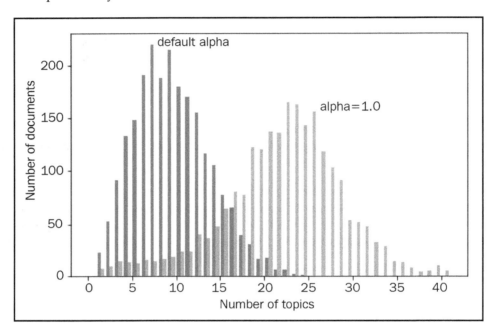

Our brains are not very good at reasoning with probability distributions, but we can readily make sense of a list of words. Therefore, it is typical to summarize topics with a list of the most highly weighted words.

In the following table, we display the first ten topics:

Topic no.	Topic
1	Dress military soviet president new state capt carlucci states leader stance government
2	Koch Zambia Lusaka oneparty orange Kochs party i government mayor new political
3	Human turkey rights abuses royal Thompson threats new state wrote garden president
4	Bill employees experiments levin taxation federal measure legislation senate president whistle blowers sponsor

5	Ohio July drought Jesus disaster percent Hartford Mississippi crops northern valley Virginia
6	United percent billion year president world years states people i bush news
7	b Hughes affidavit states united ounces squarefoot care delaying charged unrealistic bush
8	yeutter dukakis bush convention farm subsidies Uruguay percent secretary general i told
9	Kashmir government people Srinagar India dumps city two Jammu Kashmir group Mosley Pakistan
10	workers Vietnamese Irish wage immigrants percent bargaining last island police Hutton i

Although daunting at first glance, when reading through the list of words, we can clearly see that the topics are not just random words, but instead these are logical groups. We can also see that these topics refer to older news items, from when the Soviet Union still existed and Gorbachev was its general secretary. We can also represent the topics as a word cloud, making more likely words larger. For example, this is the visualization of a topic that deals with the police:

We can also see that some of the words should perhaps be removed as they are not so informative; they are stop words. When building topic modeling, it can be useful to filter out stop words, as otherwise you might end up with a topic consisting entirely of stop words. We may also wish to preprocess the text to stems in order to normalize plurals and verb forms. This process was covered in Chapter 6, *Clustering - Finding Related Posts*, and you can refer to it for details. If you are interested, you can download the code from the companion website of the book and try all these variations to draw different pictures.

Comparing documents by topic

Topics can be useful on their own to build the sort of small vignettes with words that are shown in the previous screenshot. These visualizations can be used to navigate a large collection of documents. For example, a website can display the different topics as different word clouds, allowing a user to click through to the documents. In fact, they have been used in just this way to analyze large collections of documents.

However, topics are often just an intermediate tool to another end. Now that we have an estimate for each document of how much of that document comes from each topic, we can compare the documents in topic space. This simply means that instead of comparing word to word, we say that two documents are similar if they talk about the same topics.

This can be very powerful as two text documents that share few words may actually refer to the same topic! They may just refer to it using different constructions (for example, one document may speak of the United Kingdom while the other will use the abbreviation UK).

 Topic models are good on their own to build visualizations and explore data. They are also very useful as an intermediate step in many other tasks.

At this point, we can redo the task of finding the most similar post to an input query, by using the topics to define similarity. Whereas earlier we compared two documents by comparing their word vectors directly, we can now compare two documents by comparing their topic vectors.

For this, we are going to project the documents to the topic space. That is, we want to have a vector of topics that summarizes the document. This is another example of **dimensionality reduction** of the type discussed in Chapter 5, *Dimensionality Reduction*. Here, we show you how topic models can be used for exactly this purpose; once topics have been computed for each document, we can perform operations on the topic vector and forget about the original words. If the topics are meaningful, they will be potentially more informative than the raw words. Additionally, this may bring computational advantages, as it is much faster to compare vectors of topic weights than vectors that are as large as the input vocabulary (which will contain thousands of terms).

Using gensim, we looked at how to compute the topics corresponding to all the documents in the corpus. We will now compute these for all the documents and store it in a NumPy array and compute all pairwise distances:

```
from gensim import matutils
topics = matutils.corpus2dense(model[corpus], num_terms=model.num_topics)
```

Now, topics is a matrix of topics. We can use the pdist function in SciPy to compute all pairwise distances. There are several distances available. By default, it uses the Euclidean distance. That is, with a single function call, we compute all the values of sum((topics[ti] - topics[tj])**2):

```
from scipy.spatial import distance
distances = distance.squareform(distance.pdist(topics))
```

Now, we will employ one last little trick; we will set the diagonal elements of the distance matrix to infinity to ensure that it will appear as larger than any other:

```
for ti in range(len(topics)):
    distances[ti,ti] = np.inf
```

And we are done! For each document, we can look up the closest element easily (this is a type of nearest-neighbor classifier):

```
def closest_to(doc_id):
    return distances[doc_id].argmin()
```

This will not work if we have not set the diagonal elements to a large value: the function will always return the same element as it is the one most similar to itself (except in the weird case where two elements have exactly the same topic distribution, which is very rare unless they are exactly the same).

For example, here is one possible query document (it is the second document in our collection):

```
From: geb@cs.pitt.edu (Gordon Banks)
Subject: Re: request for information on "essential tremor" and
  Indrol?

In article <1q1tbnINNnfn@life.ai.mit.edu> sundar@ai.mit.edu
  writes:

Essential tremor is a progressive hereditary tremor that gets
  worse
when the patient tries to use the effected member.  All limbs,
  vocal
cords, and head can be involved.  Inderal is a beta-blocker and
is usually effective in diminishing the tremor.  Alcohol and
  mysoline
are also effective, but alcohol is too toxic to use as a
  treatment.
--
----------------------------------------------------------------
----------
Gordon Banks  N3JXP      | "Skepticism is the chastity of the
  intellect, and
geb@cadre.dsl.pitt.edu   | it is shameful to surrender it too
  soon."
    ------------------------------------------------------------
-----------
```

If we ask for the most similar document to `closest_to(1)`, we receive the following document as a result:

```
From: geb@cs.pitt.edu (Gordon Banks)
Subject: Re: High Prolactin

In article <93088.112203JER4@psuvm.psu.edu> JER4@psuvm.psu.edu
  (John E. Rodway) writes:
>Any comments on the use of the drug Parlodel for high prolactin
  in the blood?
>

It can suppress secretion of prolactin. Is useful in cases of galactorrhea.
Some adenomas of the pituitary secret too much.

--
----------------------------------------------------------------
----------
Gordon Banks  N3JXP      | "Skepticism is the chastity of the
```

```
    intellect, and
    geb@cadre.dsl.pitt.edu    |   it is shameful to surrender it too
    soon."
```

The system returns a post by the same author discussing medication.

Modeling the whole of Wikipedia

While the initial LDA implementations can be slow, which limits their use to small document collections, modern algorithms work well with very large collections of data. Following the documentation of `gensim`, we are going to build a topic model for the whole of the English-language Wikipedia. This takes hours, but can be done with just a laptop! With a cluster of machines, we can make it go much faster, but we will look at that sort of processing environment in a later chapter.

First, we download the whole Wikipedia dump from `http://dumps.wikimedia.org`. This is a large file (currently over 14 GB), so it may take a while, unless your internet connection is very fast. Then, we will index it with a `gensim` tool:

```
python -m gensim.scripts.make_wiki enwiki-latest-pages-articles.xml.bz2
wiki_en_output
```

Run the previous line on the command shell, not on the Python shell! After several hours, the index will be saved in the same directory. At this point, we can build the final topic model. This process looks exactly like it did for the small AP dataset. We first import a few packages:

```
import logging, gensim
```

Now, we set up logging using the standard Python logging module (which `gensim` uses to print out status messages). This step is not strictly necessary, but it is nice to have a little more output to know what is happening:

```
logging.basicConfig(format='%(asctime)s : %(levelname)s : %(message)s',
level=logging.INFO)
```

Now we load the preprocessed data:

```
id2word = gensim.corpora.Dictionary.load_from_text(
                'wiki_en_output_wordids.txt')
mm = gensim.corpora.MmCorpus('wiki_en_output_tfidf.mm')
```

Finally, we build the LDA model as we did earlier:

```
model = gensim.models.ldamodel.LdaModel(
        corpus=mm,
        id2word=id2word,
        num_topics=100)
```

This will again take a couple of hours. You will see the progress on your console, which can give you an indication of how long you still have to wait.

Once it is done, we can save the topic `model` to a file, so we don't have to redo it:

```
model.save('wiki_lda.pkl')
```

If you exit your session and come back later, you can load the model again using the following command (after the appropriate imports, naturally):

```
model = gensim.models.ldamodel.LdaModel.load('wiki_lda.pkl')
```

The `model` object can be used to explore the collection of documents and build the `topics` matrix as we did earlier.

We can see that this is still a sparse model even if we have many more documents than we had earlier (over 4 million as we are writing this):

```
lens = (topics > 0).sum(axis=1)
print('Mean number of topics mentioned: {0:.4}'.format(np.mean(lens)))
print('Percentage of articles mentioning <10 topics: {0:.1%}'.format(
        np.mean(lens <= 10)))
Mean number of topics mentioned: 6.244
Percentage of articles mentioning <10 topics: 95.1%
```

So, the average document mentions `6.244` topics and `95.1` percent of them mention `10` or fewer topics.

We can ask what the most talked about topic on Wikipedia is. We will first compute the total weight for each topic (by summing up the weights from all the documents) and then retrieve the words corresponding to the most highly weighted topic. This is performed using the following code:

```
weights = topics.sum(axis=0)
words = model.show_topic(weights.argmax(), 64)
```

Using the same tools as we did earlier to build up a visualization, we can see that the most talked about topic is related to music and is a very coherent topic. A full 18 percent of Wikipedia pages are partially related to this topic (5.5 percent of all the words in Wikipedia are assigned to this topic). Take a look at the following screenshot:

 These plots and numbers were obtained when the book was being written. As Wikipedia keeps changing, your results will be different. We expect that the trends will be similar, but the details may vary.

Alternatively, we can look at the least talked about topic:

```
words = model.show_topic(weights.argmin(), 64)
```

Refer to the following screenshot:

The least talked about topic is harder to interpret, but many of its top words refer to locations in Africa. Just 2.1 percent of documents touch upon it, and it represents just 0.1 percent of the words.

Choosing the number of topics

So far in the chapter, we have used a fixed number of topics for our analysis, namely 100. This was a purely arbitrary number; we could have just as well used either 20 or 200 topics. Fortunately, for many uses, this number does not really matter. If you are going to only use the topics as an intermediate step, as we did previously when finding similar posts, the final behavior of the system is rarely very sensitive to the exact number of topics used in the model. This means that as long as you use enough topics, whether you use 100 topics or 200, the recommendations that result from the process will not be very different. However, 100 is often a good enough number (while 20 is too few for a general collection of text documents), but we could have used more if we had more documents.

The same is true of setting the `alpha` value. While playing around with it can change the topics, the final results are again robust in terms of this change. Naturally, this depends on the exact nature of your data, and should be tested empirically to make sure that the results are indeed stable.

 Topic modeling is often an end toward a goal. In that case, it is not always very important which parameter values are used exactly. A different number of topics or values for parameters such as `alpha` will result in systems whose end results are almost identical in their final results.

On the other hand, if you are going to explore the topics directly, or build a visualization tool that exposes them, you should probably try a few values and see which gives you the most useful or most appealing results. There are also statistical concepts such as perplexity that can be used to determine which of a series of models best fits the data, enabling a more informed decision.

Alternatively, there are a few methods that will automatically determine the number of topics for you, depending on the dataset. One popular model is called the **hierarchical Dirichlet process (HDP)**. Again, the full mathematical model behind it is complex and beyond the scope of this book. However, what we can tell you is that instead of having the topics fixed first, as in the LDA generative method, the topics themselves are generated along with the data, one at a time. Whenever the writer creates a new document, they have the option of using the topics that already exist or to create a completely new one. When more topics have been created, the probability of creating a new one, instead of reusing what exists, goes down, but the possibility always exists.

This means that the more documents we have, the more topics we will end up with. This is one of those statements that is unintuitive at first but makes perfect sense upon reflection. We are grouping documents and the more examples we have, the more we can break them up. If we only have a few examples of news articles, then sports will be a topic. However, as we have more, we start to break it up into the individual modalities: hockey, soccer, and so on. As we have even more data, we can start to tell nuances apart, articles about individual teams and even individual players. The same is true for people. In a group of many different backgrounds, with a few computer people, you might put them together; in a slightly larger group, you will have separate gatherings for programmers and systems administrators; and in the real-world, we even have different gatherings for Python and Ruby programmers.

HDP is available in `gensim`. Using it is trivial. To adapt the code we wrote for LDA, we just need to replace the call to `gensim.models.ldamodel.LdaModel` with a call to the `HdpModel` constructor as follows:

```
hdp = gensim.models.hdpmodel.HdpModel(mm, id2word)
```

That's it (except that it takes a bit longer to compute—there are no free lunches). Now, we can use this model in much the same way as we used the LDA model, except that we did not need to specify the number of topics.

Summary

In this chapter, we discussed topic modeling. Topic modeling is more flexible than clustering as these methods allow each document to be partially present in more than one group. To explore these methods, we used a new package, `gensim`.

Topic modeling was first developed for and is easier to understand in the case of text, but in Chapter 12, *Computer Vision*, we will see how some of these techniques may be applied to images as well. Topic models are very important in modern computer vision research. In fact, unlike the previous chapters, this chapter was very close to the cutting edge of research in machine learning algorithms. The original LDA algorithm was published in a scientific journal in 2003, but the method that `gensim` uses to be able to handle Wikipedia was only developed in 2010 and the HDP algorithm is from 2011. The research continues, and you can find many variations and models with wonderful names such as **the Indian buffet process** (not to be confused with the Chinese restaurant process, which is a different model) or **Pachinko allocation** (Pachinko being a type of Japanese game, a cross between a slot machine and pinball).

We have now gone through some of the major machine learning modes: classification, clustering, and topic modeling.

In Chapter 11, *Classification III - Music Genre Classification*, we go back to classification, but this time we will be exploring advanced algorithms and approaches.

11
Classification III – Music Genre Classification

So far, we have been lucky that every training data instance could easily be described by a vector of feature values. In the Iris dataset, for example, the flowers are represented by vectors containing values for the length and width of certain aspects of a flower. In the text-based examples, we could transform the text into bag-of-word representations and manually craft our own features that captured certain aspects of the texts.

It will be different in this chapter, when we try to classify songs by their genre. How would we, for instance, represent a three minute-long song? Should we take the individual bits of its MP3 representation? Probably not, since treating it like text and creating something like a bag of sound bites would certainly be way too complex. Somehow, we will have to convert a song into a vector of values that describe it sufficiently.

Sketching our roadmap

This chapter will show you how we can come up with a decent classifier in a domain that is outside our comfort zone. For one, we will have to use sound-based features, which are much more complex than the text-based ones we've used so far. And then we will learn how to deal with more classes than we have tackled before. In addition, we will get to know new ways of measuring classification performance.

Let's assume a scenario where, for some reason, we find a bunch of randomly-named MP3 files on our hard disk, which are assumed to contain music. Our task, to sort them according to music genre into different folders, such as jazz, classical, country, pop, rock, and metal.

Fetching the music data

We will use the GTZAN dataset, which is frequently used to benchmark music genre classification tasks. It is organized into 10 distinct genres, of which we will use only six for the sake of simplicity: classical, jazz, country, pop, rock, and metal. The dataset contains the first 30 seconds of 100 songs per genre. We can download the dataset from `http://opihi.cs.uvic.ca/sound/genres.tar.gz`.

We can download and extract it directly with Python, which has been nice especially if you're using Windows, which doesn't come with a tarball unzipper.

Throughout the Jupyter notebook, we will make use of the excellent `pathlib` library, which is part of Python since version 3.4. It allows easy path and file manipulation:

```
from pathlib import Path
DATA_DIR = "data"
if not Path(DATA_DIR).exists():
    os.mkdir(DATA_DIR)
import urllib.request
genre_fn = 'http://opihi.cs.uvic.ca/sound/genres.tar.gz'
# The division operator of Path instances is overloaded to behave
# like os.path.join(), which makes it very convenient to use.
urllib.request.urlretrieve(genre_fn, Path(DATA_DIR) / 'gen-res.tar.gz')
```

Now that we have downloaded it, we extract it using the `tarfile` module:

```
import tarfile
cwd = os.getcwd()
os.chdir(DATA_DIR)

try:
    f = tarfile.open('genres.tar.gz', 'r:gz')
    try:
        f.extractall()
    finally:
        f.close()
finally:
    os.chdir(cwd)
```

Converting into WAV format

Sure enough, if we want to test our classifier on our private MP3 collection, we would not be able to extract much meaning. This is because MP3 is a lossy music compression format that cuts out parts that the human ear cannot perceive. This is nice for storing because, with MP3, you can fit 10 times as many songs on your device. For our endeavor, however, it is not so nice. For classification, we will have an easier time with WAV files because they can be directly read by the `scipy.io.wavfile` package. We would, therefore, have to convert our MP3 files, if we want to use them with our classifier.

If don't have a conversion tool nearby, you might want to check out SoX: `http://sox.sourceforge.net`. It claims to be the Swiss Army knife of sound processing, and we agree with this bold claim.

The GTZAN dataset, however, comes with music files not in MP3 but in AU format, which means we have to convert it file by file. The following snippet is a neat trick that is possible in Jupyter notebooks: it conveniently allows us to run system commands, such as the `sox` sound converter within a Python environment. We simply prepend the command line with an exclamation mark (`!`) and use curly brackets to pass on Python expressions:

```
GENRE_DIR = Path(DATA_DIR) / 'genres'
# You need to adapt the SOX_PATH accordingly on your system
SOX_PATH = r'C:\Program Files (x86)\sox-14-4-2'
for au_fn in Path(GENRE_DIR).glob('**/*.au'):
    print(au_fn)
    !"{SOX_PATH}/sox.exe" {au_fn} {au_fn.with_suffix('.wav')}
```

Of course, all of this can be done in a normal Linux or Windows shell as well, but will require a bit more shell expertise.

One advantage of having all of our music files in WAV format is that it is directly readable by the SciPy toolkit:

```
>>> sample_rate, X = scipy.io.wavfile.read(wave_filename)
```

X now contains the samples and `sample_rate` is the rate at which they were taken. Let's use that information to peek into some music files to get an idea of what the data looks like.

Looking at music

A very convenient way to get a quick impression of what the songs of diverse genres "look" like is to draw a spectrogram for a set of songs in a genre. A spectrogram is a visual representation of the frequencies that occur in a song. It shows the intensity for the frequencies on the y axis in the specified time intervals on the x axis. In the following spectrogram, that would mean the brighter the color, the stronger the frequency in the particular time window of the song.

Matplotlib provides the convenient `specgram()` function, which performs most of the under-the-hood calculation and plotting for us:

```
>>> import scipy.io.wavfile
>>> from matplotlib.pyplot import specgram
>>> sample_rate, X = scipy.io.wavfile.read(wave_filename)
>>> print(sample_rate, X.shape)
22050, (661794,)
>>> specgram(X, Fs=sample_rate, xextent=(0,30), cmap='hot')
```

The WAV file we just read in was sampled at a rate of 22050 Hz and contains 661794 samples.

If we now plot the spectrogram for these first 30 seconds for diverse WAV files, we can see that there are commonalities between songs of the same genre, as shown in the following diagram:

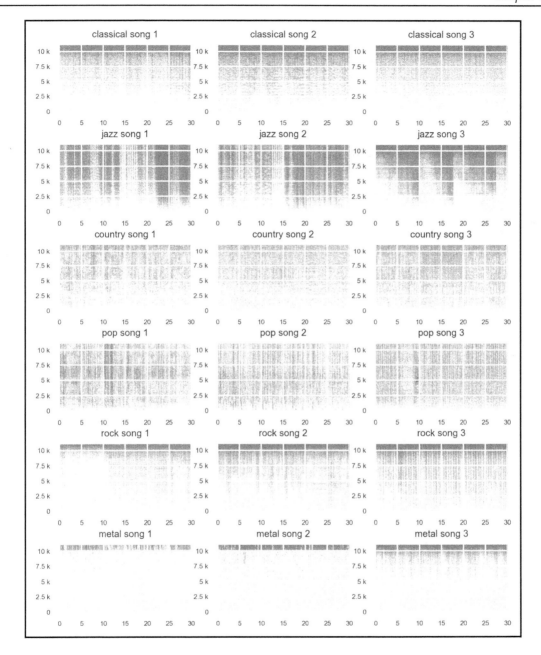

Just by glancing at the image, we immediately see the difference in the spectrum between, for example, metal and classical songs. While metal songs have high intensity over most of the frequency spectrum all the time (they're energetic!), classical songs show a more diverse pattern.

It should be possible to train a classifier that discriminates at least between metal and classical songs with high enough accuracy. Other genre pairs, such as country and rock, could pose a bigger challenge, though. This looks like a real challenge for us since we need to discern not only two classes, but six. We need to be able to distinguish between all of them reasonably well.

Decomposing music into sine-wave components

Our plan is to extract individual frequency intensities from the raw sample readings (stored in X earlier) and feed them into a classifier. These frequency intensities can be extracted by applying the **fast Fourier transform** (**FFT**), which translates the wave signal into coefficients of its frequency components. As the theory behind FFT is outside the scope of this chapter, let's just look at an example to get an idea of what it accomplishes. Later on, we will treat it as a black-box feature extractor.

For example, let's generate two WAV files, `sine_a.wav` and `sine_b.wav`, which contain the sound of 400 Hz and 3,000 Hz sine waves, respectively. The aforementioned Swiss Army knife, `sox`, is one way to achieve this on the command line (or directly from Jupyter by prepending an exclamation mark):

```
sox --null -r 22050 sine_a.wav synth 0.2 sine 400
sox --null -r 22050 sine_b.wav synth 0.2 sine 3000
```

In the following charts, we have plotted their first 0.008 seconds. In the following images, we can see the FFT of the sine waves. Not surprisingly, we see a spike at 400 Hz and 3000 Hz below the corresponding sine waves.

Now, let's mix them both, giving the 400 Hz sound half the volume of the 3,000 Hz one:

```
sox --combine mix --volume 1 sine_b.wav --volume 0.5 sine_a.wav
sine_mix.wav
```

We see two spikes in the FFT plot of the combined sound, of which the 3,000 Hz spike is almost double the size of the 400 Hz:

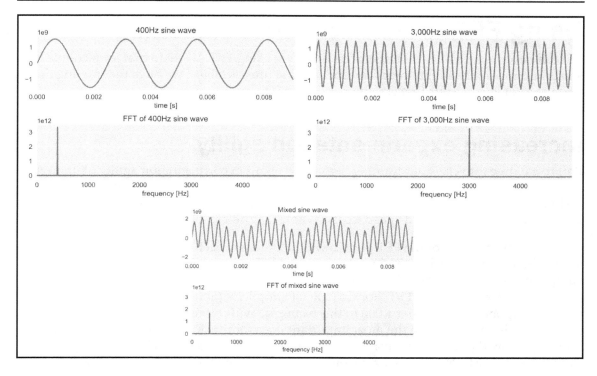

For real music, we quickly see that the FFT doesn't look as beautiful as in the preceding example:

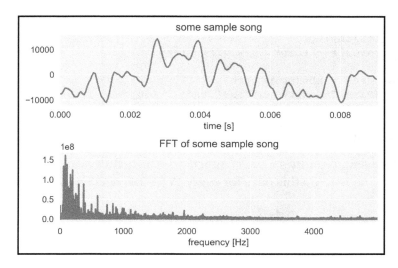

Using FFT to build our first classifier

We can now create a musical fingerprint of a song using FFT. If we do that for a couple of songs and manually assign their corresponding genres as labels, we have the training data that we can feed into our first classifier.

Increasing experimentation agility

Before we dive into classifier training, let's think about experimentation agility. Although we have the word "fast" in FFT, it is much slower than the creation of the features in our text-based chapters. And because we are still in an experimentation phase, we might want to think about how we could speed up the whole feature-creation process.

Of course, the creation of the FFT per file will be the same each time we run the classifier. We could, therefore, cache it and read the cached FFT representation instead of the complete WAV file. We do this with the `create_fft()` function, which, in turn, uses `scipy.fft()` to create the FFT. For the sake of simplicity (and speed!), let's fix the number of FFT components to the first 1,000 in this example. With our current knowledge, we do not know whether these are the most important ones for music-genre classification, only that they show the highest intensities in the preceding FFT example. If we later want to use more or fewer FFT components, we would have to recreate the FFT representations for each sound file:

```
import numpy as np
import scipy

def create_fft(fn):
    sample_rate, X = scipy.io.wavfile.read(fn)

    fft_features = abs(scipy.fft(X)[:1000])
    np.save(Path(fn).with_suffix('.fft'), fft_features)

for wav_fn in Path(GENRE_DIR).glob('**/*.wav'):
    create_fft(wav_fn)
```

We save the data using NumPy's `save()` function, which always appends `.npy` to the filename. We only have to do this once for every WAV file needed for training or predicting.

The corresponding FFT reading function is `read_fft()`:

```
def read_fft(genre_list, base_dir=GENRE_DIR):
    X = []
    y = []
    for label, genre in enumerate(genre_list):
        genre_dir = Path(base_dir) / genre
        for fn in genre_dir.glob("*.fft.npy"):
            fft_features = np.load(fn)

            X.append(fft_features[:1000])
            y.append(label)

    return np.array(X), np.array(y)
```

In our scrambled `music` directory, we expect the following music genres:

```
GENRES = ["classical", "jazz", "country", "pop", "rock", "metal"]
```

Training the classifier

Let's use the logistic regression classifier, which has already served us well in the `Chapter 9, Classification II – Sentiment Analysis`:

```
from sklearn.linear_model.logistic import LogisticRegression
def create_model():
    return LogisticRegression()
```

Just to mention one surprising aspect: the evaluation of accuracy rates when first switching from binary to multiclass classification. In binary classification problems, we have learned that an accuracy of 50% is the worst case, as it could have been achieved by random guessing. In multiclass settings, 50% can already be very good. With our six genres, for instance, random guessing would result in only 16.7% (equal class sizes assumed).

The full training procedure now looks as follows:

```
from collections import defaultdict
from sklearn.metrics import precision_recall_curve, roc_curve, \
                             confusion_matrix
from sklearn.metrics import auc
from sklearn.model_selection import ShuffleSplit

def train_model(clf_factory, X, Y):
    labels = np.unique(Y)

    cv = ShuffleSplit(n_splits=1, test_size=0.3, random_state=0)
```

```
train_errors = []
test_errors = []

scores = []
pr_scores = defaultdict(list)
precisions = defaultdict(list)
recalls = defaultdict(list)
thresholds = defaultdict(list)

roc_scores = defaultdict(list)
tprs = defaultdict(list)
fprs = defaultdict(list)

clfs = [] # used to later get the median

cms = []

for train, test in cv:
    X_train, y_train = X[train], Y[train]
    X_test, y_test = X[test], Y[test]

    clf = clf_factory()
    clf.fit(X_train, y_train)
    clfs.append(clf)

    train_score = clf.score(X_train, y_train)
    test_score = clf.score(X_test, y_test)
    scores.append(test_score)

    train_errors.append(1 - train_score)
    test_errors.append(1 - test_score)

    y_pred = clf.predict(X_test)
    cm = confusion_matrix(y_test, y_pred) # will be explained soon
    cms.append(cm)

    for label in labels:
        y_label_test = np.asarray(y_test == label, dtype=int)
        proba = clf.predict_proba(X_test)
        proba_label = proba[:, label]

        precision, recall, pr_thresholds = preci-sion_recall_curve(
            y_label_test, proba_label)
        pr_scores[label].append(auc(recall, precision))
        precisions[label].append(precision)
        recalls[label].append(recall)
        thresholds[label].append(pr_thresholds)
```

```
        fpr, tpr, roc_thresholds = roc_curve(y_label_test,
                                           pro-ba_label)
        roc_scores[label].append(auc(fpr, tpr))
        tprs[label].append(tpr)
        fprs[label].append(fpr)

    all_pr_scores = np.asarray(pr_scores.values()).flatten()
    summary = (np.mean(scores), np.std(scores),
               np.mean(all_pr_scores), np.std(all_pr_scores))
    print("%.3f\t%.3f\t%.3f\t%.3f\t" % summary)

    return np.mean(train_errors), np.mean(test_errors), np.asarray(cms)
```

The whole training invocation is as follows:

```
X, Y = read_fft(GENRES)
train_avg, test_avg, cms = train_model(create_model, X, Y)
```

Using a confusion matrix to measure accuracy in multiclass problems

With multiclass problems, we shouldn't just be interested in how well we manage to correctly classify the genres. We should also look into which genres we confuse with each other. This can be done with the appropriately named confusion matrix, which you may have noticed is part of the training procedure:

```
>>> cm = confusion_matrix(y_test, y_pred)
```

If we print out the confusion matrix, we would see something like the following:

```
[[26  1  2  0  0  2]
 [ 4  7  5  0  5  3]
 [ 1  2 14  2  8  3]
 [ 5  4  7  3  7  5]
 [ 0  0 10  2 10 12]
 [ 1  0  4  0 13 12]]
```

This is the distribution of labels that the classifier predicted for the test set for every genre. The diagonal represents the correct classifications. Since we have six genres, we have a six-by-six matrix. The first row in the matrix says that for 31 classical songs (the sum of first row), it predicted 26 to belong to the classical genre, 1 to be a jazz song, 2 to be country, and 2 to be metal. The diagonal shows the correct classifications. In the first row, we see that out of *(26+1+2+2)*=31 songs, 26 have been correctly classified as classical and 5 were misclassifications. This is actually not that bad. The second row is more sobering: only 7 out of 24 jazz songs have been correctly classified–that is, only 29%.

Of course, we follow the train/test split setup from the previous chapters, so that we actually have to record the confusion matrices per cross-validation fold. We have to average and normalize later on, so that we have a range between 0 (total failure) and 1 (everything classified correctly).

A graphical visualization is often much easier to read than NumPy arrays. The `matshow()` function of `matplotlib` is our friend:

```
from matplotlib import pylab as plt

def plot_confusion_matrix(cm, genre_list, name, title):
    plt.clf()
    plt.matshow(cm, fignum=False, cmap='Blues', vmin=0, vmax=1.0)
    ax = plt.axes()
    ax.set_xticks(range(len(genre_list)))
    ax.set_xticklabels(genre_list)
    ax.xaxis.set_ticks_position("bottom")
    ax.set_yticks(range(len(genre_list)))
    ax.set_yticklabels(genre_list)
    ax.tick_params(axis='both', which='both', bottom='off', left='off')
    plt.title(title)
    plt.colorbar()
    plt.grid(False)
    plt.show()
    plt.xlabel('Predicted class')
    plt.ylabel('True class')
    plt.grid(False)
```

When you create a confusion matrix, be sure to choose a color map (the `cmap` parameter of `matshow()`) with an appropriate color ordering so that it is immediately visible what a lighter or darker color means. Especially discouraged for these kinds of graphs are rainbow color maps, such as, `matplotlib` instance default jet or even the paired color map.

The final graph looks like the following:

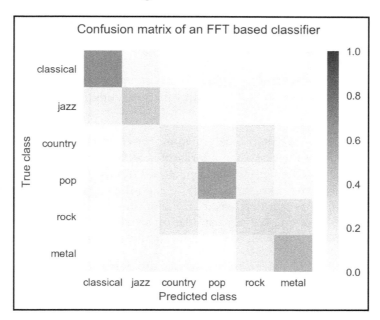

For a perfect classifier, we would have expected a diagonal of dark squares from the upper-left corner to the lower-right one, and light colors for the remaining areas. In the preceding graph, we immediately see that our FFT-based classifier is far from perfect. It only predicts classical songs correctly (dark square). For rock, for instance, it preferred the label metal most of the time.

Obviously, using FFT points us in the right direction (the classical genre was not that bad), but is not enough to get a decent classifier. Surely, we can play with the number of FFT components (fixed to 1,000). But before we dive into parameter tuning, we should do our research. There we find that FFT is indeed not a bad feature for genre classification–it is just not refined enough. Shortly, we will see how we can boost our classification performance by using a processed version of it.

Before we do that, however, we will learn another method of measuring classification performance.

An alternative way to measure classifier performance using receiver-operator characteristics

We already learned that measuring accuracy is not enough to truly evaluate a classifier. Instead, we relied on precision-recall (P/R) curves to get a deeper understanding of how our classifiers perform.

There is a sister of P/R curves, called **receiver-operator-characteristics (ROC)**, which measures similar aspects of the classifier's performance, but provides another view of the classification performance. The key difference is that P/R curves are more suitable for tasks where the positive class is much more interesting than the negative one or where the number of positive examples is much less than the number of negative ones. Information retrieval and fraud detection are typical application areas. On the other hand, ROC curves provide a better picture on how well the classifier behaves in general.

To better understand the differences, let's consider the performance of the previously trained classifier in classifying country songs correctly, as shown in the following graph:

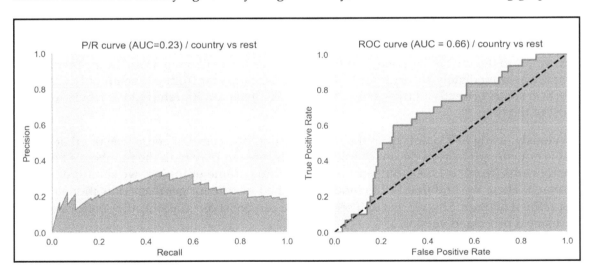

On the left, we see the P/R curve. For an ideal classifier, we would have the curve going from the top-left directly to the top-right and then to the bottom right, resulting in an **area-under-curve (AUC)** of 1.0.

The right graph depicts the corresponding ROC curve. It plots the **True Positive Rate (TPR)** over the **False Positive Rate (FPR)**. Here, an ideal classifier would have a curve going from the lower-left to the top-left, and then to the top-right. A random classifier would be a straight line from the lower-left to the upper-right, as shown by the dashed line, having an AUC of 0.5. Therefore, we cannot compare an AUC of a P/R curve with that of an ROC curve.

Independent of the curve, when comparing two different classifiers on the same dataset, we it is always safe to assume that a higher AUC of a P/R curve for one classifier also means a higher AUC of the corresponding ROC curve and vice versa. Hence, we never bother to generate both. More on this can be found in the very insightful paper *The Relationship Between Precision-Recall and ROC Curves,* by Davis and Goadrich (ICML, 2006).

The following table summarizes the differences between P/R and ROC curves:

	x axis	y axis
P/R	$Recall = \dfrac{TP}{TP + FN}$	$Precision = \dfrac{TP}{TP + FP}$
ROC	$FPR = \dfrac{FP}{FP + TN}$	$TPR = \dfrac{TP}{TP + FN}$

Looking at the definitions of the ' x and y axes, we see that the TPR in the ROC curve's y axis is the same as the Recall of the P/R graph's x axis.

The FPR measures the fraction of true negative examples that were falsely classified as positive ones, ranging from 0 in a perfect case (no `false` positives) to 1 (all are `false` positives).

Going forward, let's use ROC curves to measure our classifiers' performance to get a better feeling for it. The only challenge for our multiclass problem is that both ROC and P/R curves assume a binary classification problem. For our purpose, let's, therefore, create one chart per genre that shows how the classifier performed a one-versus-rest classification:

```
from sklearn.metrics import roc_curve
y_pred = clf.predict(X_test)for label in labels:
    y_label_test = np.asarray(y_test==label, dtype=int)
    proba = clf.predict_proba(X_test)
    proba_label = proba[:, label]

    # calculate false and true positive rates as well as the
    # ROC thresholds
    fpr, tpr, roc_thres = roc_curve(y_label_test, proba_label)

    # plot tpr over fpr ...
```

The outcomes are the following six ROC plots (again, for the full code, please follow the accompanying Jupyter notebook). As we have already found out, our first version of the classifier only performs well on classical songs. Looking at the individual ROC curves, however, tells us that we are really underperforming for most of the other genres. Only jazz and country provide some hope. The remaining genres are clearly not usable:

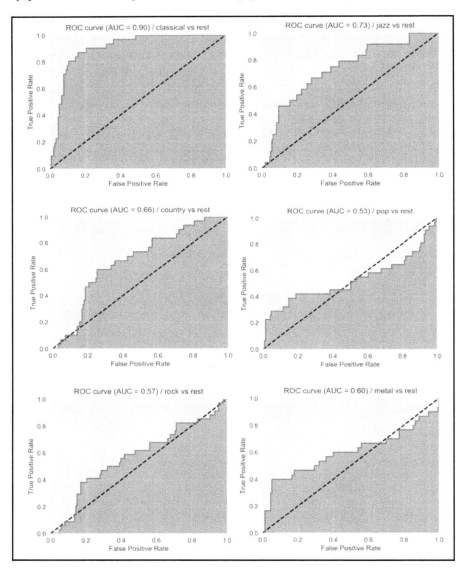

Improving classification performance with mel frequency cepstral coefficients

We already learned that FFT is pointing us in the right direction but in itself, will not be enough to finally arrive at a classifier that successfully manages to organize our scrambled directory of songs into individual genre directories. We need a more advanced version of it.

At this point, we have to do more research. Other people might have had similar challenges in the past and already found ways that might also help us. And, indeed, there is even a yearly conference dedicated to music-genre classification, organized by the International **Society for Music Information Retrieval (ISMIR)**. Apparently, **Automatic Music Genre Classification (AMGC)** is an established subfield of music information retrieval. Glancing over some of the AMGC papers, we can see that there is a bunch of work targeting automatic genre classification which might help us.

One technique that seems to be successfully applied in many cases is called **mel frequency cepstral (MFC)** coefficients. The MFC encodes the power spectrum of a sound, which is the power of each frequency the sound contains. It is calculated as the Fourier transform of the logarithm of the signal's spectrum. If that sounds too complicated, simply remember that the name cepstrum originates from spectrum, with the first four characters reversed. MFC has been successfully used in speech and speaker recognition. Let's see whether it also works for us. We are fortunate in that someone else already needed exactly this and published an implementation of it as part of the `python_speech_features` module. We can install it easily with `pip`. Afterward, we can call the `mfcc()` function, which calculates MFC coefficients, as follows:

```
>>> from python_speech_features import mfcc

>>> fn = Path(GENRE_DIR) / 'jazz' / 'jazz.00000.wav'
>>> sample_rate, X = scipy.io.wavfile.read(fn)
>>> ceps = mfcc(X)
>>> print(ceps.shape)
  (4135, 13)
```

ceps contains 13 coefficients (the default value for the num_ceps parameter of mfcc()) for each of the 4135 frames for the song. Taking all of the data would overwhelm our classifier. What we could do, instead, is an averaging per coefficient over all the frames. Assuming that the start and end of each song is possibly less genre-specific than the middle part of it, we also ignore the first and last 10 percent:

```
>>> num_ceps = ceps.shape[0]
>>> np.mean(ceps[int(num_ceps*0.1):int(num_ceps*0.9)], axis=0)
array([ 16.43787597, 7.44767565, -13.48062285, -7.49451887,
        -8.14466849, -4.79407047, -5.53101133, -5.42776074,
        -8.69278344, -6.41223865, -3.01527269, -2.75974429, -3.61836327])
```

Sure enough, the benchmark dataset we will be using contains only the first 30 seconds of each song, so we don't need to cut off the last 10 percent. We do it anyway, so that our code works on other datasets as well, which are most likely not truncated.

Similar to our work with FFT, we also want to cache the once-generated MFCC features and read them, instead of recreating them each time we train our classifier.

This leads to the following code:

```
def create_ceps(fn):
    sample_rate, X = scipy.io.wavfile.read(fn)
    np.save(Path(fn).with_suffix('.ceps'), mfcc(X))

for wav_fn in Path(GENRE_DIR).glob('**/*.wav'):
    create_fft(wav_fn)
def read_ceps(genre_list, base_dir=GENRE_DIR):
    X = []
    y = []
    for label, genre in enumerate(genre_list):
        genre_dir = Path(base_dir) / genre
        for fn in genre_dir.glob("*.ceps.npy"):
            ceps = np.load(fn)
            num_ceps = len(ceps)
            X.append(np.mean(ceps[int(num_ceps / 10):int(num_ceps * 9 /
10)], axis=0))
            y.append(label)

    return np.array(X), np.array(y)
```

We get the following promising results with a classifier that uses only 13 features per song:

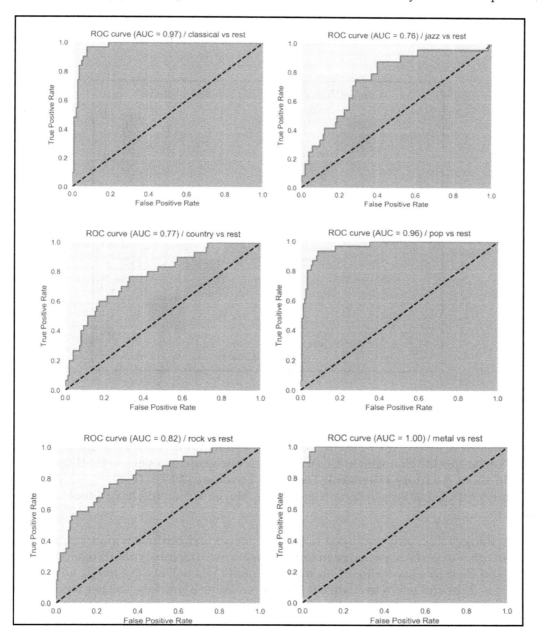

The classification performance for all genres has improved. Classical and metal are at almost 1.0 AUC. And indeed, the confusion matrix in the following plot looks much better now. We can clearly see the diagonal, showing that the classifier manages to classify the genres correctly in most cases. This classifier is actually quite usable for solving our initial task:

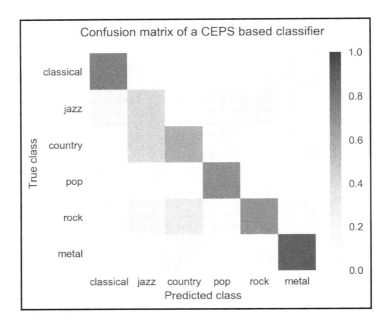

If we want to improve on this, this confusion matrix tells us quickly what to focus on: the non-white spots on the non-diagonal places. For instance, we have a darker spot where we mislabelled rock songs as being jazz with considerable probability. To fix this, we would probably need to dive deeper into the songs and extract things such as drum patterns and similar genre-specific characteristics. And then, while glancing over the ISMIR papers, we also read about **Auditory Filterbank Temporal Envelope** (**AFTE**) features, which seem to outperform MFCC features in certain situations. Maybe we should have a look at them as well?

The nice thing is that, only equipped with ROC curves and confusion matrices, we are free to pull in other experts' knowledge in terms of feature extractors without having to fully understand their inner workings. Our measurement tools will always tell us when the direction is right and when to change it. Of course, being a machine learner who is eager to learn, we will always have the feeling that there is an exciting algorithm buried somewhere in a black box of our feature extractors, just waiting for us to be understood.

Music classification using Tensorflow

Can we use our features to feed into TensorFlow? Of course! But let's try to use this opportunity to achieve two other goals:

- We will make the TensforFlow classifier behave like a `sklearn` one to be reused in all the compatible functions.
- Even if neural networks can extract any feature, they still need to be designed and trained to extract them. In this example, starting from the original sound file, we will show you that it is not enough to get better results than the cepstral coefficients.

But let's cut to the chase and set our hyperparameters:

```
import tensorflow as tf
import numpy as np

n_epochs = 50
learning_rate = 0.01
batch_size = 128
step = 32
dropout_rate = 0.2

signal_size = 1000
signal_shape = [signal_size,1]
```

We start with our 600 samples, but to add more data to the training, we will split our file into chunks:

```
def read_wav(genre_list, multiplicity=1, base_dir=GENRE_DIR):
    X = []
    y = []
    for label, genre in enumerate(genre_list):
        genre_dir = Path(base_dir) / genre
        for fn in genre_dir.glob("*.wav"):
            sample_rate, new_X = scipy.io.wavfile.read(fn)
            for i in range(multiplicity):
                X.append(new_X[i*signal_size:(i+1)*signal_size])
                y.append(label)

    return np.array(X).reshape((-1, signal_size, 1)), np.array(y)
```

From each file, we will get 20 shorter samples:

```
from sklearn.model_selection import train_test_split

X, Y = read_wav(GENRES, 20)
classes = len(GENRES)
X_train, X_test, Y_train, Y_test = train_test_split(X, Y,
                                        test_size=(1. / 6.))
```

Our network will be very similar to the image classification one. Instead of 2D convolutional layers, we will use 1D layers. We will also add a parameter for getting the pool size. The previous networks were using small 2D pools, we will probably have to use larger pools.

We will also use a dropout layer. As we don't have many samples, we have to avoid the network to generalize poorly. This will help us achieve this purpose:

```
class CNN():
    def __init__(
            self,
            signal_shape=[1000,1],
            dim_W1=64,
            dim_W2=32,
            dim_W3=16,
            classes=6,
            kernel_size=5,
            pool_size=16
            ):

        self.signal_shape = signal_shape

        self.dim_W1 = dim_W1
        self.dim_W2 = dim_W2
        self.dim_W3 = dim_W3
        self.classes = classes
        self.kernel_size = kernel_size
        self.pool_size = pool_size

    def build_model(self):
        image = tf.placeholder(tf.float32, [None]+self.signal_shape,
    name="signal")
        Y = tf.placeholder(tf.int64, [None], name="label")

        probabilities = self.discriminate(image, training)
        cost =
    tf.reduce_mean(tf.nn.sparse_softmax_cross_entropy_with_logits(labels=Y,
                logits=probabilities))
        accuracy = tf.reduce_mean(tf.cast(tf.equal(tf.argmax(probabilities,
```

```
ax-is=1),
                        Y), tf.float32), name="accuracy")

        return image, Y, cost, accuracy, probabilities
```

Here, we reuse the `sparse_softmax_cross_entropy_with_logits` cost-helper function that we saw in `Chapter 8`, *Artificial Neural Networks and Deep Learning*. As a reminder, it compares an integer target to a layer so that the node with the maximum value matches this target:

```
def create_conv1d(self, input, filters, kernel_size, name):
    layer = tf.layers.conv1d(
                inputs=input,
                filters=filters,
                kernel_size=kernel_size,
                activation=tf.nn.leaky_relu,
                name="Conv1d_" + name,
                padding="same")
    return layer
def create_maxpool(self, input, name):
    layer = tf.layers.max_pooling1d(
                inputs=input,
                pool_size=[self.pool_size],
                strides=self.pool_size,
                name="MaxPool_" + name)
    return layer

def create_dropout(self, input, name, is_training):
    layer = tf.layers.dropout(
                inputs=input,
                rate=dropout_rate,
                name="DropOut_" + name,
                training=is_training)
    return layer

def create_dense(self, input, units, name):
    layer = tf.layers.dense(
                inputs=input,
                units=units,
                name="Dense" + name,
                )
    layer = tf.layers.batch_normalization(
                inputs=layer,
                momentum=0,
                epsilon=1e-8,
                training=True,
                name="BatchNorm_" + name,
                )
```

```
        layer = tf.nn.leaky_relu(layer, name="LeakyRELU_" + name)
        return layer

    def discriminate(self, signal, training):
        h1 = self.create_conv1d(signal, self.dim_W3, self.kernel_size,
"Layer1")
        h1 = self.create_maxpool(h1, "Layer1")

        h2 = self.create_conv1d(h1, self.dim_W2, self.kernel_size,
"Layer2")
        h2 = self.create_maxpool(h2, "Layer2")
        h2 = tf.reshape(h2, (-1, self.dim_W2 * h2.shape[1]))

        h3 = self.create_dense(h2, self.dim_W1, "Layer3")
        h3 = self.create_dropout(h3, "Layer3", training)
        h4 = self.create_dense(h3, self.classes, "Layer4")
        return h4
```

As we said before, it is possible to encapsulate our network inside a sklearn object, BaseEstimator. These estimators have a set of parameters that are extracted from the constructor, as we can see here:

```
from sklearn.base import BaseEstimator

class Classifier(BaseEstimator):
    def __init__(self,
            signal_shape=[1000,1],
            dim_W1=64,
            dim_W2=32,
            dim_W3=16,
            classes=6,
            kernel_size=5,
            pool_size=16):
        self.signal_shape=signal_shape
        self.dim_W1=dim_W1
        self.dim_W2=dim_W2
        self.dim_W3=dim_W3
        self.classes=classes
        self.kernel_size=kernel_size
        self.pool_size=pool_size
```

The `fit` method is the one that creates and trains the model. Here we also save the network and the state of the variables:

```
def fit(self, X, y):
    tf.reset_default_graph()

    print("Fitting (W1=%i) (W2=%i) (W3=%i) (kernel=%i) (pool=%i)"
           % (self.dim_W1, self.dim_W2, self.dim_W3, self.kernel_size,
self.pool_size))
    cnn_model = CNN(
              signal_shape=self.signal_shape,
              dim_W1=self.dim_W1,
              dim_W2=self.dim_W2,
              dim_W3=self.dim_W3,
              classes=self.classes,
              kernel_size=self.kernel_size,
              pool_size=self.pool_size
              )

    signal_tf, Y_tf, cost_tf, accuracy_tf, output_tf =
cnn_model.build_model()
    train_step = tf.train.AdamOptimizer(learning_rate, be-
ta1=0.5).minimize(cost_tf)

    saver = tf.train.Saver()
    with tf.Session() as sess:
        sess.run(tf.global_variables_initializer())
        for epoch in range(n_epochs):
            permut = np.random.permutation(len(X_train))
            for j in range(0, len(X_train), batch_size):
                batch = permut[j:j+batch_size]
                Xs = X_train[batch]
                Ys = Y_train[batch]

                sess.run(train_step,
                        feed_dict={
                            Y_tf: Ys,
                            signal_tf: Xs
                            })
        saver.save(sess, './classifier')
    return self
```

They are then restored in the `predict` method, where we will use the trained network to classify new data:

```
def predict(self, X):
    tf.reset_default_graph()
    new_saver = tf.train.import_meta_graph("classifier.meta")
    with tf.Session() as sess:
        new_saver.restore(sess, tf.train.latest_checkpoint('./'))

        graph = tf.get_default_graph()
        training_tf = graph.get_tensor_by_name('is_training:0')
        signal_tf = graph.get_tensor_by_name('signal:0')
        output_tf =
graph.get_tensor_by_name('LeakyRELU_Layer4/Maximum:0')
        predict = sess.run(output_tf,
                        feed_dict={
                            training_tf: False,
                            signal_tf: X
                        })
        return np.argmax(predict, axis=1)
```

We haven't created a `score` method in this estimator, but we can create one from the `predict` method with the `sklearn` API.

Now we will use this estimator and do a grid search to find an appropriate set of hyperparameters. As we don't have many samples, we will use only a handful of units on each convolutional layer as well as for the dense layer. We also want to extract better filters. After all, sounds usually requires bigger filters to extract meaningful features:

```
from sklearn.model_selection import GridSearchCV
from sklearn.metrics import accuracy_score, make_scorer

param_grid = {
    "dim_W1": [4, 8, 16],
    "dim_W2": [4, 8, 16],
    "dim_W3": [4, 8, 16],
    "kernel_size":[7, 11, 15],
    "pool_size":[8, 12, 16],
}

cv = GridSearchCV(Classifier(), param_grid, scor-
ing=make_scorer(accuracy_score), cv=6)
```

```
cv.fit(X, Y)
print(cv.best_params_)

{'dim_W1': 4, 'dim_W2': 4, 'dim_W3': 16, 'kernel_size': 15, 'pool_size':
12}
```

Now that we have spent hours finding an adequate set of hyperprameters, we can use it to check the confusion matrix:

```
clf = Classifier(**cv.best_params_)
clf.fit(X_train, Y_train)

Y_train_predict = clf.predict(X_train)
Y_test_predict = clf.predict(X_test)

from sklearn.metrics import confusion_matrix
cm = confusion_matrix(Y_train, Y_train_predict)
plot_confusion_matrix(cm / np.sum(cm, axis=0), GENRES, "CNN",
    "Confusion matrix of a CNN based classifier (train)")
cm = confusion_matrix(Y_test, Y_test_predict)
plot_confusion_matrix(cm / np.sum(cm, axis=0), GENRES, "CNN",
    "Confusion matrix of a CNN based classifier (test)")
```

Refer to the following graphs:

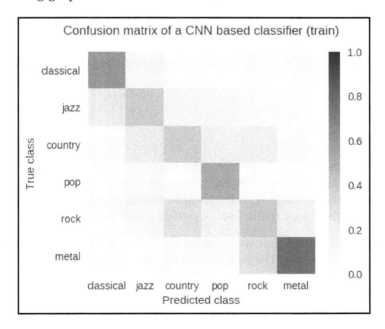

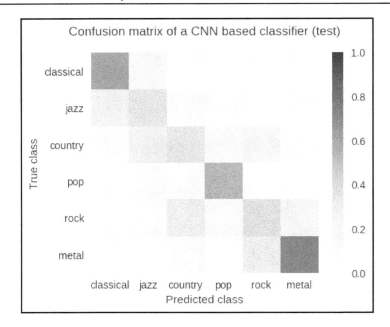

Even with the best parameters, this shows what we said before: you also need to have adequate features. You can throw computer power to train a fancier network, but you will also need more data.

Try this network (or one with a different layer configuration) on the cepstral features. Can it achieve a better classification? Can it match the best `LogisticRegression` classifier we created earlier? Let's find out!

Summary

In this chapter, we stepped out of our comfort zone when we built a music-genre classifier. Not having a deep understanding of music theory, at first we failed to train a classifier that predicts the music genre of songs with reasonable accuracy using FFT. But, then, we created a classifier that showed really usable performance using MFC features.

In both cases, we used features that we understood only enough to know how and where to put them in our classifier setup. The first one failed, and the second succeeded. The difference between them is that in the second case, we relied on features that were created by experts in the field.

And that is totally OK. If we are mainly interested in the result, we sometimes simply have to take shortcuts–we just have to make sure that these shortcuts are from domain-specific experts. And because we've learned how to correctly measure performance in this new multi-class classification problem, we took these shortcuts with confidence.

In Chapter 12, *Computer Vision*, will take a look at image processing, feature representations, CNN, and GAN.

12
Computer Vision

Image analysis and computer vision have always been important in industrial and scientific applications. With the popularization of cell phones with powerful cameras and internet connections, images are now increasingly generated by consumers. Therefore, there are opportunities to make use of computer vision to provide a better user experience in new contexts.

In this chapter, we will look at how to apply several techniques you have learned about in the rest of this book to this specific type of data. In particular, we will learn how to use the `mahotas` computer vision package to extract features from images. These features can then be used as input to the same classification methods we studied in other chapters. We will apply these techniques to publicly available datasets of photographs. We will also see how the same features can be used for finding similar images. We will also learn about using local features. These are relatively generic and achieve very good results in many tasks (although they have a higher computational cost).

Finally, at the end of the chapter, we will use Tensorflow to generate new images based on an existing dataset. In particular, in this chapter we will do the following:

- Learn how to represent and manipulate images as NumPy arrays
- Learn how to represent images as a small set of features so that standard classification and clustering methods can be used on this data type
- Learn how to use visual words to generate another type of feature
- Learn how to generate new images similar to existing ones

Introducing image processing

From the point of view of the computer, an image is a large rectangular array of pixel values. Our goal is to process one or more image and to arrive at a decision for our application.

Depending on the setting, it may be a classification problem, a clustering problem, or any of the other problem classes we have seen in the book.

The first step will be to load the image from disk, where it is typically stored in an image-specific format such as PNG or JPEG, the former being a lossless compression format and the latter a lossy compression, one that is optimized for visual assessment of photographs. Then, we may wish to perform preprocessing on the images (for example, normalizing them for illumination variations).

Loading and displaying images

In order to manipulate images, we will use a package called `mahotas`. You can obtain `mahotas` through anaconda and read its manual at `https://mahotas.readthedocs.io`. Mahotas is an open source package (it has an MIT license, so it can be used in any project) and was developed by one of the authors of this book. It is based on NumPy. Thus, the NumPy knowledge you have acquired so far can be used for image processing. There are other image packages, such as **scikit-image** (**skimage**), the **n-dimensional image** (**ndimage**) module in SciPy, and the Python bindings for OpenCV. All of these work natively with NumPy arrays, so you can even mix and match functionality from different packages to build a combined pipeline.

We start by importing `mahotas` with the `mh` abbreviation, which we will use throughout this chapter, as follows:

```
import mahotas as mh
```

Now, we can load an image file using `imread` as follows:

```
image = mh.imread('scene00.jpg')
```

The `scene00.jpg` file (this file is contained in the dataset available in this book's companion code repository) is a color image of height `h` and width `w`; the image will be an array of shape `(h, w, 3)`. The first dimension is the height, the second is the width, and the third is red/green/blue. Other systems put the width in the first dimension, but this is the convention that is used by all NumPy-based packages. The type of array will typically be `np.uint8` (an unsigned 8-bit integer). These are the images that your camera takes and that your monitor can fully display.

Some specialized equipment, used in scientific and technical applications, can take images with a higher bit resolution (that is, with more sensitivity to small variations in brightness). 12 or 16 bits are common in this type of equipment. Mahotas can deal with all these types, including floating point images. In many computations, even if the original data is composed of unsigned integers, it is advantageous to convert to floating point numbers in order to simplify the handling of rounding and overflow issues.

Mahotas can use a variety of different input/output backends. Unfortunately, none of them can load all image formats that exist (there are hundreds, with several variations of each). However, the loading of PNG and JPEG images is supported by all of them. We will focus on these common formats and refer you to the `mahotas` documentation on how to read uncommon formats.

We can display the image on screen using `matplotlib`, and the `plotting` library we have already used several times, as follows:

```
from matplotlib import pyplot as plt
fig,ax = plt.subplots()
ax.imshow(image)
```

As shown in the following screenshot, this code shows the image using the convention that the first dimension is the height and the second the width. It correctly handles color images as well. When using Python for numerical computation, we benefit from the whole ecosystem working well together: `mahotas` works with NumPy arrays, which can be displayed with matplotlib. Later, we will compute features from images to use with scikit-learn:

Thresholding

We start this chapter with some simple image processing manipulations. These will not use machine learning, but the goal is to demonstrate that images can be manipulated as arrays. This will later be useful when we introduce new features.

Thresholding is a very simple operation: we transform all pixel values above a certain threshold to 1 and all those below it to 0 (or by using Booleans, transform them to `True` and `False`). The important question in thresholding is to select a good value to use as the threshold limit. Mahotas implements a few methods for choosing a threshold value from the image. We will use a method called `Otsu` after its inventor. The first necessary step is to convert the image to grayscale, with `rgb2gray` in the `mahotas.colors` submodule.

Instead of `rgb2gray`, we could also have just the mean value of the red, green, and blue channels, by calling `image.mean(2)`. The result, however, would not be the same, as `rgb2gray` uses different weights for the different colors to give a subjectively more pleasing result. Our eyes are not equally sensitive to the three basic colors:

```
image = mh.colors.rgb2grey(image, dtype=np.uint8)
fig,ax = plt.subplots()
ax.imshow(image) # Display the image
```

By default, matplotlib will display this single-channel image as a false color image, using red for high values and blue for low values. For natural images, grayscale is more appropriate. You can select it with:

```
plt.gray()
```

Now the image is shown in grayscale. Note that only the way in which the pixel values are interpreted and shown has changed and the image data is untouched. We can continue our processing by computing the threshold value. Thresholding is a form of two-class clustering and there are several methods for this task. `Otsu` is one such `thresholding` method, which attempts to find two compact groups of pixels, those above and those below the threshold:

```
thresh = mh.thresholding.otsu(image)
print('Otsu threshold is {}.'.format(thresh))
Otsu threshold is 138.

fig,ax = plt.subplots()
ax.imshow(image > thresh)
```

When applied to the previous image, this method finds the `threshold` to be `138`, which separates the ground from the sky above, as shown in the following screenshot:

Gaussian blurring

Blurring your image may seem odd, but it often serves to reduce noise, which helps with further processing. With `mahotas`, it is just a function call:

```
im16 = mh.gaussian_filter(image, 16)
```

Notice that we did not convert the grayscale image to unsigned integers; we just made use of the floating point result as is. The second argument to the `gaussian_filter` function is the size of the filter (the standard deviation of the filter). Larger values result in more blurring, as shown in the following screenshot:

We can use the preceding screenshot and the `threshold` with `Otsu` (using the previous code). Now, the boundaries are smoother, without the jagged edges, as shown in the following screenshot:

Putting the center in focus

The final example shows you how to mix NumPy operators with a tiny bit of filtering to get an interesting result. We start with a photo of a path in the forest:

```
im = mh.imread('forest')
```

To split the red, green, and blue channels, we use the following code. The NumPy transpose method changes the order of axes in a multi-dimensional array:

```
r,g,b = im.transpose(2,0,1)
```

Now, we filter the three channels separately and build a composite image out of it with mh.as_rgb. This function takes three two-dimensional arrays, performs contrast stretching to make each an 8-bit integer array, and then stacks them, returning a color RGB image:

```
r24 = mh.gaussian_filter(r, 24.)
g24 = mh.gaussian_filter(g, 24.)
b24 = mh.gaussian_filter(b, 24.)
im24 = mh.as_rgb(r24, g24, b24)
```

Now, we blend the two images from the center away to the edges. First, we need to build a weights array W, which will contain at each pixel a normalized value, which is its distance to the center:

```
h, w = r.shape # height and width
Y, X = np.mgrid[:h, :w]
```

We used the `np.mgrid` object, which returns arrays of size (h, w), with values corresponding to the *y* and *x* coordinates, respectively. The next steps are as follows:

```
Y = Y - h/2. # center at h/2
Y = Y / Y.max() # normalize to -1 .. +1

X = X - w/2.
X = X / X.max()
```

We now use a Gaussian function to give the center region a high value:

```
C = np.exp(-2.*(X**2+ Y**2))

# Normalize again to 0..1
C = C - C.min()
C = C / C.ptp()
C = C[:,:,None] # This adds a dummy third dimension to C
```

Notice that all of these manipulations are performed using NumPy arrays and not some `mahotas`-specific methodology:

```
ringed = mh.stretch(im*C + (1-C)*im24)
```

Finally, we can combine the two images to have the center be in sharp focus and the edges softer:

Basic image classification

We will start with a small dataset that was collected especially for this book. It has three classes: buildings, natural scenes (landscapes), and pictures of text. There are 30 images in each category, and they were all taken using a cell phone camera with minimal composition. The images are similar to those that would be uploaded to a modern website by users with no photography training. This dataset is available in the companion code repository. Later in this chapter, we will look at a larger dataset with more images and more categories that are more difficult to classify.

When classifying images, we start with a large rectangular array of numbers (pixel values). Nowadays, millions of pixels are common. We could try to feed all these numbers as features into the learning algorithm. This is not a very good idea unless you have a lot of data. This is because the relationship of each pixel (or even each small group of pixels) to the final result is very indirect. Also, having millions of pixels, but only as a small number of example images, results in a very hard statistical learning problem. This is an extreme form of the P greater than N type of problem we discussed in `Chapter 3`, *Regression*. Instead, a good approach for smaller problems is to compute features from the image and use those features for classification.

We previously used an example of the scene class. The following are examples of the text and building classes:

Computing features from images

With `mahotas`, it is very easy to compute features from images. There is a submodule named `mahotas.features`, where feature computation functions are available.

A commonly used set of texture features is the Haralick set. As with many methods in image processing, the name honors its inventor. These features are texture-based; they distinguish between images that are smooth and those that are patterned, and between different patterns. With `mahotas`, it is very easy to compute them as follows:

```
haralick_features = mh.features.haralick(image)
haralick_features_mean = np.mean(haralick_features, axis=0)
haralick_features_all = np.ravel(haralick_features)
```

The `mh.features.haralick` function returns a 4 x 13 array. The first dimension refers to four possible directions in which to compute the features (vertical, horizontal, diagonal, and anti-diagonal). If we are not interested in the direction specifically, we can use the average over all the directions (shown in the earlier code as `haralick_features_mean`). Otherwise, we can use all the features separately (using `haralick_features_all`). This decision should be informed by the properties of the dataset. In our case, we reason that the horizontal and vertical directions should be kept separately. Therefore, we will use `haralick_features_all`.

There are a few other feature sets implemented in `mahotas`. Linear binary patterns are another texture-based feature set, which is very robust against illumination changes. There are other types of features, including local features, which we will discuss later in this chapter.

With these features, we use a standard classification method such as `logistic regression`, as follows:

```
from glob import glob
images = glob('SimpleImageDataset/*.jpg')
features = []
labels = []
for im in images:
    labels.append(im[:-len('00.jpg')])
    im = mh.imread(im)
    im = mh.colors.rgb2gray(im, dtype=np.uint8)
    features.append(mh.features.haralick(im).ravel())

features = np.array(features)
labels = np.array(labels)
```

The three classes have very different textures. Buildings have sharp edges and big blocks where the color is similar (the pixel values are rarely exactly the same, but the variation is slight). Text is made of many sharp dark-light transitions, with small black areas in a sea of white. Natural scenes have smoother variations with fractal-like transitions. Therefore, a classifier based on texture is expected to do well.

We are going to use a logistic regression classifier as a classifier, with preprocessing of the features, as follows:

```
from sklearn.pipeline import Pipeline
from sklearn.preprocessing import StandardScaler
from sklearn.linear_model import LogisticRegression
clf = Pipeline([('preproc', StandardScaler()),
                ('classifier', LogisticRegression())])
```

Since our dataset is small, we can use leave-one-out regression as follows:

```
from sklearn import model_selection
cv = model_selection.LeaveOneOut()
scores = model_selection.cross_val_score(clf, features, labels, cv=cv)
print('Accuracy: {:.1%}'.format(scores.mean()))
Accuracy: 81.1%
```

81 percent is not bad for the three classes (random guessing would correspond to 33 percent). We can do better by writing our own features.

Writing your own features

A feature is nothing magical. It is simply a number that we computed from an image. There are several feature sets already defined in literature. These often have the added advantage that they have been designed and studied to be invariant to many unimportant factors. For example, linear binary patterns are completely invariant to multiplying all pixel values by a number or adding a constant to all these values. This makes this feature set robust against illumination changes.

However, it is also possible that your particular use case would benefit from a few specially designed features.

A simple type of feature that is not shipped with mahotas is a color histogram. Fortunately, this feature is easy to implement. A color histogram partitions the color space into a set of bins, and then counts how many pixels fall into each of the bins.

The images are in RGB format, that is, each pixel has three values: R for red, G for green, and B for blue. Since each of these components is an 8-bit value, the total is 17 million different colors. We are going to reduce this number to only 64 colors by grouping colors into bins. We will write a function to encapsulate this algorithm as follows:

```
def chist(im):
```

To bin the colors, we first divide the image by `64`, rounding down the pixel values as follows:

```
im = im // 64
```

This makes the pixel values range from zero to three, which gives us a total of `64` different colors.

Separate the red, green, and blue channels as follows:

```
r,g,b = im.transpose((2,0,1))
pixels = 1 * r + 4 * b + 16 * g
hist = np.bincount(pixels.ravel(), minlength=64)
hist = hist.astype(float)
```

Convert to log scale, as seen in the following code snippet. This is not strictly necessary, but makes for better features. We use `np.log1p`, which computes *log(h+1)*. This ensures that zero values are kept as zero values (mathematically, the logarithm of zero is not defined, and NumPy prints a warning if you attempt to compute it):

```
hist = np.log1p(hist)
return hist
```

We can adapt the previous processing code to use the function we wrote very easily:

```
features = []
for im in images:
    image = mh.imread(im)
    features.append(chist(im))
```

Using the same cross-validation code we used earlier, we obtain 90 percent accuracy. The best results, however, come from combining all the features, which we can implement as follows:

```
features = []
for im in images:
    imcolor = mh.imread(im)
    im = mh.colors.rgb2gray(imcolor, dtype=np.uint8)
    features.append(np.concatenate([
            mh.features.haralick(im).ravel(),
```

```
        chist(imcolor),
    ]))
```

By using all of these features, we get 95.6 percent accuracy, as shown in the following code snippet:

```
scores = model_selection.cross_val_score(
    clf, features, labels, cv=cv)
print('Accuracy: {:.1%}'.format(scores.mean()))
Accuracy: 95.6%
```

This is a perfect illustration of the principle that good algorithms are the easy part. You can always use an implementation of state-of-the-art classification from scikit-learn. The real secret and added value often comes in feature design and engineering. This is where knowledge of your dataset is valuable.

Using features to find similar images

The basic concept of representing an image by a relatively small number of features can be used for more than just classification. For example, we can also use it to find similar images to a given query image (as we did before with text documents).

We will compute the same features as before, with one important difference: we will ignore the bordering area of the picture. The reason is that, due to the amateur nature of the compositions, the edges of the picture often contain irrelevant elements. When the features are computed over the whole image, these elements are taken into account. By simply ignoring them, we get slightly better features. In the supervised example, it is not as important, as the learning algorithm will then learn which features are more informative and weigh them accordingly. When working in an unsupervised fashion, we need to be more careful to ensure that our features are capturing important elements of the data. This is implemented in a loop as follows:

```
features = []
for im in images:
    imcolor = mh.imread(im)
    # ignore everything in the 200 pixels closest to the borders
    imcolor = imcolor[200:-200, 200:-200]
    im = mh.colors.rgb2gray(imcolor, dtype=np.uint8)
    features.append(np.concatenate([
            mh.features.haralick(im).ravel(),
            chist(imcolor),
        ]))
```

We now normalize the features and compute the distance matrix as follows:

```
sc = StandardScaler()
features = sc.fit_transform(features)
from scipy.spatial import distance
dists = distance.squareform(distance.pdist(features))
```

We will plot just a subset of the data (every 10th element) so that the query will be on top and the returned nearest neighbor at the bottom, as shown in the following code :

```
fig, axes = plt.subplots(2, 9)
for ci,i in enumerate(range(0,90,10)):
    query = images[i]
    dists_query = dists[i]
    closest = dists_query.argsort()
    # closest[0] is same as the query image, so pick next closest
    closest = closest[1]
    result = images[closest]
    query = mh.imread(query)
    result = mh.imread(result)
    axes[0, ci].imshow(query)
    axes[1, ci].imshow(result)
```

The result is shown in the following screenshot (the top image is the query image and the bottom image the returned result):

It is clear that the system is not perfect, but can find images that are at least visually similar to the queries. In all but one case, the image found comes from the same class as the query.

Classifying a harder dataset

The previous dataset was an easy dataset for classification using texture features. In fact, many of the problems that are interesting from a business point of view are relatively easy. However, sometimes we may be faced with a tougher problem and need better and more modern techniques to get good results.

We will now test a public dataset, which has the same structure: several photographs split into a small number of classes. The classes are animals, cars, transportation, and natural scenes.

When compared to the three-class problem we discussed previously, these classes are harder to tell apart. Natural scenes, buildings, and text have very different textures. In this dataset, however, texture and color are not clear markers of the image class. The following is one example from the animal class:

And here is another example from the car class:

Both objects are against natural backgrounds, and with large, smooth areas inside the objects. This is a harder problem than the previous dataset, so we will need to use more advanced methods. The first improvement will be to use a slightly more powerful classifier. The logistic regression that scikit-learn provides is a penalized form of logistic regression, which contains an adjustable parameter, C. By default, C = 1.0, but this may not be optimal. We can use a grid search to find a good value for this parameter as follows:

```
from sklearn.grid_search import GridSearchCV
C_range = 10.0 ** np.arange(-4, 3)
grid = GridSearchCV(LogisticRegression(), param_grid={'C' : C_range})
clf = Pipeline([('preproc', StandardScaler()),
                ('classifier', grid)])
```

The data is not organized in a random order inside the dataset: similar images are close together. Thus, we use a cross-validation schedule that considers the data shuffled so that each fold has a more representative training set, as shown in the following code:

```
cv = model_selection.KFold(n_splits=5,
                    shuffle=True, random_state=123)
scores = model_selection.cross_val_score(
    clf, ifeatures, labels, cv=cv)
print('Accuracy: {:.1%}'.format(scores.mean()))
Accuracy: 73.4%
```

This is not so bad for four classes, but we will now see if we can do better by using a different set of features. In fact, we will see that we need to combine these features with other methods to get the best possible results.

Local feature representations

Unlike the previous features we used, local features are computed on a small region of the image. Mahotas supports computing types of features called **Speeded Up Robust Features** (**SURF**). These features are designed to be robust against rotational or illumination changes (that is, they only change their values slightly when illumination changes).

When using these features, we have to decide where to compute them. There are three possibilities that are commonly used:

- Randomly
- In a grid
- Detecting interesting areas of the image (a technique known as keypoint detection or interest point detection)

All of these are valid and will, under the right circumstances, give good results. Mahotas supports all three. Using interest point detection works best if you have a reason to expect that your interest point will correspond to areas of importance in the image.

We will be using the `interest point` method. Computing the features with `mahotas` is easy: import the right submodule and call the `surf.surf` function as follows:

```
descriptors = surf.surf(im, descriptor_only=True)
```

The `descriptors_only=True` flag means that we are only interested in the local features themselves, and not in their pixel location, size, or orientation (the word `descriptor` is often used to refer to these local features). Alternatively, we could have used the `dense sampling` method, using the `surf.dense` function as follows:

```
from mahotas.features import surf
descriptors = surf.dense(im, spacing=16)
```

This returns the value of the descriptors computed on points that are at a distance of 24 pixels from each other. Since the position of the points is fixed, the meta information on the interest points is not very interesting and is not returned by default. In either case, the result (descriptors) is an nx 64 array, where *n* is the number of points sampled. The number of points depends on the size of your images, their content, and the parameters you pass to the functions. In this example, we are using the default settings, and we obtain a few hundred descriptors per image.

We cannot directly feed these descriptors to a support vector machine, logistic regressor, or similar classification system. In order to use the descriptors from the images, there are several solutions. We could just average them, but the results of doing so are not very good as they throw away all location-specific information. In that case, we would have just another global feature set based on edge measurements.

The solution we will use here is the **bag of words** model. It was published first in 2004, but this is one of those obvious-in-hindsight ideas; it is very simple to implement and achieves very good results.

It may seem strange to speak of *words* when dealing with images. It may be easier to understand if you think that you don't have written words, which are easy to distinguish from each other, but orally spoken audio. Now, each time a word is spoken, it will sound slightly different, and different speakers will have their own pronunciation. Thus, a word's waveform will not be identical every time it is spoken. However, by using clustering on these waveforms, we can hope to recover most of the structure so that all the instances of a given word are in the same cluster. Even if the process is not perfect (and it will not be), we can still talk of grouping the waveforms into words.

We perform the same operation with image data: we cluster together similar-looking regions from all images and call these **visual words**.

The number of words used does not usually have a big impact on the final performance of the algorithm. Naturally, if the number is extremely small (10 or 20, when you have a few thousand images), then the overall system will not perform well. Similarly, if you have too many words (many more than the number of images, for example), the system will also not perform well. However, in between these two extremes, there is often a very large plateau, where you can choose the number of words without a big impact on the result. As a rule of thumb, using a value such as 256, 512, or 1,024 if you have many images should give you a good result.

We are going to start by computing the features as follows:

```
alldescriptors = []
for im in images:
    im = mh.imread(im, as_grey=True)
    im = im.astype(np.uint8)
    alldescriptors.append((surf.surf(im, descriptor_only=True))
# get all descriptors into a single array
concatenated = np.concatenate(alldescriptors)
```

Now, we use k-means clustering to obtain the centroids. We could use all the descriptors, but we are going to use a smaller sample for extra speed. We have several million descriptors and it would not be wrong to use them all. However, it would require much more computation for little extra benefit. The sampling and clustering is as shown in the following code:

```
# use only every 64th vector
concatenated = concatenated[::64]
from sklearn.cluster import KMeans
k = 256
km = KMeans(k)
km.fit(concatenated)
```

After this is done (which will take a while), the km object contains information about the centroids. We now go back to the descriptors and build feature vectors as follows:

```
sfeatures = []
for d in alldescriptors:
    c = km.predict(d)
    sfeatures.append(np.bincount(c, minlength=256))
# build single array and convert to float
sfeatures = np.array(sfeatures, dtype=float)
```

The end result of this loop is that `sfeatures[fi, fj]` is the number of times that the image `fi` contains the element `fj`. The same could have been computed faster with the `np.histogram` function, but getting the arguments just right is a little tricky. We convert the result to floating point as we do not want integer arithmetic (with its rounding semantics).

The result is that each image is now represented by a single array of features of the same size (the number of clusters in our case is 256). Therefore, we can use our standard classification methods as follows:

```
scores = model_selection.cross_val_score(
    clf, sfeatures, labels, cv=cv)
print('Accuracy: {:.1%}'.format(scores.mean()))
Accuracy: 62.4%
```

This is worse than before! Have we gained nothing?

In fact, we have, as we can combine all features together to obtain `76.7` percent accuracy, as follows:

```
allfeatures = np.hstack([ifeatures, sfeatures]) scores =
model_selection.cross_val_score( clf, allfeatures, labels, cv=cv)
print('Accuracy: {:.1%}'.format(scores.mean()))
Accuracy: 76.7%
```

This is the best result we have, better than any single feature set. This is due to the fact that the local SURF features are different enough to add new information to the global image features we had before and improve the combined result.

Image generation with adversarial networks

Generative Adversarial Networks (GANs) are a new, trendy type of network. Their main attraction is the Generative side. This means that we can train a network to generate a new sample of data that is similar to a reference.

A few years ago, researchers used **Deep Belief Networks (DBN)** for this task, consisting of a visible layer and then a set of internal layers that ended up recurrent. Training such networks was quite difficult, so people thought about new architectures.

Enter our GAN. How can we train a network to generate samples that are similar to a reference? First, we need to design a generator network. Typically, we need a set of random variables that will be fed inside a set of dense and `conv2d_transpose` layers. The latter do the opposite of the `conv2d` layer, going from an input that looks like a convoluted output to an output that looks like a convolution input.

Now, to train this network, we use the Adversarial part. The trick is to train another network, a discriminator, to detect whether a sample is a real sample or a generated sample. One iteration will train the discriminator to enhance its discrimination power, and the iteration after will train the generator to get an image closer to a real one.

Let's try to generate realistic handwritten digits; we will reuse parts of our previous CNN classifier. We need to add a generator there and change the layers to take into account the additional random input that will generate our images.

Let's start with some helper functions: a match helper for our `cost` function as well as a function to write our newly generated samples to disk and display then during our training session. We also create our own layer for batch normalization to simplify the underlying computation:

```
import tensorflow as tf
import numpy as np

def match(logits, labels):
    logits = tf.clip_by_value(logits, 1e-7, 1. - 1e-7)
    return tf.reduce_mean(tf.nn.softmax_cross_entropy_with_logits_v2(
        logits=logits, labels=labels))
```

 We use the non-sparse version of the `cost` function helper we used before, `softmax_cross_entropy_with_logits_v2`. We could have used the sparse version as well, but at the cost of additional code. As there is only one output value, this is simple to handle.

Let's explain the batch normalize layer. We compute the mean and the standard deviation of the input tensor. Then, we normalize this matrix (this way, the matrix has a mean of 0 and a standard deviation of 1). We have an explicit handling of 2D and 4D matrices because we need to handle the difference in the axis explicitly:

```
def batchnormalize(X, eps=1e-8, g=None, b=None):
    if X.get_shape().ndims == 4:
        mean = tf.reduce_mean(X, [0,1,2])
        std = tf.reduce_mean( tf.square(X-mean), [0,1,2] )
        X = (X-mean) / tf.sqrt(std+eps)

        if g is not None and b is not None:
```

```
            g = tf.reshape(g, [1,1,1,-1])
            b = tf.reshape(b, [1,1,1,-1])
            X = X*g + b

    elif X.get_shape().ndims == 2:
        mean = tf.reduce_mean(X, 0)
        std = tf.reduce_mean(tf.square(X-mean), 0)
        X = (X-mean) / tf.sqrt(std+eps)

        if g is not None and b is not None:
            g = tf.reshape(g, [1,-1])
            b = tf.reshape(b, [1,-1])
            X = X*g + b

    else:
        raise NotImplementedError

    return X

def save_visualization(X, nh_nw, save_path='./sample.jpg'):
    from imageio import imwrite
    from matplotlib import pyplot as plt
    h,w = X.shape[1], X.shape[2]
    img = np.zeros((h * nh_nw[0], w * nh_nw[1], 3))

    for n,x in enumerate(X):
        j = n // nh_nw[1]
        i = n % nh_nw[1]
        img[j*h:j*h+h, i*w:i*w+w, :] = x

    img = img.astype(np.uint8)
    imwrite(save_path, img)
    plt.imshow(img)
    plt.show()
```

 As we are using the `sigmoid mapping` function for probabilities, we need to remove values 0 and 1 from the mapping (as they map from infinity). We do that by adding `1e-7` to 0 and subtracting it from 1.

We can now create our class, creating our model. The constructor will have additional new parameters, the number of classes Y, as well as the size of a random state Z:

```
class DCGAN():
    def __init__(
            self,
            image_shape=[28,28,1],
            dim_z=100,
            dim_y=10,
            dim_W1=1024,
            dim_W2=128,
            dim_W3=64,
            dim_channel=1,
            ):

        self.image_shape = image_shape
        self.dim_z = dim_z
        self.dim_y = dim_y

        self.dim_W1 = dim_W1
        self.dim_W2 = dim_W2
        self.dim_W3 = dim_W3
        self.dim_channel = dim_channel
```

This is now our new special layer for the generator that will create good images—the convolution transpose layer we talked about earlier:

```
def create_conv2d_transpose(self, input, filters, kernel_size, name,
with_batch_norm):
        layer = tf.layers.conv2d_transpose(
                inputs=input,
                filters=filters,
                kernel_size=kernel_size,
                strides=[2,2],
                name="Conv2d_transpose_" + name,
                padding="SAME")
        if with_batch_norm:
            layer = batchnormalize(layer)
            layer = tf.nn.relu(layer, name="RELU_" + name)
        return layer
```

Our discriminator should return a probability between 0 and 1 of being a real image. To accomplish this and to allow the generator to create various types of images, we drive into the discriminator the image, and also their classes on each layer:

```
def discriminate(self, image, Y, reuse=False):
    with tf.variable_scope('discriminate', reuse=reuse):
        Y = tf.one_hot(Y, dim_y)
        yb = tf.reshape(Y, tf.stack([-1, 1, 1, self.dim_y]))
        image = tf.concat(axis=3, values=
            [image, yb*tf.ones([1, 28, 28, self.dim_y])])
        h1 = self.create_conv2d(image, self.dim_W3, 5, "Lay-er1", True)
        h1 = tf.concat(axis=3, values=
            [h1, yb*tf.ones([1, 14, 14, self.dim_y])])
        h2 = self.create_conv2d(h1, self.dim_W2, 5, "Layer2", True)
        h2 = tf.reshape(h2, tf.stack([-1, 7*7*128]))
        h2 = tf.concat(axis=1, values=[h2, Y])
        h3 = self.create_dense(h2, self.dim_W1, "Layer3", True)
        h3 = tf.concat(axis=1, values=[h3, Y])
        h4 = self.create_dense(h3, 1, "Layer4", True)
    return h4
```

As we said before, the generator does the opposite, going from our class variables and random state to the final generated image with values between 0 and 1:

```
def generate(self, Z, Y, reuse=False):
    with tf.variable_scope('generate', reuse=reuse):

        Y = tf.one_hot(Y, dim_y)
        yb = tf.reshape(Y, tf.stack([-1, 1, 1, self.dim_y]))
        Z = tf.concat(axis=1, values=[Z,Y])
        h1 = self.create_dense(Z, self.dim_W1, "Layer1", False)
        h1 = tf.concat(axis=1, values=[h1, Y])
        h2 = self.create_dense(h1, self.dim_W2*7*7, "Layer2", False)
        h2 = tf.reshape(h2, tf.stack([-1,7,7,self.dim_W2]))
        h2 = tf.concat(axis=3, values=
            [h2, yb*tf.ones([1, 7, 7, self.dim_y])])

        h3 = self.create_conv2d_transpose(h2, self.dim_W3, 5, "Layer3",
True)
        h3 = tf.concat(axis=3, values=
            [h3, yb*tf.ones([1, 14,14,self.dim_y])] )

        h4 = self.create_conv2d_transpose(
            h3, self.dim_channel, 7, "Layer4", False)
        x = tf.nn.sigmoid(h4)
    return x
```

It is now time to assemble the pieces. We create placeholders for the generators, as well as for the real images inputs. We then create our image generator (which we will use to show our generated images) and then our discriminators. Here lies the trick. We create two of them at the same time. One is used for the real images and should return 1; the other will be fed the generated images and should return 0. As the two share the same weights, we pass the reuse flag for the second discriminator.

The cost we try to optimize for the discriminator step is the sum of the discrepancies of the two discriminators and for the generator. As we said, we optimize the generator to get a 1 on the discriminator:

```
def build_model(self):
    Z = tf.placeholder(tf.float32, [None, self.dim_z])
    Y = tf.placeholder(tf.int64, [None])

    image_real = tf.placeholder(tf.float32, [None]+self.image_shape)
    image_gen = self.generate(Z, Y)

    raw_real = self.discriminate(image_real, Y, False)
    raw_gen = self.discriminate(image_gen, Y, True)

    discrim_cost_real = match(raw_real, tf.ones_like(raw_real))
    discrim_cost_gen = match(raw_gen, tf.zeros_like(raw_gen))
    discrim_cost = discrim_cost_real + discrim_cost_gen

    gen_cost = match( raw_gen, tf.ones_like(raw_gen) )

    return Z, Y, is_training, image_real, image_gen, dis-crim_cost,
gen_cost
```

We can now start setting up the graph with the hyperparameters:

```
n_epochs = 10
learning_rate = 0.0002
batch_size = 1024
image_shape = [28,28,1]
dim_z = 10
dim_y = 10
dim_W1 = 1024
dim_W2 = 128
dim_W3 = 64
dim_channel = 1

visualize_dim=196
step = 200
```

As before, we read the MNIST dataset:

```
from sklearn.datasets import fetch_mldata
mnist = fetch_mldata('MNIST original')
mnist.data.shape = (-1, 28, 28)
mnist.data = mnist.data.astype(np.float32).reshape( [-1, 28, 28, 1]) / 255.
mnist.num_examples = len(mnist.data)
```

And we create our graph. We split the variables into two lists (as they have a prefix), with an Adam optimizer for each of them. We also create the variables for our samples to check if whether our generator has started generating recognizable images:

```
from sklearn.datasets import fetch_mldata
mnist = fetch_mldata('MNIST original')
mnist.data.shape = (-1, 28, 28)
mnist.data = mnist.data.astype(np.float32).reshape( [-1, 28, 28, 1]) / 255.
mnist.num_examples = len(mnist.data)
tf.reset_default_graph()
dcgan_model = DCGAN(
        image_shape=image_shape,
        dim_z=dim_z,
        dim_W1=dim_W1,
        dim_W2=dim_W2,
        dim_W3=dim_W3,
        )
Z_tf, Y_tf, iimage_tf, image_tf_sample, d_cost_tf, g_cost_tf, =
dcgan_model.build_model()
discrim_vars = list(filter(lambda x: x.name.startswith('discriminate'),
    tf.trainable_variables()))
gen_vars = list(filter(lambda x: x.name.startswith('generate'),
tf.trainable_variables()))

train_op_discrim = tf.train.AdamOptimizer(learning_rate,
beta1=0.5).minimize(
    d_cost_tf, var_list=discrim_vars)
train_op_gen = tf.train.AdamOptimizer(learning_rate, beta1=0.5).minimize(
    g_cost_tf, var_list=gen_vars)

Z_np_sample = np.random.uniform(-1, 1, size=(visualize_dim,dim_z))
Y_np_sample = np.random.randint(10, size=[visualize_dim])
```

In our session, we first transform the labels to one-hot encoding with Tensorflow and then we use the same pattern as for our previous networks. We generate random numbers for the generated images for each batch, and we optimize the discriminator and then the generator, as we planned:

```
with tf.Session() as sess:
    mnist.target = tf.one_hot(mnist.target.astype(np.int8), dim_y).eval()
    Y_np_sample = tf.one_hot(Y_np_sample, dim_y).eval()
    sess.run(tf.global_variables_initializer())
    for epoch in range(n_epochs):
        permut = np.random.permutation(mnist.num_examples)
        trX = mnist.data[permut]
        trY = mnist.target[permut]
        Z = np.random.uniform(-1, 1, size=[mnist.num_examples,
dim_z]).astype(np.float32)

        print("epoch: %i" % epoch)
        for j in range(0, mnist.num_examples, batch_size):
            if j % step == 0:
                print(" batch: %i" % j)

            batch = permut[j:j+batch_size]

            Xs = trX[batch]
            Ys = trY[batch]
            Zs = Z[batch]

            sess.run(train_op_discrim,
                    feed_dict={
                        Z_tf:Zs,
                        Y_tf:Ys,
                        image_tf:Xs,
                        })

            sess.run(train_op_gen,
                    feed_dict={
                        Z_tf:Zs,
                        Y_tf:Ys,
                        })

            if j % step == 0:
                generated_samples = sess.run(
                        image_tf_sample,
                        feed_dict={
                            Z_tf:Z_np_sample,
                            Y_tf:Y_np_sample,
                            })
                generated_samples = generated_samples * 255
```

```
save_visualization(generated_samples, (7,28),
        save_path='./sample_%03d_%04d.jpg' %
                (epoch, j / step))
```

epoch: 0
  batch: 0

...
epoch: 3
  batch: 0

epoch: 9
 batch: 64000

We can see quite early shapes that resemble digits. The way they evolve is very interesting. They go from smooth to crispy to noisy (for a high number of epochs). This is understandable because there is no convergence for these networks. As they are adversarial, each time one learns a trick that works on the other, the other will counter it. For instance, if the images are not smooth enough, the discriminator may discriminate on this difference, and if the generator generates smooth images, then the discriminator will move on to other differences. The problem is that the generator will forget about past known tricks, so there is no way to stop at a meaningful point!

Summary

We learned the classical feature-based approach to handling images in a machine learning context; by converting from a million pixels to a few numeric features, we were able to directly use a logistic regression classifier. All of the technologies that we learned in the other chapters suddenly became directly applicable to image problems. We saw one example in the use of image features to find similar images in a dataset.

We also learned how to use local features in a bag of words model for classification. This is a very modern approach to computer vision and achieves good results, while being robust enough for many irrelevant aspects of the image, such as illumination, and even uneven illumination in the same image. We also used clustering as a useful intermediate step in classification, rather than as an end in itself.

We focused on `mahotas`, which is one of the major computer vision libraries in Python. There are others that are equally well maintained. Skimage is similar in spirit, but has a different set of features. OpenCV is a very good C++ library with a Python interface. All of these can work with NumPy arrays and you can mix and match functions from different libraries to build complex computer vision pipelines.

We also tried a new way of generating similar images with Tensorflow (which can be used on non-image domains) with the current trendy type of network named GAN.

In `Chapter 13`, *Reinforcement Learning,* we will explore reinforcement learning, a hot topic for deep learning. We will see how we can make a neural network learn a set of rules without telling it anything.

13
Reinforcement Learning

Deepmind marked the year 2017 by creating the best Go player in the world. How did they achieve this? With deep learning, of course, but more precisely with reinforcement learning.

Deep Blue beat human chess players with traditional game analysis. It would build a tree of possible outcomes and prune it with different strategies (like alpha/beta, but adapted to the space of possible outcomes of chess). But this was not possible with Go, which was never solvable by computers until Deepmind created their network and its training methods. Because without training, the network is useless!

In this chapter, we will do the following:

- Look at different types of reinforcement learning
- Explore the concept of Q-learning
- Estimate a Q function via a table and via a neural network
- Make a network play an Atari game using Q-learning

Types of reinforcement learning

Reinforcement learning is part of the unsupervised learning space. Its goal is to make a model behave better and better, but we don't have the ground truth, a set of labeled data, for instance, to train our model. This only thing we can do is to use the network, and if the network gets a good result, then we use it to enhance our model with backpropagation. Otherwise, we try some more.

We can also use this approach in finance to optimize a portfolio; this can also be used for robots. In the past, people use genetic algorithms to train a walking robot, but now we can also use reinforcement learning for this task!

Now we have neural networks that can come to the rescue. Let's look at a few of the main types of networks that have been given attention in the last few years.

Policy and value network

We can start with solving Go. Go is a simple game that is thousands of years old. It's a two player game with full information, meaning that two players face each other and there is no hidden knowledge; everything is contained on the board (contrary to, say, card games like poker). At each turn, the player places one of their stones (either white for the first player or black for the second) on the board, possibly changing the color of other stones in the process, and the games ends with whoever has the most stones of their color.

The issue is that the board is quite big, 19 x 19 squares, meaning that at the beginning you have a very big set of possible options. Which one leads to winning the game?

For chess, this was solved without neural networks. There are only a subset of possible moves, and a fast computer can now analyze all of these moves up to a given depth. At the leaves of this analysis tree, it is possible in chess to know if we are closer to winning or if we are on the verge of losing. For Go, it's not possible.

Enter deep learning. For Go, we still need to analyse different possible moves, but we won't try to be as exhaustive as in chess; we will instead use **Monte-Carlo Tree Search** (**MCTS**). This means that we will draw a random uniform number and from this number we will play one move. We do this for several moves in advance and then we assess whether we are closer to winning or not.

But as we saw before, we can't measure this is Go, so how do we select a move for the search and how can we decide if we are winning or losing? This is why we have two networks. The policy network will provide the probabilities for the next move, and the value network will provide one value—either it thinks we are winning or we are losing.

Combined together, it is possible to generate a set of possible moves with their odds of success, and we can play them. At the end of the game, we use the information to reinforce the two networks.

Later, the new AlphaGo Zero merged these networks together. There was no longer a policy and a value network, and it got far better at playing than the original AlphaGo. So we don't have to have a dichotomy for such problems, as it is possible to design an architecture that does both.

Q-network

Actually, Deepmind started making a name for themselves before Go. They were using what is called a Q-network to solve Atari games. These are a set of simple games where the gamer can play only up to 10 moves at each stage.

With these networks, the goal is to estimate a long-term reward function (like the number of points) and which move will maximize it. By feeding in enough options at the beginning, the network will progressively learn how to play better and better. The reward function is the following:

$$Q(s,a) = r + \gamma(max(Q(s',a')))$$

r is the reward, γ is a discounting factor (future gains are not as important as the immediate reward), s is the current state of the game, and a is the action we could take.

Of course, as it is continuously learning, it is also continuously forgetting, and the network will have to be fed with past training as well. To use a metaphor, it will end up running without being able to walk, which is quite useless.

Excelling at games

In the remainder of this chapter, we will use Q-games with the `gym` package. It offers a standard API for playing different types of games, so it's the perfect test case for what we want to show you.

A small example

Anaconda doesn't ship this package, so it has to be installed though `pip`:

```
>>> pip install gym[atari]
```

 We won't use the Atari part of the `gym`, but it will be required for the breakout game.

From this package, we can create an environment for different games, like this:

```
env = gym.make('FrozenLake-v0')
```

This creates a new environment for the text game FrozenLake. It consists of four four-character strings, starting with S and ending up at G, the goal. But there are holes (H) on the way to this goal, and ending up there makes you lose the game:

- SFFF
- FHFH
- FFFH
- HFFG

From the environment, we can get the size of the observation space, env.observation_space.n, which is 16 here (where the player is located) and the size of the action space env.action_space.n, which is 4 here.

As this is a small toy example, we can create an estimation of Q(s, a):

```
# Inspired by https://github.com/tensorlayer/tensorlayer/
#       blob/master/example/tutorial_frozenlake_q_table.py
Q = np.zeros((env.observation_space.n, env.action_space.n))
# Set learning hyperparameters
lr = .8
y = .95
num_episodes = 2000

# Let's run!
for i in range(num_episodes):
    # Reset environment and get first new observation (top left)
    s = env.reset()
    # Do 100 iterations to update the table
    for i in range(100):
        # Choose an action by picking the max of the table
        # + additional random noise ponderated by the episode
        a = np.argmax(Q[s,:]
            + np.random.randn(1, env.action_space.n) / (i + 1))
        # Get new state and reward from environment after chosen step
        s1, r, d,_ = env.step(a)
        # Update Q-Table with new knowledge
        Q[s,a] = Q[s,a] + lr*(r + y*np.max(Q[s1,:]) - Q[s,a])
        s = s1
        if d == True:
            break
```

We can now display the content of the table Q:

```
[[0.18118924 0.18976168 0.19044738 0.18260069]
 [0.03811294 0.19398589 0.18619181 0.18624451]
 [0.16266812 0.13309552 0.14401865 0.11183018]
 [0.02533285 0.12890984 0.02641699 0.15121063]
 [0.20015578 0.00201834 0.00902377 0.03619787]
 [0. 0. 0. 0. ]
 [0.1294778 0.04845176 0.03590482 0.13001683]
 [0. 0. 0. 0. ]
 [0.02543623 0.05444387 0.01170018 0.19347353]
 [0.06137181 0.43637431 0.00372395 0.00830249]
 [0.25205174 0.00709722 0.00908675 0.00296389]
 [0. 0. 0. 0. ]
 [0. 0. 0. 0. ]
 [0. 0.15032826 0.43034276 0.09982157]
 [0. 0.86241133 0. 0. ]
 [0. 0. 0. 0. ]]
```

We can see all the entries that have 0 in some of our rows; these are the holes and the final goal stage. Starting from the first step, we can go through this table to a next step with probabilities given by these rows (after normalization).

Of course, this is not a network, so let's use Tensorflow to make a network learn this table.

Using Tensorflow for the text game

Let's think of the type of architecture we need here. We have the state of the game as the input, and we want one of four values as the output. The game is simple enough that there is an optimal strategy, a unique path to get from the start to the goal. This means that the network can be very simple, with just one layer and a linear output:

```
inputs = tf.placeholder(shape=[None, 16], dtype=tf.float32, name="input")
Qout = tf.layers.dense(
    inputs=inputs,
    units=4,
    use_bias=False,
    name="dense",
    kernel_initializer=
        tf.random_uniform_initializer(minval=0, maxval=.0125)
)
predict = tf.argmax(Qout, 1)

# Our optimizer will try to optimize
nextQ = tf.placeholder(shape=[None, 4], dtype=tf.float32, name="target")
loss = tf.reduce_sum(tf.square(nextQ - Qout))
```

```
trainer = tf.train.GradientDescentOptimizer(learning_rate=learning_rate)
updateModel = trainer.minimize(loss)
```

For our training, we need to reintroduce new options, like the randomness we had in our table before. To accomplish this, for every 10 predictions, we sample a random action (this is called an epsilon-greedy strategy, and we will reuse a variation of it later with the Atari games). Otherwise, we compute the actual Q value and we train our network to match this result (updating the dense layer weights):

```
# To keep track of our games and our results
with tf.Session() as sess:
    sess.run(tf.global_variables_initializer())

    for i in range(num_episodes):
        s = env.reset()
        for j in range(100):
            a, targetQ = sess.run([predict, Qout],
                feed_dict={inputs:np.identity(16)[s:s+1]})
            # We randomly choose a new state
            # that we may have not encountered before
            if np.random.rand(1) < e:
                a[0] = env.action_space.sample()

            s1, r, d, _ = env.step(a[0])
            # Obtain the Q' values by feeding
            # the new state through our network
            Q1 = sess.run(Qout,
                feed_dict={inputs:np.identity(16)[s1:s1 + 1]})
            # Obtain maxQ' and set our target value for chosen action.
            targetQ[0, a[0]] = r + y*np.max(Q1)
            # Train our network using target and predicted Q values
            sess.run(updateModel,
                feed_dict={inputs:np.identity(16)[s:s+1], nextQ:targetQ})
            s = s1
            if d == True:
                # Reduce chance of random action as we train the model.
                e = 1 / ((i // 50) + 10)
                break
```

With this strategy, the layer gets around 40% success, but this value is biased. If we plot the evolution of the reward (averaged through time over 20 episodes), the network improves drastically over time:

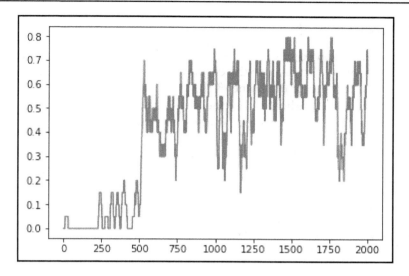

And the same happens with the alive time:

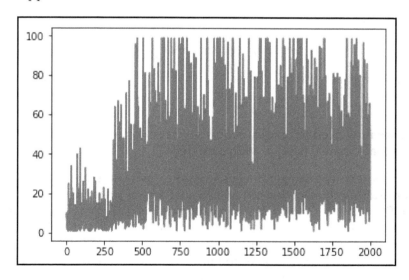

We can see that when the network started to get better at rewards, it also managed to keep the player alive longer. Unfortunately, the network is still not the best at this task. A human would take only eight steps to finish the game.

We can now use a similar strategy for the Atari games.

Playing breakout

The Atari games can be played in several ways. The first is the interaction way. Either we can use a memory view, or we can use the displayed image (which is always the same). On top of this, the −v? at the end of the name of the game indicates if the step is repeated and how often. v0 for breakout indicates that the step is taken two, three, or four times before we ask for a new one. For v4, it skips four frames deterministically.

We can start with an empty, simple breakout game:

```
# Import the gym module
import gym

# Create a breakout environment
env = gym.make('BreakoutDeterministic-v4')
# Reset it, returns the starting frame
frame = env.reset()
# Render
env.render()

is_done = False
while not is_done:
    # Perform a random action, returns the new frame, reward and whether
the game is over
    frame, reward, is_done, _ = env.step(env.action_space.sample())
    # Render
    env.render()
```

The only thing we now need to modify is how we get the new step for the game. Well, we need more than that: first we need to train a model!

Let's look at the context. We can get images from the environment (they are 160 x 210 pixels), and considering the fact that we will require lots of previous images, this size may be too much to fit on one computer. We can drop one pixel out of two in all directions, for instance, so this is what preprocess will achieve. We will also add two functions that transpose our internal state. The reason is that we have images that are 84 x 105 with one channel, but we need to use past images to know in which direction the ball moves. To achieve this, we transpose this state on the fly to have an image that is *84 x 105 x state_length*:

```
import gym
import os
import six
import numpy as np
import tensorflow as tf
import random
```

```
from collections import deque , namedtuple

Transition = namedtuple("Transition",
    ["state", "action", "re-ward", "next_state", "done"])

def to_grayscale(img):
    return np.mean(img, axis=2).astype(np.uint8)

def downsample(img):
    return img[::2, ::2]

def preprocess(img):
    return to_grayscale(downsample(img))[None,:,:]

def adapt_state(state):
    return [np.float32(np.transpose(state, (2, 1, 0)) / 255.0)]

def adapt_batch_state(state):
    return np.transpose(np.array(state), (0, 3, 2, 1)) / 255.0

def get_initial_state(frame):
    processed_frame = preprocess(frame)
    state = [processed_frame for _ in range(state_length)]
    return np.concatenate(state)
```

 Although we can make all the Atari games work with the network we are building, there is one issue. We are just taking every other pixel in each direction. But what happens if we are playing space invaders with a one-pixel-width missile? There is a 50/50 chance that we will die without seeing the missile!

To make this better, we could use `skimage.rescale` instead. For breakout, we don't need it, so this is left as an exercise for the reader.

We are now going to write a set of hyperparameters, as well as some constants for the game, like the name of the environment and the size of the image:

```
env_name = "Breakout-v4"
width = 80 # Resized frame width
height = 105 # Resized frame height
```

We need to train the network for a very long time, so let's play 12000 games. To predict a new action, we will use the past 4 images:

```
n_episodes = 12000 # Number of runs for the agent
state_length = 4 # Number of most frames we input to the network
```

We are also going to need to set our parameters for the Q function:

```
gamma = 0.99 # Discount factor
```

At the beginning, we want to test very often a random action (left or right for breakout). Then during the training, we will progressively remove the randomness (this is our epsilon-greedy strategy). Each time we run the network, we consider this one step, so let's reduce this random factor by over 1 million steps:

```
# During all these steps, we progressively lower epsilon
exploration_steps = 1000000
initial_epsilon = 1.0 # Initial value of epsilon in epsilon-greedy
final_epsilon = 0.1 # Final value of epsilon in epsilon-greedy
```

We need to fill in our collection of actions, so at the beginning we don't train, we just let the game play with random actions. This is going to be our initial training set, and over time we will add all our games to this set of training set. When it hits 400000 elements, we start dumping the old, more random training states:

```
# Number of steps to populate the replay memory before training starts
initial_random_search = 20000
replay_memory_size = 400000 # Number of states we keep for training
batch_size = 32 # Batch size
network_update_interval = 10000 # The frequency with which the target
network is updated
```

We will use RMSProp to train our network, so we set a very low learning rate with momentum:

```
learning_rate = 0.00025 # Learning rate used by RMSProp
momentum = 0.95 # momentum used by RMSProp
# Constant added to the squared gradient in the denominator
# of the RMSProp update
min_gradient = 0.01
```

Finally, we will store the trained network through time (with some checkpoints so that we can restart the training at some partially trained state), and we will store some information to Tensorboard, like the reward that we found and the length of a game:

```
network_path = 'saved_networks/' + env_name
tensorboard_path = 'summary/' + env_name
save_interval = 300000 # The frequency with which the network is saved
```

We can now create our network class. We will create one instance for each network. Yes, we need two networks—one to estimate the next action to take and one to estimate the Q values or targets. From time to time, we will update the network for action (named `q_estimator` here) to the target estimator (named `target_estimator`):

```
class Estimator():
    """Q-Value Estimator neural network.
    This network is used for both the Q-Network and the Target Network.
    """

    def __init__(self, env, scope="estimator", summar-ies_dir=None):
        self.scope = scope
        self.num_actions = env.action_space.n
        self.epsilon = initial_epsilon
        self.epsilon_step = \
            (initial_epsilon - final_epsilon) / exploration_steps
        # Writes Tensorboard summaries to disk
        self.summary_writer = None
        with tf.variable_scope(scope):
            # Build the graph
            self.build_model()
        if summaries_dir:
            summary_dir = os.path.join(summaries_dir,
                "summaries_%s" % scope)
            if not os.path.exists(summary_dir):
                os.makedirs(summary_dir)
            self.summary_writer = tf.summary.FileWriter(summary_dir)

    def build_model(self):
        """
        Builds the Tensorflow graph.
        """
        self.X = tf.placeholder(shape=[None, width, height, state_length],
            dtype=tf.float32, name="X")
        # The TD target value
        self.y = tf.placeholder(shape=[None], dtype=tf.float32, name="y")
        # Integer id of which action was selected
        self.actions = tf.placeholder(shape=[None], dtype=tf.int32,
    name="actions")

        model = tf.keras.Sequential()
        model.add(tf.keras.layers.Convolution2D(filters=32, kernel_size=8,
            strides=(4, 4), activation='relu',
            input_shape=(width, height, state_length), name="Layer1"))
        model.add(tf.keras.layers.Convolution2D(filters=64, kernel_size=4,
            strides=(2, 2), activation='relu', name="Layer2"))
        model.add(tf.keras.layers.Convolution2D(filters=64, kernel_size=3,
```

```
            strides=(1, 1), activation='relu', name="Layer3"))
model.add(tf.keras.layers.Flatten(name="Flatten"))
model.add(tf.keras.layers.Dense(512, activation='relu',
    name="Layer4"))
model.add(tf.keras.layers.Dense(self.num_actions, name="Output"))
self.predictions = model(self.X)

a_one_hot = tf.one_hot(self.actions, self.num_actions, 1.0, 0.0)
q_value = tf.reduce_sum(tf.multiply(self.predictions, a_one_hot),
    reduction_indices=1)
# Calculate the loss
self.losses = tf.squared_difference(self.y, q_value)
self.loss = tf.reduce_mean(self.losses)

# Optimizer Parameters from original paper
self.optimizer = tf.train.RMSPropOptimizer(learning_rate,
    momentum=momentum, epsilon=min_gradient)
self.train_op = self.optimizer.minimize(self.loss,
    global_step=tf.train.get_global_step())

# Summaries for Tensorboard
self.summaries = tf.summary.merge([
    tf.summary.scalar("loss", self.loss),
    tf.summary.histogram("loss_hist", self.losses),
    tf.summary.histogram("q_values_hist", self.predictions),
    tf.summary.scalar("max_q_value",
        tf.reduce_max(self.predictions))
])
```

We used `keras` in this case to build our network. It stacks three convolutional layers (without max pool layers, although we do drop some nodes to reduce the number of parameters) and then two dense layers. All of them use a `relu` activation later.

 Note that`keras` is a high-level interface. In this example, we use `Sequential` which means that each layer connects to the previous one. It is then built by passing a placeholder to the model and getting an output tensor.

With the network, we can now create a `cost` function and feed it to an optimizer. We also add some summary reports to check the distribution of Q or loss values:

```
def predict(self, sess, s):
    return sess.run(self.predictions, { self.X: s })

def update(self, sess, s, a, y):
    feed_dict = { self.X: s, self.y: y, self.actions: a }
    summaries, global_step, _, loss = sess.run(
```

```
        [self.summaries, tf.train.get_global_step(), self.train_op,
self.loss], feed_dict)
        if self.summary_writer:
            self.summary_writer.add_summary(summaries, glob-al_step)
        return loss

    def get_action(self, sess, state):
        if self.epsilon >= random.random():
            action = random.randrange(self.num_actions)
        else:
            action = np.argmax(self.predict(sess, adapt_state(state)))
        # Decay epsilon over time
        if self.epsilon > final_epsilon:
            self.epsilon -= self.epsilon_step
        return action

    def get_trained_action(self, state):
        action = np.argmax(self.predict(sess, adapt_state(state)))
        return action
```

We add a method to wrap the prediction, as we will use it in several places—firstly in an update method that will actually train this estimator. We also have two methods to retrieve an action, either with an epsilon-greedy strategy or without (after the training):

```
    def copy_model_parameters(estimator1, estimator2):
        """
        Copies the model parameters of one estimator to another.
        Args:
          estimator1: Estimator to copy the paramters from
          estimator2: Estimator to copy the parameters to
        """
        e1_params = [t for t in tf.trainable_variables()
             if t.name.startswith(estimator1.scope)]
        e1_params = sorted(e1_params, key=lambda v: v.name)
        e2_params = [t for t in tf.trainable_variables()
             if t.name.startswith(estimator2.scope)]
        e2_params = sorted(e2_params, key=lambda v: v.name)

        update_ops = []
        for e1_v, e2_v in zip(e1_params, e2_params):
            op = e2_v.assign(e1_v)
            update_ops.append(op)
        return update_ops
```

This is our function that we will call to update one estimator from another. This creates a set of operations that we will run in our session later:

```
def create_memory(env):
    # Populate the replay memory with initial experience
    replay_memory = deque()
    frame = env.reset()
    state = get_initial_state(frame)

    for i in range(replay_memory_init_size):
        action = np.random.choice(np.arange(env.action_space.n))
        frame, reward, done, _ = env.step(action)
        next_state = np.append(state[1:, :, :], preprocess(frame), axis=0)
        replay_memory.append(
            Transition(state, action, reward, next_state, done))
        if done:
            frame = env.reset()
            state = get_initial_state(frame)
        else:
            state = next_state
    return replay_memory
```

This function creates an empty replay memory. This is required so that the game can learn something. Without this set of initial states, we cannot train the network. So we just play random moves for a while and hope it will make our network gain some first-hand knowledge of the game. Of course, we also have our epsilon-greedy strategy that will add new moves to the game later. This will also help us a lot:

```
def setup_summary():
    with tf.variable_scope("episode"):
        episode_total_reward = tf.Variable(0., name="EpisodeTotalReward")
        tf.summary.scalar('Total Reward', episode_total_reward)
        episode_avg_max_q = tf.Variable(0., name="EpisodeAvgMaxQ")
        tf.summary.scalar('Average Max Q', episode_avg_max_q)
        episode_duration = tf.Variable(0., name="EpisodeDuration")
        tf.summary.scalar('Duration', episode_duration)
        episode_avg_loss = tf.Variable(0., name="EpisodeAverageLoss")
        tf.summary.scalar('Average Loss', episode_avg_loss)
        summary_vars = [episode_total_reward, episode_avg_max_q,
            episode_duration, episode_avg_loss]
        summary_placeholders =
            [tf.placeholder(tf.float32) for _ in range(len(summary_vars))]
        update_ops = [sum-mary_vars[i].assign(summary_placeholders[i])
            for i in range(len(summary_vars))]
    summary_op = tf.summary.merge_all(scope="episode")
    return summary_placeholders, update_ops, summary_op
```

We defined here all the variables we want to visualize in Tensorboard on top of the histograms from the estimator.

 During the training, use `tensorboard --logdir=summary` to visualize the evolution of the training and the performance of your network.

We can start our main training loop by setting up the environment, estimators, and help functions:

```
if __name__ == "__main__":
    from tqdm import tqdm

    env = gym.make(env_name)
    tf.reset_default_graph()

    # Create a global step variable
    global_step = tf.Variable(0, name='global_step', traina-ble=False)
    # Create estimators
    q_estimator = Estimator(env, scope="q",
        summaries_dir=tensorboard_path)
    target_estimator = Estimator(env, scope="target_q")
    copy_model = copy_model_parameters(q_estimator, tar-get_estimator)
    summary_placeholders, update_ops, summary_op = setup_summary()
    replay_memory = create_memory(env)
```

We can start our Tensorflow session and restore the network if there is a previous version stored in our save location:

```
with tf.Session() as sess:
    sess.run(tf.global_variables_initializer())
    saver = tf.train.Saver()
    # Load a previous checkpoint if we find one
    latest_checkpoint = tf.train.latest_checkpoint(network_path)
    if latest_checkpoint:
        print("Loading model checkpoint %s...\n" % lat-est_checkpoint)
        saver.restore(sess, latest_checkpoint)
    total_t = sess.run(tf.train.get_global_step())
```

From here, we can start playing games. We do that first by saving the network if we need to, and then we set up the game state:

```
for episode in tqdm(range(n_episodes)):
    if total_t % save_interval == 0:
        # Save the current checkpoint
        saver.save(tf.get_default_session(), network_path)

    frame = env.reset()
    state = get_initial_state(frame)
    total_reward = 0
    total_loss = 0
    total_q_max = 0
```

We iterate forever in this game, taking an action and saving the state of this action in our replay memory. This way, when the network learns to play better, we also save these better moves to learn them even better later:

```
for duration in itertools.count():
    # Maybe update the target estimator
    if total_t % network_update_interval == 0:
        sess.run(copy_model)

    action = q_estimator.get_action(sess, state)
    frame, reward, terminal, _ = env.step(action)
    processed_frame = preprocess(frame)
    next_state = np.append(state[1:, :, :], processed_frame, axis=0)
    reward = np.clip(reward, -1, 1)
    replay_memory.append(
        Transition(state, action, reward, next_state, terminal))
    if len(replay_memory) > replay_memory_size:
        replay_memory.popleft()
```

We get a set of states from our replay memory, with the reward, the action that was used, to estimate our Q value. Once we have this, we optimize the network to enhance its behavior. This is now where we can update our network to play better, based on the target Q-network:

```
samples = random.sample(replay_memory, batch_size)
states_batch, action_batch, reward_batch, next_states_batch, done_batch = \
                map(np.array, zip(*samples))
# Calculate q values and targets (Double DQN)
adapted_state = adapt_batch_state(next_states_batch)
q_values_next = q_estimator.predict(sess, adapted_state)
best_actions = np.argmax(q_values_next, axis=1)
q_values_next_target = tar-get_estimator.predict(sess, adapted_state)
targets_batch = reward_batch + np.invert(done_batch).astype(np.float32) *
```

```
        gamma * q_values_next_target[np.arange(batch_size), best_actions]
    # Perform gradient descent update
    states_batch = adapt_batch_state(states_batch)
    loss = q_estimator.update(sess, states_batch, action_batch, targets_batch)
    total_q_max += np.max(q_values_next)
    total_loss += loss
    total_t += 1
    total_reward += reward
    if terminal:
        break
```

Once the game is finished, we save our variables to Tensorboard as well as capture a screenshot of the endgame:

```
stats = [total_reward, total_q_max / duration, dura-tion, total_loss /
duration]
for i in range(len(stats)):
    sess.run(update_ops[i], feed_dict={
        summary_placeholders[i]: float(stats[i])
    })
summary_str = sess.run(summary_op, )
q_estimator.summary_writer.add_summary(summary_str, episode)
env.env.ale.saveScreenPNG(six.b('%s/test_image_%05i.png' % (CHART_DIR,
episode)))
```

We can train our network over our 12,000 games with this final loop. For each iteration, we get a new action from the trained network (starting with lots of random ones) and we train our network.

Here is an example of the Tensorboard graphs for the previous code:

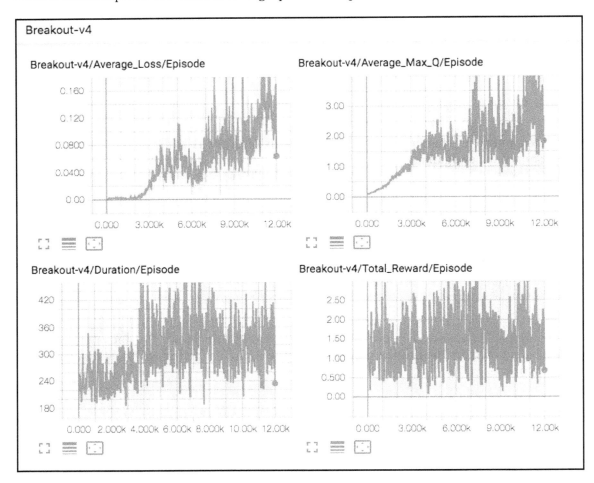

After a long time, we can see the average Q slowly improving, although the reward stays low. We can see that after the training the network is a bit better, but it will still require lots of games to be good!

On top of the graphs displaying the evolution of the training, Tensorboard also provides a view of the graph that supports our network. This is very useful to check that it is correct and fits what we designed. It shows for instance the different weights that we use for a certain cost. If they are reused, this will be very clear from the graph.

This is another view available in Tensorboard when we called
`summary_writer.add_graph(sess.graph)`:

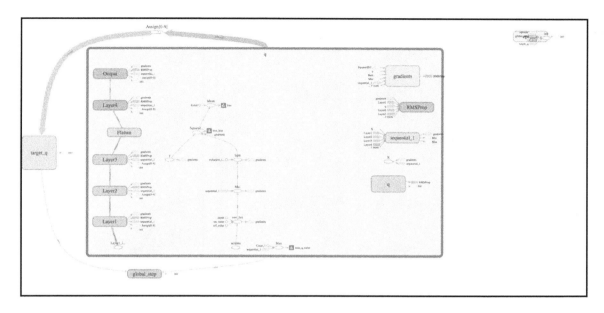

TIP

The next step is now to try different hyper parameters. After all, we don't know if the network will end up learning the game. For instance, adding more episodes will enhance the ability to train, but what would changing the epsilon-greedy strategy do? Or the memory size? Or simply the batch size?

Summary

We saw here that reinforcement learning is a very powerful tool to train a model on data where we don't have a ground truth or the optimal strategy. This still takes lots of time to achieve on a single processor, especially without GPU.

In Chapter 14, *Bigger Data*, we will see how we can harness the power of the cloud for even more complex models.

14
Bigger Data

It's not easy to say what big data is. We will adopt an operational definition: when data is so large that it becomes cumbersome to work with, we refer to it as **big data**. In some cases, this might mean petabytes of data or trillions of transactions: data that will not fit into a single hard drive. In other cases, it may be one hundred times smaller, but still difficult to work with.

Why has data itself become an issue? While computers keep getting faster and gaining more memory, the size of the data has grown as well. In fact, data has grown faster than computational speed and few algorithms scale linearly with the size of the input data taken together; this means that data has grown faster than our ability to process it.

We will first build on some of the experience of the previous chapters and work with what we can call medium data setting (not quite big data, but not small either). For this, we will use a package called `jug`, which allows us to perform the following tasks:

- Break up your pipeline into tasks
- Cache (memorize) intermediate results
- Make use of multiple cores, including multiple computers on a grid

The next step is to move on to true big data, and we will see how to use the cloud for computation purpose. In particular, you will learn about the Amazon Web Services infrastructure. In this section, we introduce another Python package called `cfncluster` to manage clusters.

Learning about big data

The expression big data does not mean a specific amount of data, neither in the number of examples nor in the number of gigabytes, terabytes, or petabytes occupied by the data. It means that data has been growing faster than processing power. This implies the following:

- Some of the methods and techniques that worked well in the past now need to be redone or replaced as they do not scale well to the new size of the input data
- Algorithms cannot assume that all the input data can fit in memory
- Managing data becomes a major task in itself
- Using computer clusters or multicore machines becomes a necessity and not a luxury

This chapter will focus on this last piece of the puzzle: how to use multiple cores (either on the same machine or on separate machines) to speed up and organize your computations. This will also be useful in other medium-sized data tasks.

Using jug to break up your pipeline into tasks

Often, we have a simple pipeline: we preprocess the initial data, compute features, and then call a machine learning algorithm with the resulting features.

Jug is a package developed by Luis Pedro Coelho, one of the authors of this book. It's open source (using the liberal MIT license) and can be useful in many areas, but was designed specifically around data analysis problems. It simultaneously solves several problems, for example:

- It can memoize results to disk (or a database), which means that if you ask it to compute something you have already computed before, the result is instead read from disk.
- It can use multiple cores or even multiple computers on a cluster. Jug was also designed to work very well in batch computing environments, which use queuing systems such as **Portable Batch System** (**PBS**), **Load Sharing Facility** (**LSF**), or **Grid Engine**. It will be used in the second half of the chapter when we build online clusters and dispatch jobs to them.

An introduction to tasks in jug

Tasks are the basic building blocks of jug. A task is composed of a function and values for its arguments. Consider this simple example:

```
def double(x):
    return 2*x
```

In this chapter, the code examples will generally have to be typed in script files. Commands that should be typed at the shell will be indicated by prefixing them with $.

A task could be call `double` with argument 3. Another task would be call `double` with argument 642.34. Using jug, we can build these tasks as follows:

```
from jug import Task
t1 = Task(double, 3)
t2 = Task(double, 642.34)
```

Save this to a file called `jugfile.py` (which is just a regular Python file). Now, we can run `jug execute` to run the tasks. This is something you type on the command line, not at the Python prompt, so we show it marked with a dollar sign ($):

$ jug execute

You will also get some feedback on the tasks (jug will say that two tasks named `double` were run). Run `jug execute` again and it will tell you that it did nothing! It does not need to. In this case, we gained little, but if the tasks took a long time to compute, it would have been very useful.

You may notice that a new directory also appeared on your hard drive named `jugfile.jugdata`, with a few weirdly named files. This is the memorization cache. If you remove it, `jug execute` will run all your tasks again.

Often, it's good to distinguish between pure functions, which simply take their inputs and return a result from more general functions that can perform actions (such as reading from files, writing to files, accessing global variables, modifying their arguments, or anything that the language allows). Some programming languages, such as Haskell, even distinguish pure from impure functions in the type system.

With jug, your tasks do not need to be perfectly pure. It's even recommended that you use tasks to read in your data or write out your results. However, accessing and modifying global variables will not work well: the tasks may be run in any order on different processors. The exceptions are global constants, but even this may confuse the memorization system (if the value is changed between runs). Similarly, you should not modify the input values. Jug has a debug mode (use `jug execute --debug`), which slows down your computation, but will give you useful error messages if you make this sort of mistake.

The preceding code works, but is a bit cumbersome. You are always repeating the `Task(function, argument)` construct. Using a bit of Python magic, we can make the code even more natural as follows:

```python
from jug import TaskGenerator
from time import sleep

@TaskGenerator
def double(x):
    sleep(4)
    return 2*x

@TaskGenerator
def add(a, b):
    return a + b

@TaskGenerator
def print_final_result(oname, value):
    with open(oname, 'w') as output:
        output.write('Final result: {}n'.format(value))


y = double(2)
z = double(y)
y2 = double(7)
z2 = double(y2)
print_final_result('output.txt', add(z,z2))
```

Except for the use of `TaskGenerator`, the preceding code could be a standard Python file! However, using `TaskGenerator`, it actually creates a series of tasks, and it is now possible to run it in a way that takes advantage of multiple processors. Behind the scenes, the decorator transforms your functions so that they do not actually execute when called, but create a `Task` object. We also take advantage of the fact that we can pass tasks to other tasks and this results in a dependency being generated.

You may have noticed that we added a few `sleep(4)` calls in the preceding code. This simulates running a long computation. Otherwise, this example is so fast that there is no point in using multiple processors.

We start by running `jug status`, which results in the output shown in the following screenshot:

Waiting	Ready	Finished	Running	Task name
1	0	0	0	jugfile.print_final_result
1	0	0	0	jugfile.add
2	2	0	0	jugfile.double
4	2	0	0	Total

Now, we start two processes simultaneously (using the `&` operator, which is the traditional Unix way of starting processes in the background):

```
$ jug execute &
$ jug execute &
```

Now, we run `jug status` again:

Waiting	Ready	Finished	Running	Task name
1	0	0	0	jugfile.print_final_result
2	0	0	2	jugfile.double
1	0	0	0	jugfile.add
4	2	0	0	Total

We can see that the two initial double operators are running at the same time. After about 8 seconds, the whole process will finish and the `output.txt` file will be written.

By the way, if your file was called anything other than `jugfile.py`, you would then have to specify it explicitly on the command line. For example, if your file was called `analysis.py`, you would run the following command:

```
$ jug execute analysis.py
```

This is the only disadvantage of not using the name `jugfile.py`. So, feel free to use more meaningful names.

Looking under the hood

How does jug work? At the basic level, it's very simple. `Task` is a function plus its argument. Its arguments may be either values or other tasks. If a task takes other tasks, there is a dependency between the two tasks (and the second one cannot be run until the results of the first task are available).

Based on this, jug recursively computes a hash for each task. This hash value encodes the whole computation to get the result. When you run `jug execute`, for each task, there is a little loop that runs the logic, depicted in the following flowchart:

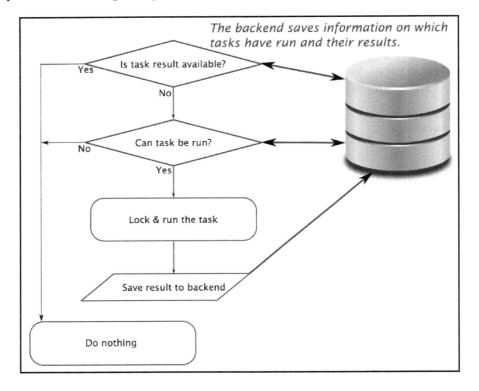

The default backend writes the file to disk (in this funny folder named `jugfile.jugdata/`). Another backend is available, which uses a Redis database. With proper locking, which jug takes care of, this also allows for many processes to execute tasks; each process will independently look at all the tasks and run the ones that have not run yet and then write them back to the shared backend. This works on either the same machine (using multicore processors) or in multiple machines as long as they all have access to the same backend (for example, using a network disk or the Redis databases). In the second half of this chapter, we will discuss computer clusters, but for now let's focus on multiple cores.

You can also understand why it's able to memoize intermediate results. If the backend already has the result of a task, it's not run again. On the other hand, if you change the task, even in minute ways (by altering one of the parameters), its hash will change. Therefore, it will be rerun. Furthermore, all tasks that depend on it will also have their hashes changed and they will be rerun as well.

Using jug for data analysis

Jug is a generic framework, but it's ideally suited for medium-scale data analysis. As you develop your analysis pipeline, it's good to have intermediate results automatically saved. If you have already computed the preprocessing step before and are only changing the features you compute, you do not want to recompute the preprocessing step. If you have already computed the features but want to try combining a few new ones into the mix, you also do not want to recompute all your other features.

Jug is also specifically optimized to work with NumPy arrays. Whenever your tasks return or receive NumPy arrays, you are taking advantage of this optimization. Jug is another piece of this ecosystem where everything works together.

We will now look back at `Chapter 12`, *Computer Vision*. In that chapter, we learned how to compute features on images. Remember that the basic pipeline consisted of the following features:

- Loading image files
- Computing features
- Combining these features
- Normalizing the features
- Creating a classifier

We are going to redo this exercise, but this time with the use of jug. The advantage of this version is that it's now possible to add a new feature or classifier without having to recompute all of the pipeline:

1. We start with a few imports as follows:

```
from jug import TaskGenerator import mahotas as mh from glob
import glob
```

2. Now, we define the first task generators and feature computation functions:

```
@TaskGenerator
def compute_texture(im):
    from features import texture
    imc = mh.imread(im)
    return texture(mh.colors.rgb2gray(imc))

@TaskGenerator
def chist_file(fname):
    from features import chist
    im = mh.imread(fname)
    return chist(im)
```

> The features module we import is the one from Chapter 12, *Computer Vision*.

> We write functions that take the filename as input instead of the image array. Using the full images would also work, of course, but this is a small optimization. A filename is a string, which is small if it gets written to the backend. It's also very fast to compute a hash if needed. It also ensures that the images are only loaded by the processes that need them.

3. We can use TaskGenerator on any function. This is true even for functions we did not write, such as np.array, np.hstack or the following command:

```
import numpy as np
to_array = TaskGenerator(np.array)
hstack = TaskGenerator(np.hstack)
haralicks = []
chists = []
labels = []

# Change this variable to point to
# the location of the dataset on disk
basedir = '../SimpleImageDataset/'
# Use glob to get all the images
images = glob('{}/*.jpg'.format(basedir))
```

```
for fname in sorted(images):
    haralicks.append(compute_texture(fname))
    chists.append(chist_file(fname))
    # The class is encoded in the filename as xxxx00.jpg
    labels.append(fname[:-len('00.jpg')])

haralicks = to_array(haralicks)
chists = to_array(chists)
labels = to_array(labels)
```

4. One small inconvenience of using jug is that we must always write functions to output the results to files, as shown in the preceding examples. This is a small price to pay for the extra convenience of using jug:

```
@TaskGenerator
def accuracy(features, labels):
    from sklearn.linear_model import LogisticRegression
    from sklearn.pipeline import Pipeline
    from sklearn.preprocessing import StandardScaler
    from sklearn import model_selection

    clf = Pipeline([('preproc', StandardScaler()),
                    ('classifier', LogisticRegression())])
    cv = model_selection.LeaveOneOut()
    scores = model_selection.cross_val_score(
        clf, features, labels, cv=cv)
    return scores.mean()
```

5. Note that we are only importing sklearn inside this function. This is a small optimization. This way, sklearn is only imported when it's really needed:

```
scores_base = accuracy(haralicks, labels)
scores_chist = accuracy(chists, labels)
combined = hstack([chists, haralicks])
scores_combined = accuracy(combined, labels)
```

6. Finally, we write and call a function to print out all results. It expects its argument to be a list of pairs with the name of the algorithm and the results:

```
@TaskGenerator
def print_results(scores):
    with open('results.image.txt', 'w') as output:
        for k,v in scores:
            output.write('Accuracy [{}]: {:.1%}n'.format(
                k, v.mean()))

print_results([
        ('base', scores_base),
        ('chists', scores_chist),
        ('combined' , scores_combined),
        ])
```

7. That's it. Now, on the shell, run the following command to run this pipeline using `jug`:

```
$ jug execute image-classification.py
```

Reusing partial results

For example, let's say you want to add a new feature (or even a set of features). As we saw in `Chapter 12`, *Computer Vision*, this is easy to do by changing the feature computation code. However, this would imply recomputing all the features again, which is wasteful, particularly if you want to test new features and techniques quickly.

We now add a set of features, that is, another type of texture feature called linear binary patterns. This is implemented in mahotas; we just need to call a function, but we wrap it in `TaskGenerator`:

```
@TaskGenerator
def compute_lbp(fname):
    from mahotas.features import lbp
    imc = mh.imread(fname)
    im = mh.colors.rgb2grey(imc)
    # The parameters 'radius' and 'points' are set to typical values
    # check the documentation for their exact meaning
    return lbp(im, radius=8, points=6)
```

We replace the previous loop with an extra function call:

```
lbps = []
for fname in sorted(images):
    # the rest of the loop as before
    lbps.append(compute_lbp(fname))
lbps = to_array(lbps)
```

We call `accuracy` with these newer features:

```
scores_lbps = accuracy(lbps, labels)
combined_all = hstack([chists, haralicks, lbps])
scores_combined_all = accuracy(combined_all, labels)

print_results([
        ('base', scores_base),
        ('chists', scores_chist),
        ('lbps', scores_lbps),
        ('combined' , scores_combined),
        ('combined_all' , scores_combined_all),
        ])
```

Now, when you run `jug execute` again, the new features will be computed, but the old features will be loaded from the cache. This is when jug can be very powerful. It ensures that you always get the results you want while saving you from unnecessarily recomputing cached results. You will also see that adding this feature set improves on the previous methods.

Not all features of jug will be mentioned in this chapter, but here is a summary of the most potentially interesting ones we didn't cover in the main text:

- `jug invalidate`: This declares that all results from a given function should be considered invalid and in need of recomputation. This will also recompute any downstream computation, which depended (even indirectly) on the invalidated results
- `jug status --cache`: If `jug status` takes too long, you can use the `--cache` flag to cache the status and speed it up. Note that this will not detect any changes to the `jugfile`, but you can always use `--cache --clear` to remove the cache and start again
- `jug cleanup`: This removes any extra files in the memorization cache. This is a garbage collection operation

There are other, more advanced features, which allow you to look at values that have been computed inside the `jugfile`. Read up on features such as barriers in the jug documentation online at `http://jug.rtfd.org`.

Using Amazon Web Services

When you have a lot of data and a lot of computation to be performed, you might start to crave more computing power. Amazon (`http://aws.amazon.com`) allows you to rent computing power by the hour. Thus, you can access a large amount of computing power without having to commit to purchasing a large number of machines (including the cost of managing the infrastructure). There are other competitors in this market, but Amazon is the largest player, so we briefly cover it here.

Amazon Web Services (**AWS**) is a large set of services. We will focus only on the **Elastic Compute Cloud** (**EC2**) service. This service offers you virtual machines and disk space, which can be allocated and deallocated quickly.

There are three modes of use. The first is a reserved mode, whereby you prepay to have cheaper per-hour access, a fixed per-hour rate, and a variable rate, which depends on the overall compute market (when there is less demand, the costs are lower; when there is more demand, the prices go up).

On top of this general system, there are several types of machines available with varying costs, from a single core to a multicore system with a lot of RAM or even **graphical processing units** (**GPUs**). We will later see that you can also get several of the cheaper machines and build yourself a virtual cluster. You can also choose to get a Linux or Windows server (with Linux being slightly cheaper). In this chapter, we will work on our examples on Linux, but most of this information will be valid for Windows machines as well.

For testing, you can use a single machine in the **free tier**. This allows you to play around with the system, get used to the interface, and so on. Note, though, that this machine contains a slow CPU.

The resources can be managed through a web interface. However, it's also possible to do so programmatically and to write scripts that allocate virtual machines, format hard disks, and perform all operations that are possible through the web interface. In fact, while the web interface changes very frequently (and some of the screenshots we show in the book may be out of date by the time it goes to press), the programmatic interface is more stable, and the general architecture has remained stable since the service was introduced.

Access to AWS services is performed through a traditional username/password system, although Amazon calls the username an *access key* and the password a secret key. They probably do so to keep it separate from the username/password you use to access the web interface. In fact, you can create as many access/secret key pairs as you wish and give them different permissions. This is helpful for a larger team, where a senior user with access to the full web panel can create other keys for developers with fewer privileges.

Amazon.com has several regions. These correspond to physical regions of the world: West Coast US, East Coast US, several Asian locations, a South American one, and two European ones. If you are transferring data, it's best to keep it close to where you will be transferring to and from. Additionally, keep in mind that if you are handling user information, there may be regulatory issues regarding transfer to another jurisdiction. In this case, do check with an informed counsel on the implications of transferring data about European customers to the US or any other similar transfer.

AWS is a very large topic and there are various books exclusively available covering it. The purpose of this chapter is to give you an overall impression of what is available and what is possible with AWS. In the practical spirit of this book, we do this by working through examples, but we will not exhaust all possibilities.

Creating your first virtual machines

The first step is to go to `http://aws.amazon.com/` and create an account. These steps are similar to any other online service. A single machine is free, but to get more you will need a credit card. In this example, we will use a few machines, so it may cost you a few dollars if you want to run through it. If you are not ready to take out a credit card just yet, you can certainly read the chapter to learn what AWS provides, without going through the examples. Then you can make a more informed decision on whether to sign up:

1. Once you sign up for AWS and log in, you will be taken to the console. Here, you will see the many services that AWS provides, as depicted in the following screenshot (this is the panel shown as it was when this book was written. Amazon regularly makes minor changes, so you may see something slightly different from what we present in the book):

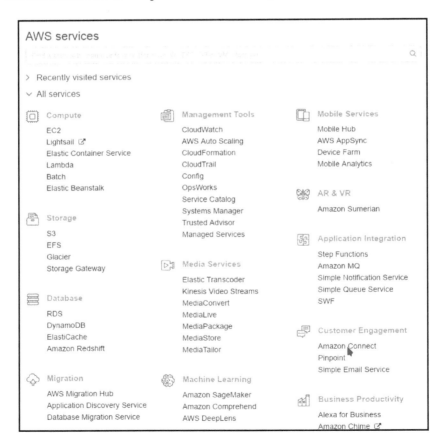

2. You must first create a user using the **Identity and Access Management** service. Add a user, which in the screenshot is called `aws_ml`, and assign it programmatic access:

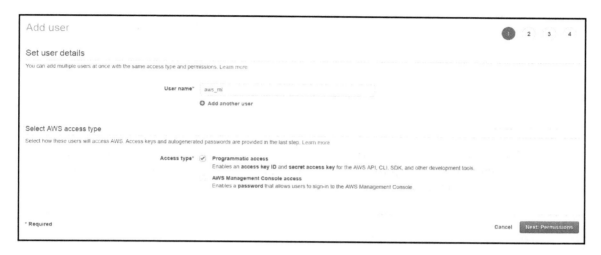

3. We create a group for the user (called `EC2_FULL` in the following screenshot) and give it the **AmazonEC2FullAccess** permissions. Assigning the right permissions is very important, or later steps will fail with permission errors:

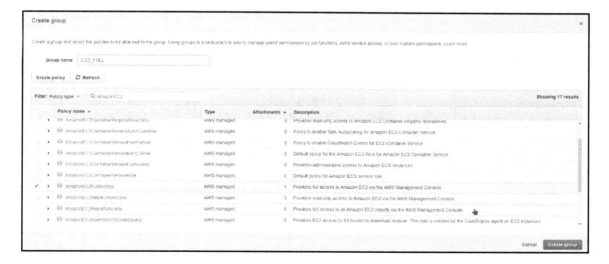

4. Finally, at the very end, you must copy the information, namely, the access key. You can simply download the CSV file and save. Again, if you do not save this information, later steps will fail:

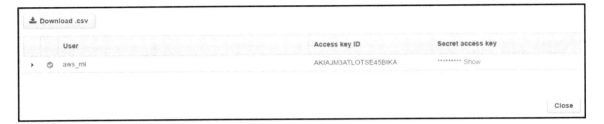

5. Now, we go back to the console and this time, we pick and click on **EC2** (the top element in the **Compute** column). We now see the EC2 management console, as shown in the following screenshot:

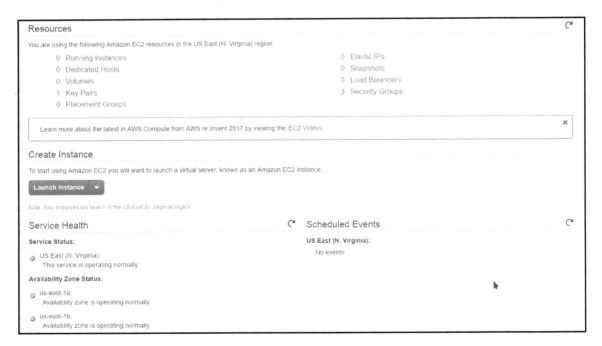

6. In the top-right corner, you can pick your region (see the Amazon regions information box). Note that you will only see information about the region that you have selected. Thus, if you mistakenly select the wrong region (or have machines running in multiple regions), your machines may not appear (this seems to be a common pitfall of using the EC2 web management console).

7. In EC2 parlance, a running server is called an **instance**. We select **Launch Instance**, which leads to the following screen asking us to select the operating system to use:

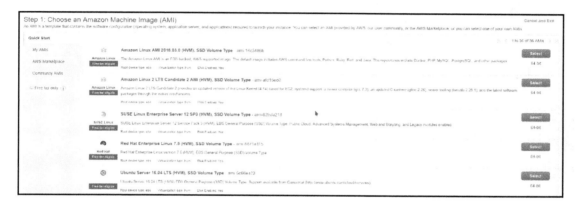

8. Select the **Amazon Linux** option (if you are familiar with one of the other offered Linux distributions, such as Red Hat, SUSE, or Ubuntu, you can also select one of them, but the configurations will be slightly different). Now that you have selected the software, you will need to select the hardware. On the next screen, you will be asked to select which type of machine to use:

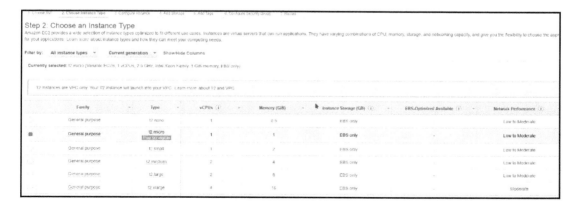

9. We will start with one instance of the `t2.micro` type (the `t1.micro` type was an older, even less powerful machine). This is the smallest possible machine and it's free. Keep clicking on **Next** and accept all of the defaults until you come to the screen mentioning a key pair:

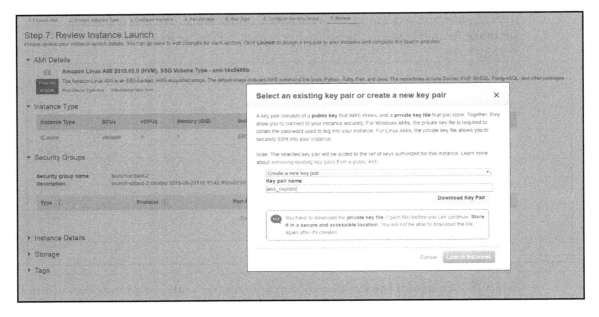

10. We will pick the name `awskeys` for the key pair. Then check **Create a new key pair**. Name the key pair file `awskeys.pem`. Download and save this file somewhere safe! This is the **Secure Shell (SSH)** key that will enable you to log in to your cloud machine. Accept the remaining defaults and your instance will launch.

11. You will now need to wait a few minutes for your instance to come up. Eventually, the instance will be shown in green with the status as **running**:

12. In the preceding screenshot, you should see the **Public IP** which can be used to log in to the instance as follows:

```
$ ssh -i awskeys.pem ec2-user@54.93.165.5
```

13. Therefore, we will be calling the `ssh` command and passing it the key files that we downloaded earlier as the identity (using the `-i` option). We are logging in as the user `ec2-user` on the machine with the IP address `54.93.165.5`. This address will, of course, be different in your case. If you choose another distribution for your instance, the username may also change. In this case, try logging in as `root`, `ubuntu` (for Ubuntu distribution), or `fedora` (for Fedora distribution).

14. Finally, if you are running a Unix-style operating system (including macOS), you may have to tweak its permissions by calling the following command:

```
$ chmod 600 awskeys.pem
```

This sets the read/write permission for the current user only. SSH will otherwise give you an ugly warning.

15. Now you should be able to log in to your machine. If everything is okay, you should see the banner, as shown in the following screenshot:

```
$ ssh -i aws_explore.pem ec2-user@34.201.68.154

Last login: Wed May 23 16:14:17 2018 from 94.252.95.61

      __|  __|_  )
      _|  (     /    Amazon Linux AMI
     ___|\___|___|

https://aws.amazon.com/amazon-linux-ami/2018.03-release-notes/
6 package(s) needed for security, out of 7 available
Run "sudo yum update" to apply all updates.
[ec2-user@ip-172-30-0-118 ~]$ ▮
```

This is a regular Linux box where you have `sudo` permission: you can run any command as a superuser by prefixing it with `sudo`. You can run the `update` command it recommends to get your machine up to speed.

Installing Python packages on Amazon Linux

If you prefer another distribution, you can use your knowledge of that distribution to install Python, NumPy, and others. Here, we will do it on the standard Amazon distribution:

1. We start by installing several basic Python packages as follows:

```
$ curl -O
https://repo.continuum.io/miniconda/Miniconda3-latest-Linux-x86
_64.sh
$ chmod +x ./Miniconda3-latest-Linux-x86_64.sh
$ bash ./Miniconda3-latest-Linux-x86_64.sh
```

2. Now, follow the basic instructions and set the `PATH` variable as instructed:

```
$ export PATH=/home/ec2-user/miniconda3/bin:$PATH
```

3. Now, we can create a new environment, which we call py3.6 (as it is a Python 3.6 environment) and activate it:

```
$ conda create -n py3.6 python=3.6 numpy scikit-learn
$ source activate py3.6
```

4. To install mahotas and jug, we add the conda-forge channel (it is generally a good idea to do so; it has many well-maintained packages):

```
$ conda config --add channels conda-forge
$ conda install mahotas imread jug git
```

Running jug on our cloud machine

We can now download the data and code for the book by cloning the code repository to your machine:

```
$ git clone \
https://github.com/PacktPublishing/Building-Machine-Learning-Systems-with-P
ython-Third-edition
$ cd BuildingMachineLearningSystemsWithPython
$ cd ch14
```

Finally, we run this following command:

```
$ jug execute
```

This would work just fine, but we would have to wait a long time for the results. Our free tier machine (of type t2.micro) is not very fast and only has a single processor. So, we will upgrade our machine!

We go back to the EC2 console and right-click on the running instance to get the pop-up menu. We need to first stop the instance. This is the virtual machine equivalent to powering off. You can stop your machines at any time. At this point, you stop paying for them. Note that you are still using disk space, which also has a cost, billed separately. You can terminate the instance, which will also destroy the disk. This means you lose any information saved on the machine.

Once the machine is stopped, the **Change instance type** option becomes available. Now, we can select a more powerful instance, for example, a c5.xlarge instance with eight cores. The machine is still off, so you need to start it again (the virtual equivalent to booting up).

AWS offers several instance types at different price points. As this information is constantly being revised as more powerful options are introduced and prices change (generally, getting cheaper), we cannot give you many details in the book, but you can find the most up-to-date information on Amazon's website.

We need to wait for the instance to come back up. Once it has, look up its IP address in the same fashion as we did before. When you change instance run on types, your instance will get a new address assigned to it.

 You can assign a fixed IP to an instance using Amazon.com's Elastic IPs functionality, which you will find on the left-hand side of the EC2 console. This is useful if you find yourself creating and modifying instances very often. There is a small cost associated with this feature.

With 8 cores, you can run 8 jug processes simultaneously, as illustrated in the following code:

```
$ # the loop below runs 8 times
$ for counter in $(seq 8); do
> jug execute &
> done
```

Use `jug status` to check whether these eight jobs are, in fact, running. After your jobs are finished (which should now happen pretty fast), you can stop the machine and downgrade it again to a `t2.micro` instance to save money. The micro instance can be used for free (within certain limits), while the `c5.xlarge` one we used costs 0.170 US dollars per hour (as of June, 2018—check the AWS website for up-to-date information).

Automating the generation of clusters with cfncluster

As we just learned, we can spawn machines using the web interface, but it quickly becomes tedious and error prone. Fortunately, Amazon has an API. This means that we can write scripts that perform all the operations we discussed earlier, automatically. Even better, others have already developed tools that can be used to mechanize and automate many of the processes you want to perform with AWS.

Amazon themselves provide many command-line tools for their own infrastructure. For cluster provision, the tool is called `cfncluster`. If you are using `conda`, you can install it with:

```
$ conda install cfncluster
```

You can run this from your local machine: it will use the Amazon API.

The first step is to go back to the AWS Console in your web browser and add the **AdministratorAccess** permission to your AWS user. This is a brute-force approach; it gives the user all administration rights, and while it is useful when learning about AWS, it is not recommended for production use:

Now, we create a new virtual private cloud on AWS using the VPC service. Choose all the default options:

```
$ cfncluster configure
```

Pick from the options listed. It is important that you choose the right key (which we generated earlier). This will generate a configuration file in `~/.cfncluster/config`. For the moment, we will use all the defaults, but this is where you can later change them to suit your needs.

Keys, keys, and more keys:
There are three completely different types of keys that are important when dealing with AWS. First, there is a standard username/password combination, which you use to log in to the website. Second, there is the SSH key system, which is a public/private key system implemented with files; with your public key file, you can log in to remote machines. Third, there is the AWS access key/secret key system, which is just a form of username/password that allows you to have multiple users on the same account (including adding different permissions to each one, but we will not cover these advanced features in this book). To look up our access/secret keys, we go back to the AWS Console, click on our name in the top right, and select **Security Credentials**. Now, at the bottom of the screen, we should see our access key, which may look something like this: `AAKIIT7HHF6IUSN3OCAA`.

We can now create the cluster:

```
$ cfncluster create public
```

This may take a few minutes. This will allocate two compute nodes to our cluster and a main master node (these are default values; you can change them in the `cfncluster` configuration file). Once the process is finished, you should see output:

```
Output:"MasterPublicIP"="52.86.118.172"
Output:"MasterPrivateIP"="172.30.2.146"
Output:"GangliaPublicURL"="http://52.86.118.172/ganglia/"
Output:"GangliaPrivateURL"="http://172.30.2.146/ganglia/"
```

Note the IP address of the master node that is printed out (in this case `52.86.118.172`). If you forget it, you can look it up again with the command:

```
$ cfncluster status public
```

All of these nodes have the same filesystem, so anything we create on the master node will also be seen by the worker nodes. This also means that we can use jug on these clusters.

These clusters can be used as you wish, but they come equipped with a job queue engine, which makes them ideal for batch processing. The process of using them is simple:

1. You log into the master node.
2. You prepare your scripts on the master (or better yet, have them prepared beforehand).
3. You submit jobs to the queue. A job can be any Unix command. The scheduler will find free nodes and run your job.

4. You wait for the jobs to finish.

5. You read the results on the master node. You can also now kill all the slave nodes to save money. In any case, do not leave your system running when you do not need it anymore! Otherwise, this will cost you (in dollars and cents).

As we said earlier, `cfncluster` provides a batch queuing system for its clusters; you write a script to perform your actions, put it on the queue, and it will run in any available node.

As before, we use our key to log into the master node:

```
$ ssh -i awskeys.pem ec2-user@52.86.118.172
```

Set up miniconda as before (the setup—`aws.txt` file in the code repository has all the necessary commands). We can use the same `jugfile` system as before, except that now, instead of running it directly on the master, we schedule it on the cluster:

1. First, write a very simple wrapper script as follows:

```
#!/usr/bin/env bash
export PATH=$HOME/miniconda3/bin:$PATH
source activate py3.6
jug execute jugfile.py
```

2. Call it `run-jugfile.sh` and use `chmod +x run-jugfile.sh` to give it executable permission. Now, we can schedule jobs on the cluster by using the following command:

```
$ qsub -cwd ./run-jugfile.sh
```

This will create two jobs, each of which will run the `run-jugfile.sh` script, which we will simply call jug. You can still use the master as you wish. In particular, you can, at any moment, run `jug status` and see the status of the computation. In fact, jug was developed in exactly such an environment, so it works very well in it.

3. Eventually, the computation will finish. At this point, we need to first save our results. Then, we can kill off all the nodes. We create a directory, `~/results`, and copy our results there:

```
# mkdir ~/results
# cp results.image.txt ~/results
```

4. Now, log off the cluster and go back to our worker machine:

```
# exit
```

5. Now we are back at our original AWS machine or your local computer (notice the $ sign in the next code examples):

```
$ scp -i awskeys.pem -pr ec2-user@52.86.118.172:results .
```

6. Finally, we should kill all the nodes to save money as follows:

```
$ cfncluster stop public
Stopping the cluster will destroy the compute nodes, but keep
the master node running as well as the disk space. This reduces
costs to a minimum, but to really destroy all
$ cfncluster delete public
```

Terminating will really destroy the filesystem and all your results. In our case, we have copied the final results to safety manually. Another possibility is to have the cluster write to a filesystem, which is not allocated and destroyed by `cfncluster`, but is available to you on a regular instance; in fact, the flexibility of these tools is immense. However, these advanced manipulations cannot all fit in this chapter.

Summary

We looked at how to use jug, a little Python framework, to manage computations in a way that takes advantage of multiple cores or multiple machines. Although this framework is generic, it was built specifically to address the data analysis needs of its author (who is also an author of this book). Therefore, it has several aspects that make it fit in with the rest of the Python machine learning environment.

You also learned about AWS and the Amazon cloud. Using cloud computing is often a more effective use of resources than building in-house computing capacity. This is particularly true if your needs are not constant and are changing. Furthermore `cfncluster` even allows for clusters that automatically grow as you launch more jobs and shrink as they terminate.

This is the end of the book. We have come a long way. You learned how to perform classification and clustering. You learned about dimensionality reduction and topic modeling to make sense of large datasets. Toward the end, we looked at some specific applications (such as music genre classification and computer vision). For implementations, we relied on Python. This language has an increasingly expanding ecosystem of numeric computing packages built on top of NumPy. Whenever possible, we relied on scikit-learn, but used other packages when necessary. Due to the fact that they all use the same basic data structure (the NumPy multidimensional array), it's possible to mix functionalities from different packages seamlessly. All of the packages used in this book are open source and available for use in any project.

Naturally, we did not cover every machine learning topic. In the appendix, we provide a selection of other resources that will help interested readers learn more about machine learning.

Where to Learn More About Machine Learning

We are at the end of our book. Now let's take a moment to look at what else is out there that could be useful to our readers.

There are many wonderful resources out there for learning more about machine learning—way too many to cover them all here. The following therefore represents only a small, and very biased, sample of resources the authors think are best at the time of writing.

Online courses

Andrew Ng is a professor at Stanford who runs an online course in machine learning at Coursera (http://www.coursera.org). It is free of charge, but may represent a significant time investment.

Books

This book is focused on the practical side of machine learning. We did not present the thinking behind the algorithms or the theory that justify them. If you are interested in that aspect of machine learning, we recommend *Pattern Recognition and Machine Learning*, by Christopher Bishop. This is a classical introductory text in the field. It will teach you the nitty-gritty of most of the algorithms we used in this book.

If you want to move beyond the introduction and learn all the gory mathematical details, *Machine Learning: A Probabilistic Perspective*, by Kevin P. Murphy, is an excellent option (www.cs.ubc.ca/~murphyk/MLbook). It's very recent (published in 2012) and contains the cutting edge of ML research. This 1,100-page book can also serve as a reference, as very little of machine learning has been left out.

Specific to deep learning, you probably want to read *Deep Learning*, by Ian Goodfellow et al. (http://www.deeplearningbook.org). The book is more on the theoretical side, but still very accessible. Its web version is free of charge, but some books are just worth the investment.

Blogs

Here is an obviously non-exhaustive list of blogs, which would be of interest for someone working in machine learning:

- Cross Validated: `http://stats.stackexchange.com` (OK, it is not really blog, but rather a question-and-answer site. The answers, though, are often so good that they could be published as blog posts as well.)
- Machine Learning Theory: `http://hunch.net`. The average pace is one post per month, very practical, always surprising approaches
- Edwin Chen's Blog: `http://blog.echen.me`. The average pace is one post per month, covering more applied topics
- Machined Learnings: `http://www.machinedlearnings.com`. The average pace is one post per month, covering more applied topics
- FlowingData: `http://flowingdata.com`. The average pace is one post per day, with the posts centering on statistics
- Simply Statistics: `http://simplystatistics.org`. Several posts per month, focusing on statistics and big data
- Statistical Modeling, Causal Inference, and Social Science: `http://andrewgelman.com`. One post per day, often often funny reads when the author points out flaws in popular media, using statistics

Data sources

If you want to play around with algorithms, you can obtain many datasets from the Machine Learning Repository at the **University of California at Irvine** (**UCI**). You can find it at `http://archive.ics.uci.edu/ml`.

Getting competitive

An excellent way to learn more about machine learning is by trying out a competition! Kaggle (http://www.kaggle.com) is a marketplace of ML competitions and was already mentioned in the introduction. On the website, you will find several different competitions with different structures, and often cash prizes.

The supervised learning competitions almost always follow this format: you (and every other competitor) are given access to labeled training data and testing data (without labels). Your task is to submit predictions for testing data. When the competition closes, whoever has the best accuracy wins. The prizes range from glory to cash.

Of course, winning something is nice, but you can gain a lot of useful experience just by participating. So, you have to stay tuned after the competition is over as participants start sharing their approaches in the forum. Most of the time, winning is not about developing a new algorithm, but cleverly preprocessing, normalizing, and combining existing methods.

All that was left out

We did not cover every machine learning package available for Python. Given the limited space, we chose to focus on scikit-learn. However, there are other options and we list a few of them here:

- pandas (https://pandas.pydata.org) – If you decide to fall in love with just one Python package in your whole life, choose this one! It provides a convenience layer on top of NumPy and speeds up common tasks, such as interactive data preprocessing, tremendously.
- Of course, all the other exciting deep learning toolkits, such as CNTK (http://cntk.ai), PyTorch (https://pytorch.org/), MXNet (https://mxnet.apache.org/), Chainer (https://chainer.org/), DSSTNE (https://github.com/amzn/amazon-dsstne), or DyNet (https://github.com/clab/dynet).
- Keras (https://keras.io/), which is a convenient library on top of TensorFlow and CNTK. Often, people start with a "real quick trying-out" version of Keras, only to find out that it is already good enough.
- MissingNo (https://github.com/ResidentMario/missingno), which is a Python module dedicated to analyzing and pruning missing values.
- Machine Learning Toolkit (Milk) (http://luispedro.org/software/milk) – This package was developed by one of the authors of this book and covers some algorithms and techniques that are not included in scikit-learn.

Summary

We are now truly at the end. We hope you enjoyed the book and feel well-equipped to start your own machine learning adventure.

We also hope you learned the importance of carefully testing your methods. In particular, we hope you've understood the importance of using the correct cross-validation method and not reporting training test results, which are an overinflated estimate of how good your method really is.

Other Books You May Enjoy

If you enjoyed this book, you may be interested in these other books by Packt:

Mastering Machine Learning Algorithms

Giuseppe Bonaccorso

ISBN: 978-1-78862-111-3

- Explore how a ML model can be trained, optimized, and evaluated
- Understand how to create and learn static and dynamic probabilistic models
- Successfully cluster high-dimensional data and evaluate model accuracy
- Discover how artificial neural networks work and how to train, optimize, and validate them
- Work with Autoencoders and Generative Adversarial Networks
- Apply label spreading and propagation to large datasets
- Explore the most important Reinforcement Learning techniques

Machine Learning Solutions

Jalaj Thanaki

ISBN: 978-1-78839-004-0

- Select the right algorithm to derive the best solution in ML domains
- Perform predictive analysis effciently using ML algorithms
- Predict stock prices using the stock index value
- Perform customer analytics for an e-commerce platform
- Build recommendation engines for various domains
- Build NLP applications for the health domain
- Build language generation applications using different NLP techniques
- Build computer vision applications such as facial emotion recognition

Leave a review - let other readers know what you think

Please share your thoughts on this book with others by leaving a review on the site that you bought it from. If you purchased the book from Amazon, please leave us an honest review on this book's Amazon page. This is vital so that other potential readers can see and use your unbiased opinion to make purchasing decisions, we can understand what our customers think about our products, and our authors can see your feedback on the title that they have worked with Packt to create. It will only take a few minutes of your time, but is valuable to other potential customers, our authors, and Packt. Thank you!

Index

www.ingramcontent.com/pod-product-compliance
Lightning Source LLC
Chambersburg PA
CBHW060651060326
40690CB00020B/4600